COCO CHANEL

JOHN BROWN

Rabbit Books

A Bookopedia Imprint

Copyright © John Brown 2023

Contents

Introduction

Humble beginnings

The Emergence of Coco

Why Two Cs

Coco the pioneer

World War I

The Inter-War Years

The 1950s

The 1960s

The 1970s

The 1980s

The !990s

2000 & Karl

Goodbye Coco

Final quotes of Coco Chanel

Conclusion

Introduction

When it comes to researching and discussing the life and times of Coco Chanel, her successes and failures, her loves and losses, there are countless records and biographical accounts available.

The difficulty I encountered when researching Chanel was in much part due to Coco Chanel herself. For a long time, historians and biographers had some difficulty in finding any information concerning her early. This was due in no small part to a genuine clerical error at the time of her birth. Her family name was recorded as "Chasnel" rather than Chanel.

This error on her birth certificate suited Coco, as she liked to change or rather reinvent certain facts about the origins of her youth.

She worked hard to conceal, distort and often embellish her early life. She was not adverse to supplying alternative facts to distort the actual truth of those early years.

Emonde Charles Roux was a longtime editor of French Vogue and a personal friend of Chanel. Unbeknown to Coco, he was about to publish a biography about Chanel.

When she discovered that Edmonde was writing a biography about her, she flew into a rage and never spoke to him again, such was the passion with which she guarded her early private life.

My purpose in writing this compact appraisal of her life, is more a handy reference point, a sort of pocket guide to this extraordinary woman and her unique achievements.

How she rose from the humblest of beginnings to the supreme star of couture.

I hope you find it informative and useful.

John Brown.

Gabrielle "Coco" Chanel

Humble Beginnings

Gabrielle "Coco" Chanel was a French fashion designer and businesswoman. She was born on August 19, 1883, in Saumur, Loire Valley, France and died on January 10, 1971, in Paris, France. She is famous for revolutionizing women's fashion in the early 20th century by introducing relaxed, comfortable designs inspired by men's clothing. Some of her most iconic designs include the "little black dress," tweed suits, and the Chanel No. 5 perfume. She opened her first boutique in Paris in 1910, and the Chanel brand continues to be a major player in the fashion industry today.

Coco Chanel was the daughter of Albert Chanel and Jeanne Devolle. Gabrielle Bonheur "Coco" Chanel was born on August 19, 1883, in Saumur, France. She was the second of five children born to Albert Chanel, a street vendor, and Jeanne Devolle, a laundrywoman. Coco's early life was marked by poverty and hardship, Her father was a street vendor, and her mother died in the winter of 1895, when Gabrielle was just twelve years old.

Following her mother's death, her father sent his sons to a nearby farm and his three daughters to the nearby orphanage, the Aubazine convent to be raised by nuns. She never saw her father again.

During her time at the orphanage, Chanel received a strict education, which included training in sewing, embroidery, and other needlework skills. She learned how to make clothing, and this experience helped lay the foundation for her future as a fashion designer. Despite the strict and austere environment of the convent, Chanel remembered her time there as an important period in her life, and she later said that the habits she wore at the convent had influenced the design of her famous "little black dress."

The only respite from this strict regime came during the summer months, when she was allowed to stay with her aunt Adrianne Louise. They spent their precious days sewing and making clothes. The major difference being, the nuns taught her the regimented basics, Louise gave her the freedom to create, She, taught her how to embellish with lace, banding and even frills. These were precious times for Gabrielle but at the end of the summer, it was back to the orphanage.

The Emergence of Coco

Once Gabrielle reached the age of eighteen, she was given a choice, leave the orphanage or become a nun. There was little chance of the latter happening, so she duly left. She went directly to her aunt Louise in Moulins. From there she went to the Notre Dame finishing school as a Free Space Pupil. After two years she ventured out into the world.

She got a job as a seamstress with a local tailor. This was considered a good position for a girl of her class and background.

Moulins was a garrison town and it wasn't long before she was being invited, along with her aunt to the music hall. This was a revelation to Gabrielle. The glamour, the colour, the gaiety, were a revelation to Gabrielle. One of the more unusual aspects of this particular venue, was the chance for ordinary members of the audience to take the stage between acts. Very soon she was on the other side of the footlights – singing. She had a reasonable voice by all accounts but a rather limited repertoire. In fact, she only knew two songs – Coco Rico and Cikaboo Coco, so she soon became known as La Petite Coco – Coco Chanel had arrived.

Coco was just 21 when a chance meeting at the music hall with Etienne Balsan, an army officer set her on a path to independence. Coco saw her chance. She knew with her orphan background she would never be a suitable candidate for marriage but there was a strong chemistry between her and Etienne and Coco was fully aware of the help he could offer.

Balsan was a wealthy textile heir and horse breeder who introduced Chanel to high society and provided financial support for her fashion endeavors. Within twelve months of their meeting, Coco had moved into the grand estate of Etienne Balsan's - Royallieu, located in the town of Chantilly, in the Oise department of France. The estate was large and luxurious, with property that included a chateau, stables, and extensive grounds for horse breeding and hunting. Balsan was a well-known figure in the French horse racing and equestrian world, and his estate was a popular destination for the wealthy and elite of the time.

Here the little girl from the orphanage mixed with the great and the good of French aristocracy. She also became a very accomplished horse-woman This was something that Balsan noticed she could do with consummate ease.

Coco had very set ideas about fashion, that sat in complete contrast to the norm. Female fashion in 1909 was still Victorian/ Edwardian in style, with billowing skirts, ultra-tight corset tops and restrictive in the extreme. Coco shocked society and the world of fashion when she attended a summer race event that year and instead of the usual over-ornate outfits considered the norm for such events, she instead, borrowed a shirt and tie from Etienne's wardrobe and over it, she wore a loose gents coat, finally she topped it off with a boater that she had made herself. Shock waves reverberated around the Parisian fashion houses. Coco cared not a jot, she had a style and she would play it to the max'.

Around this time another man entered her life - Arthur "Boy" Capel. Like Balsan, Capel was wealthy but there was one difference, Capel was English and worked for a living. Capel saw something unique in Coco and took a genuine interest in her creative ambitions. Now Coco was involved with two men, something had to give.

Coco Chanel and Arthur "Boy" Capel entered into a close and complicated relationship that influenced Chanel's personal and professional life. They first met when Capel, a patron of the Parisian café, discovered Coco was also a member.

Once Coco was sure of Capel's feelings for her, she simply wrote Balsan a note and moved out of the chateau the same day. Her destination, Paris and the waiting arms of Capel. They began an affair that lasted for several years, despite the fact that Capel was married.

Capel was a significant influence on Chanel's early career, providing financial support for her to open her first shop in 1910 in Deauville, a seaside resort in the Normandy region of France.

The area around Deauville became a popular tourist destination among the upper class and aristocracy. At the time, Emperor Napoleon II had begun visiting the city (1860) bringing his royal court with him. Luxury hotels, houses and palaces sprung up, as did the necessary infrastructure to host these elite members of society, who were looking for a place near the coast to enjoy the health benefits of fresh sea air.

Capel played an important role in the early years of Coco Chanel's fashion career. Deauville's popularity with the wealthy made the perfect backdrop for Coco's venture and it was there that Chanel opened her first boutique in 1913, once again with the help of her lover, Arthur "Boy" Capel.

The boutique was located on the fashionable Rue Gontaut-Biron, and it offered a range of simple and elegant clothes made from jersey, a fabric that was then mainly used for men's underwear. Chanel's designs were a stark departure from the heavily corseted and ornate women's fashion of the time, and they quickly caught the attention of stylish women, including Coco Chanel's close friend, the actress Gabrielle Dorziat.

Chanel continued to spend time in Deauville, where she drew inspiration from the sporty and casual style of the town's wealthy visitors. She also began to expand her business, opening a second boutique in the resort of Biarritz in 1915.

By the late 1920's all of fashion's finest houses had a presence in Deauville; Hermes, Schiaparell etc but Coco Chanel reigned supreme. Her ground breaking, wide leg trousers and striped jersey tops, that she herself had worn, when she first opened her shop, were now a staple of the fashionable set.

DEAUVILLE - Plage Fleurie. — La Promenade sur les Planches.

Deauville an early image

Chanel's success in Deauville helped to establish her reputation as a designer, and she went on to become one of the most influential figures in the fashion world. Today, Deauville continues to be a popular destination for fashion-conscious travellers, and the town still celebrates its connection to Chanel with a museum dedicated to her life and work.

'Boy' introduced her to the fashion industry and helped her establish contacts that would become important to her business. Capel's fashion sense also influenced Chanel's designs, and many of her early creations were inspired by his tailored and ultra-groomed style.

Despite their closeness, Chanel and Capel never married. It is believed that Capel intended to divorce his wife and marry Chanel, but tragically he died in a car accident in 1919 before he could do so. Chanel was devastated by his death and mourned him for many years after.

Capel's influence on Chanel can still be seen in her designs today, with the masculine-feminine aesthetic that she pioneered remaining a key feature of the Chanel brand. Their relationship also serves as a reminder of the complex and sometimes challenging personal relationships that can shape artistic and creative expression.

Despite the end of their romantic involvement, Coco and Balsan, had remained friends and he even provided some financial assistance to Chanel throughout her career.

It's hard to understand from the comfort of a 21st century perspective, just how far Coco had come in such a short time. Those difficult childhood experiences obviously helped shape her independent spirit and drive to succeed.

Chanel approximately 20 years old.

Coco The Style

Despite the fact, that Coco had left Balsan for Capel, the two men came together in a joint venture, enabling Coco to open her first shop on Rue Cambon, Paris in 1910. Chanel started out selling hats but these weren't the overblown fanciful hats of the Edwardian Paris'. The simple boaters she created, featured striped bands and compact decoration, they were a runaway success. Three years later she opened a store in Deauville a wealthy seaside resort.

This time it wasn't to sell just hats, this was a complete bespoke clothing range. At last, she could put her unique style into practice. No longer did women have to suffer being corseted to death, Coco's loose fit, stylishly cut clothes were an instant success.

Gradually she expanded its reach to include clothing, accessories, and fragrances, this was the start of the iconic fashion brand we know today.

Her first taste of clothing success came from a dress she fashioned out of an old jersey on a chilly day. In response to the many people who asked about where she got the dress, she offered to make one for them. "My fortune is built on that old

Coco at Deauville, France 'notice the hat'

jersey that I'd put on because it was cold in Deauville," she once told author Paul Morand

Her unique and simple designs, which included the iconic "little black dress," quickly caught the attention of the fashion elite and garnered her a reputation as an innovative and talented designer. In the 1920s, Chanel expanded her business to include clothing, accessories, and fragrances, solidifying her status as a major force in the fashion world. Her influence on women's fashion, particularly the popularization of a more comfortable and practical style, still remains significant to women. The original boutique on rue Cambon remains open to this day and is considered a historic landmark in the fashion world.

What set Chanel apart from other fashion designers of her time was her focus on comfort and simplicity. She broke away from the restrictive, corseted styles that were popular at the time and introduced designs that were relaxed and comfortable, yet still stylish. Her famous "little black dress" and tweed suits were part of a broader effort to create clothing that was functional and easy to wear, yet still chic and sophisticated.

In the 1920s, Chanel's fashion empire continued to grow, and she became one of the most influential figures in fashion. She opened a couture house in Paris, and her designs were sought after by women the world over. She was also an early adopter of new technologies, such as synthetic fabrics, which she used to create innovative and distinctive garments.

Despite the success of her fashion empire, Chanel faced many challenges over the years. She was forced to close her couture house during World War II, and her business suffered as a result. However, she bounced back in the 1950s, and her designs continued to be popular until her death in 1971.

Overall, Coco Chanel's early years laid the foundation for one of the most successful and influential fashion empires of all time. She will always be remembered as a pioneering figure who challenged traditional norms and paved the way for a new era in women's fashion.

Her designs were revolutionary for their time, as she incorporated masculine elements into women's fashion, such as pants and jersey fabrics. Coco's influence on the fashion world cannot be overstated, as she is credited with popularizing the "little black dress" and making it a staple in women's wardrobes.

Despite the success of her boutiques, Coco's life was far from perfect. Coco Chanel was a complex and driven individual. She was known for her independent spirit, pioneering attitude towards women's fashion, and her strong will. Chanel was also a businesswoman and marketing genius who revolutionized the fashion industry by popularizing a more comfortable, casual, and practical style for women. She had a sense of style and simplicity that simply emanated from every dress or accessory she created – it was and still is known simply, as, 'Chanel Style'.

She was a pioneering figure in the fashion industry and is widely considered as one of the most influential fashion designers of the 20th century.

Coco Chanel had many friends around Europe and particularly in London. She was a socialite and a prominent figure in the fashion world, and she had a wide network of acquaintances and friends in Europe and beyond. During her trips to London, she likely socialized with members of high society, fellow designers, and others in the fashion industry. Although it's not confirmed, it's

Chanel and ?

thought she stayed at the Ritz when in London –
she loved luxury and there was none more
sumptuous than the Ritz.

Chanel was known for her strong personality and her ability to charm those around her, so it is likely that she made many new friends during her visits to London and cultivated close relationships with those she met. Her connections in London would have also given her the opportunity to learn about new trends and gain inspiration for her designs, helping her to stay at the forefront of fashion during her career.

In terms of her character, Coco Chanel was known for her strong and independent spirit. She was a self-made woman who rose to fame and success in a male-dominated industry. She was a rebel who defied traditional gender roles and expectations, and she was not afraid to challenge the status quo.

Coco Chanel was also known for her impeccable sense of style and her attention to detail. She was a perfectionist and was known for being highly selective about the materials she used in her designs. She had a minimalist approach to fashion and was known for her use of clean lines, simple shapes, and neutral colors.

She also possessed a strong work ethic and an innovative spirit. She was always experimenting with new ideas and pushing the boundaries of what was considered fashionable. She was a visionary who transformed the fashion industry and paved the way for many other designers.

Coco Chanel is credited with creating the LBD (The Little Black Dress) in the 1920s and it has since become a symbol of elegance, sophistication, and femininity. The LBD is versatile and can be worn to a variety of events, from casual gatherings to formal parties, and can be paired with different accessories to create a range of different looks – in short, the perfect accessory.

While the origins of the black can be traced back to the Victorian era, it was primarily known as the colour of mourning, popularized by 'The Little Lady in Black' – Queen Victoria. Coco once again, turned tradition on its head and made it a fashion must have.

Coco Chanel introduced the little black dress in the 1920s, during a time when fashion was beginning to evolve from the restrictive and ornate styles of the past to more practical, streamlined designs. The LBD was a departure from the brightly coloured, heavily embellished garments of the time, and instead was simple, elegant, and understated.

Chanel's first little black dress was a simple, knee-length shift dress made from wool or crepe fabric, with long sleeves and a straight silhouette. It was a departure from the frilly, voluminous dresses that were popular at the time and was designed to be versatile enough to be worn to a variety of occasions.

The little black dress quickly became a hit, as women embraced its simplicity, versatility, and timeless elegance. Over the years, the LBD has been reinvented and reinterpreted by countless designers, but the basic concept remains the same. Today, it is a wardrobe staple that is synonymous with effortless chic and is considered an essential piece for any stylish woman's wardrobe.

In the 1920s, Chanel took her thriving business to new heights. She launched her first perfume, Chanel No. 5, which was the first to feature a designer's name. This quote from Coco became her most profound statement - Perfume "is the unseen, unforgettable, ultimate accessory of fashion. . . . that heralds your arrival and prolongs your departure."

A rare early advert for Chanel's iconic No 5

The fragrance was in fact backed by department store owner Théophile Bader and businessmen Pierre and Paul Wertheimer, with Chanel developing a close friendship with Pierre.

A deal was ultimately negotiated where the Wertheimer business would take in 70 percent of Chanel No. 5 profits for producing the perfume at their factories, with Bader receiving 20 percent and Chanel herself, receiving just 10 percent.

This may seem a rather derisory sum to receive but the impact on her core business, in what we now call PR terms, was beyond price.

Overall, Coco Chanel was a complex and multifaceted individual who left a lasting impact on the fashion world. She was a trailblazer who challenged traditional norms and paved the way for a new era of fashion.

Despite her success, she was often surrounded by controversy, including her relationships with high-ranking members of the Nazi party during World War II. However, despite these controversies, she remains one of the most influential figures in fashion history.

Here are just a few of this lady's sharper quotes:

"A girl should be two things: classy and fabulous.
"

"A woman has the age she deserves."

"A women who doesn't wear perfume has no future."

"I don't know why women want any of the things men have when one the things that women have is men."

"Look for the woman in the dress. If there is no woman, there is no dress."

"Dress shabbily and they remember the dress; dress impeccably and they remember the woman." -Coco Chanel

"A woman is closest to being naked when she is well dressed." -Coco Chanel.

Why Two Cs

The essence of any good logo or business brand is its recognition. In most cases, these established company logos were the brainchild of the original owner or the work of a clever advertising company.

Take a random selection of household names and you will see they all have one quality in common, they are almost invisible in their approach to marketing, They, are somehow, almost subliminally embedded in our consciousness.

For instance, the flowing script of Coca Cola or Pepsi, the twin Rs of Rolls Royce, VW, the smooth script of Cadburys or the daisy of Mary Quant. These brand insignias follow through the product line. Take Ford for instance, no matter the size of a vehicle, be it a family saloon or a truck, the logo is still the smooth Ford text, as created by its founder Henry Ford. There are endless examples of clever, instinctive logos, that somehow sum up the brand they. so cleverly. represent.

With most of the known brands their origins are easy to trace. There are always, of course, exceptions to the rule and none more so than the famous double C - the distinctive trademark of Chanel.

As with so many things in Chanel's life, there is always a very clear demarcation between public and private information.

We know that the double C logo was first used by Coco on or around the launch time of her famous No 5 perfume. Though there is little visible evidence that it formed part of the initial packaging.

What is less clear and was never revealed by Chanel, was why the back-to-back letter C, was actually chosen. We know that Chanel had a life-long love of emblems and heraldic patterns but what was the driving force behind this choice?

The origin of this iconic logo was, is and will probably, always remain a subject of intrigue and speculation.

With Chanel's visionary designs and innovative approach, it comes as no surprise that her logo would be equally special. It's worth remembering, that by the early 1920s, Coco was moving in very lofty social circles. Her connection with 'Boy' Capel and later, the duke of Westminster, meant she would have been heavily influenced by tradition. Many of these people could trace their coat of arms, cyphers and heraldic shields back as far as the 16th century. Chanel had no such lineage, in fact, her background couldn't have been further from these entitled people.

She sought to create a logo that would capture the essence of her brand and establish a lasting visual identity and also, in some way, become her own 'coat of arms'.

Over the years there have been several attempts to establish the origins of this clever logo.

The first explanation seemed totally plausible, the double C logo, simply represented Coco Chanel's initials. The fact that it was never denied or confirmed, left this explanation hanging in the air.

The second explanation was equally believable, the intertwined initials of her and her lover, Arthur Edward Capel, known as "Boy." Capel, who we know, played such a significant role in Chanel's life and career, both as a romantic partner and as a financial backer. The intertwining Cs were a personal homage to Capel and served as a constant reminder of their relationship, following his tragic death.

A further explanation goes back to the Aubazine Abbey Convent, where she spent several of her formative years. Chanel claimed her logo was inspired by the shapes she saw in the stained-glass windows at the orphanage. On closer inspection, this may have some creedence. Unlike most ecclesiastical buildings, there was no colour, instead, the swirling patterns were plain black, set against clear glass. They do indeed look vaguely reminiscent of the C logo.

Others have suggested that Chanel simply copied Catherine de Medicis Monogram which also happens to be interlocking C's. Whilst there is speculation that she loved the initials used at Chateau de Cremat, the home of her friend Irène Bretz in Nice, where Coco was a frequent visitor in the 1920s.

As with most things with Coco Chanel, you were only told what, she wanted you to know,

One thing is well documented however, as Coco Chanel's influence grew, so did the prominence of the double C logo. It became a defining element of her brand and was incorporated into various designs. The logo appeared on clothing, accessories, and even on the buttons of Chanel's iconic tweed suits around 1924.

The simplicity and symmetry of the interlocking Cs lend a sense of balance and timeless elegance to the logo and by extension the company itself. Devoid of excessive ornamentation, the logo has withstood the test of time and remains relevant in the ever-changing world of fashion.

Coco The Pioneer

Coco was a feminist long before the phrase was invented. Strong and determined, she carried herself well and found little problem in attracting wealthy members of the opposite sex. Her personal life has been well documented and it's known that she had several love affairs throughout her life.

Following Capel's death, Chanel had a brief fling with Pavlovich of Russia, who was a cousin of Tsar Nicholas II. Chanel also had an affair with the composer Igor Stravinsky, which reportedly inspired one of his ballets, "The Rite of Spring."

One of the most notable and significant relationships in Coco Chanel's life however, was her love affair with the Duke of Westminster, Hugh Richard Arthur Grosvenor. The Duke of Westminster was one of the richest men in the world at the time and was known for his extravagance and flamboyant lifestyle.

Apart from owning great swathes of property in London (including the American Embassy, Grosvenor Square), he owned a 700 acre estate in Scotland (Rosehall) and a stately pile outside

Chester, Cheshire (Eaton Hall). This was the scene of many shooting or house parties. His reputation as a generous host was legendary.

The estate was his ancestral home, Eaton Hall in Cheshire, a 54-bedroomed, red brick, stately homeset in 11,000 acres (45 km2) of parkland, plus extensive gardens and stables. The main residence was equally impressive. There were major works of art on display including paintings by: Goya, Rubens, Rembrandt and Raphael.

The Duke held a lifetime interest in hunting and owned several lodges, both in Scotland and France. He also regularly attended the races, including the famous Chester Racecourse (known as the Roodie).

The love affair between Coco Chanel and the Duke of Westminster is said to have begun in the 1920s, when the two first met in London, though others say it was Monte Carlo. The relationship was a whirlwind romance, and the two became inseparable. At the time, Chanel was at the height of her fame as a fashion designer and was known for her sleek, minimalist designs that were in stark contrast to the frilly, ornate fashions of the time.

The Duke of Westminster, who was actually between marriages, was drawn to Chanel's independence and creative spirit, and the two quickly became romantically involved.

They were often seen together at high-end social events and were considered to be one of the most glamorous couples of their time.

When not in the glare of publicity, the couple shared their quieter moments at Rosehall in the Scottish highlands. Here they would ride, fish and hunt.

As an aside to the happier association and in complete contrast, the Estate fell into disrepair and remained abandoned for 60 years – it was recently sold for three million pounds and is expected to become a country house hotel – what goes round etc.

Coco Chanel & Winston Churchill

The relationship between Coco Chanel and the Duke of Westminster was an unconventional one, as Chanel was known for her strong, assertive personality and was not afraid to challenge societal norms. She was also fiercely independent and was not interested in being seen as just another of the Duke's many mistresses. Instead, she wanted to be seen as an equal partner in the relationship and was not afraid to speak her mind and assert her opinions.

Despite their differences, the Duke and Coco had a passionate and long-lasting love affair that lasted for the best part of a decade. They travelled the world together, visiting exotic locations and enjoying the luxurious lifestyle that came with the Duke's immense wealth and status. On one occasion the Duke presented her with a basket of specially grown exotic fruits, lovingly grown in glass houses at Eaton Hall. Beneath the exotic fruit, was an even more exotic gift, a sparkling green emerald, a token of his profound love.

Eaton Hall, Chester, Cheshire.

Chanel was also introduced to the high society of Europe and became friends with many of the era's most influential figures, including writers, artists, and politicians such as Winston Churchill.

Even during this period, Coco was looking at the world of the English aristocracy with a commercial eye. As previously stated, Coco was an excellent horsewoman and she attended hunts and weekend parties. Her imagination was fired by the traditional attire worn at these country weekends. The traditional tweed, hacking jackets and coats, became the basis of her tweed two-piece suits and over-capes. Another prime example of the mind that never stopped.

However, the relationship between Chanel and the Duke of Westminster was not without its challenges. The Duke's marriage and the societal constraints of the time put pressure on the couple to keep their relationship a secret, which was difficult for Coco, who was used to being in the public eye. Additionally, the Duke's playboy reputation and his many other romantic entanglements caused friction in the relationship.

Despite these challenges, the affair between Coco Chanel and the Duke of Westminster continued until the early 1930s. After the Duke's death, Chanel continued to be one of the most influential figures in the fashion world and remained a key figure in the fashion industry for many years to come. Her relationship with the Duke of Westminster may have been unconventional, but it was an important part of her life and a testament to her strength, independence, and creativity.

In conclusion, Coco Chanel's love affair with the Duke of Westminster was a significant event in both of their lives and in the world of fashion and society. Their relationship was a testament to the power of love and the ability of two people from vastly different backgrounds to come together and against all the odds, create something rather meaningful.

Fast forward to the mid 1930s, this was not a good decade for Chanel. First came the depression, then the outbreak of war. She was forced to close her salon and effectively went into forced retirement for the duration of the hostilities. More controversially, her close 'friendship' with the powerful businessman and Nazi spy Hans Gunther von Dincklage (you'd have thought the name would have given him away), which was widely criticized in France due to von Dincklage's affiliation with the Nazi party, did her reputation no good.

Despite these relationships, Chanel lived much of her life as a single woman and never married. She dedicated her life to her work and her fashion empire, which remains one of the most iconic and successful fashion brands in the world today.

The pictures of the day show Coco Chanel as a small fine-featured woman, attractive but not a radiant beauty is somewhat misleading. Whilst research this book, I stumbled upon some earlier images of Coco, her face was fuller, her eyes wide and the mouth more sensual, it was easy to see the attraction. That coupled with such a strong personality obviously appealed to these men.

I have a theory when it comes to rich men and strong women. How often do we see eminent men, tycoons, film stars, even royalty, totally brought to heel by what some would say, strong and determined women. I can only assume that, when life has gifted you with every material advantage, the fascination of a self-made woman, must hold a powerful sway.

Witness the actions of Hugh Grosvenor, he was a serial womanizer – why Coco? The same question arises with the Duke of Windsor and Wallace Simpson. Fast forward to the present day and witness the complete emasculation of one Harry Windsor – Duke of Sussex. There is a pattern, quite what it is? I'm not sure but Coco had it in spades.

She was known to have a passion for the finer things in life, including travel, food, and wine, so this would chime with her relationships with wealthy and powerful men.

Here are just some of her favorite places and food:

Places:

Paris:
Coco Chanel lived in Paris for much of her life and considered it her home. She opened her first boutique in the city and was considered a leading figure in the Parisian fashion scene.

Deauville:
Chanel was a frequent visitor to the seaside town of Deauville, where she had a summer home. She was known to enjoy the town's relaxed atmosphere, beaches, and horse racing events.

Monte-Carlo-Monaco:
Coco Chanel loved to travel, and Monte Carlo was one of her favorite destinations. She was known to enjoy the glamour and luxury of the town and was often seen at the casino.

Food:
French-cuisine:
Coco Chanel was a big fan of traditional French cuisine and was known to enjoy dishes such as coq au vin, bouillabaisse, and croissants.

Seafood:
Chanel loved seafood and was often seen enjoying oysters and other shellfish.

Wine:
Coco Chanel was known to be a fan of wines in general, though it's documented that Champagne and red wines were her favourite tipple.

These were just some of Coco Chanel's favorite places and food. She was a true lover of the finer things in life, and her impeccable taste certainly impacted on her life.

Here are a few more 'Coco' quotes:

"There is no fashion for the old." -Coco Chanel

"I don't do fashion, I am fashion." -Coco Chanel

"I like fashion to go down to the street, but I can't accept that it should originate there." -

"I was the one who changed, it wasn't fashion. I was the one who was in fashion."

"There goes a woman who knows all the things that can be taught and none of the things that cannot be taught."

"Fashion is not something that exists in dresses only. Fashion is in the sky, in the street, fashion has to do with ideas, the way we live, what is happening."

"Fashion is made to become unfashionable." -

"The best things in life are free. The second best things are very, very expensive."

Coco was adored in many circles and certainly respected for her vision and determination. On the flip side, not everyone loved her and she certainly didn't love certain notable figures – one person who fell squarely into this category was Elsa Schiaparelli.

Coco Chanel and Elsa Schiaparelli were both prominent fashion designers during the interwar period, and their styles and philosophies were totally different from one another. Chanel was known for her sleek, understated designs that emphasized comfort and practicality, while Schiaparelli was known for her more whimsical designs that incorporated elements of art and surrealism into her work. Almost the Dali of fashion.

The rivalry between Chanel and Schiaparelli was rooted in their differences and their desire to be the preeminent fashion designer of their time. Chanel saw Schiaparelli as a threat to her dominance in the industry, and Schiaparelli felt that Chanel's designs were too simple and boring.

In addition, the two women had different views on femininity and the role of women in society, which contributed to their dislike of one another. Chanel was a strong, independent woman who challenged traditional gender roles, while Schiaparelli, who had a privileged upbringing in Italy, was known for her more playful, fantastical designs that celebrated women's creativity and imagination.

Ultimately, the rivalry between Chanel and Schiaparelli was a testament to the competitiveness and creativity of the fashion industry during the interwar period, and their differing styles and philosophies continue to influence fashion today. Chanel mocked her lack of any formal training or real dressmaking skills, calling her 'The Draper'. This was a reference to the way she simply draped materials over a model, then instructed her workers to follow the fashion line. Schiaparelli in turn, called Chanel the 'The Little Hat Maker'.

Additionally, Chanel was known for her temper and sharp tongue, so it's likely that there were many people she simply did not get along with.

World War I

During the World War I , Coco Chanel closed down her famous fashion house in Paris and relocated to the resort town of Deauville in Normandy, France. It was during this time that she began designing and selling simple, practical clothing for women, as a response to the severe shortages and restrictions of materials caused by the war.

She introduced comfortable, casual pieces such as jersey dresses, trousers, and comfortable hats, which were a stark contrast to the tight corsets and heavy skirts that were fashionable at the time. Her designs were a hit with the wealthy women of Deauville and she soon became known for her minimalist, yet elegant style.

In addition to her fashion work, it is alleged that Chanel also became involved in espionage during the war, working as a spy for both the British and German intelligence services.

While this has been questioned, one thing was in no doubt, Coco knew how to socialize and enjoy herself.

During the time that Coco Chanel was in Deauville, she found ways to entertain herself and socialise with the wealthy and fashionable people who visited the town. Deauville was a popular destination for the rich and famous during this time, and Chanel was able to network and make connections with influential people. She also became involved in the local horse racing scene and was a regular at the races, where she could watch the horse races and mingle with the other spectators.

In addition, Chanel was known to attend the local casino, where she could gamble and meet with others. She was also an avid bridge player and would host bridge parties at her villa.

Overall, while in Deauville, Chanel was able to stay active and engaged with the fashionable and wealthy social scene, and these experiences likely played a role in shaping her personal style and her understanding of what people wanted in their fashion and lifestyle.

Despite the challenges and controversies of the war years, Coco Chanel continued to innovate and inspire in the fashion world. After the war, she reopened her fashion house in Paris and introduced her iconic perfume, Chanel No. 5, which remains popular to this day.

It was during this time that Chanel established her reputation as one of the most influential fashion designers of the 20th century, and her iconic style, blending practicality and sophistication, continues to inspire designers and fashion lovers around the world.

The Inter-War Years

The years between the first and second world wat found Chanel in Hollywood. In February 1931 at the invitation of Goldwyn Films. She was asked to create several outfits for two films – Tonight or Never in 1931 and The Greeks Had a Word For It in 1932.

The original offer from Sam Goldwyn was a million-dollar contract to make costumes twice a year. As you would expect, the designs were very chic, obviously too chic for Hollywood, as she was never invited back.

There was a rub off from this adventure though. In 1938 she worked on a series of French films, they included;

1938 Quai e brumes (Port of Shadows)

1939 La re'gle du jeu 9The Rules of The Game)

And much later in 1961-

L'Anne'e demiere a' Marienbad (Last Year at Marianbad)

In these inter-war years, Chanel busied herself on many projects but probably non dearer to her heart than building Villa La Pausa on the cliffs of the exclusive neighbourhood of La Toracca near the town of Roquebrune-Cap-Martin, on the beautiful French Riviera. This was the only building she was known to have project managed.

Discreetly tucked away between Monte Carlo and Menton, towards the eastern tip of the Côte d'Azur, Roquebrune-Cap-Martin was once the private hunting grounds of Monaco's reigning family.

The villa was built for Coco Chanel and the Duke of Westminster in 1928 by the architect Robert Streitz. The brief was for a sophisticated but simple residence. La Pausa has all the hallmarks of Chanels design and creative input. The design was said to be inspired by the convent orphanage she attended in her early years. In particular, she insisted on a replica of the stone staircase she remembered from the orphanage of her youth.

Chanel made repeated trips from Paris to the South of France to supervise the work, paying attention to every detail of its interior design.

Some things remained in the memory of Coco, like the austere black and white of the convent. This she applied to many aspects of the villa, not least, the white walls, the ironwork, the small paned glass windows and doors. Whether this was done in homage, or a simple form of comfort, is not known. Once again, she took all her secrets and inner thoughts with her when she left this world.

The villa was built over four levels and had a floor space of approx. 10,000 sq feet, perched high on a hill, with panoramic views, overlooking the coast and nearby Menton, Monaco, Cap d'Ail and Saint-Jean-Cap-Ferrat.

This became her principal residence on the French Riviera from 1929 to 1953.

The small entrance has a Romanesque vaulted brick ceiling and lights decorated with the crown from the Dukes' Westminster's coat of arms.

La Pausa contains three wings that face onto a shaded courtyard. The property was set out over three living rooms, a dining room, seven en-suite bedrooms, two kitchens, a covered terrace and staff quarters.

Quite an impressive dwelling even by local standards. The rooms featured a number of 16th-century English oak pieces, these were gifted to her by the Duke of Westminster. English oak was also used for floors and panelling. The large reception rooms were lit by wrought-iron chandeliers from Spain.

On the lower level, she built changing rooms for the swimming pool (though no pool was visible) bath and laundry room. And of course, the obligatory staff quarters.

The interior was best described as cool and neutral with sumptuous sofas and carefully selected pieces, that simply complemented such a fine house. The garden is equally simple. Planted with lavender and rosemary and filtered with smoky light through centuries-old olives, it had an established and wistful feeling to it.

American Vogue carried a profile on La-Pausa in 1938, in which the garden was described as containing "groves of orange trees, great slopes of lavender, masses of purple iris, and huge clusters of climbing roses." The designer Roderick Cameron said that at La Pausa, Chanel was the first to cultivate lavender and other flora previously regarded as "poor plants".

It would be inconceivable, having built such a glorious residence, that Coco wouldn't want to share it with her friends. Coco was known to have a wide circle of friends, they included figures from the world of art, literature, music, politics, and society. They included such names as:

Pablo Picasso: The renowned Spanish painter and sculptor visited Chanel's villa, bringing his unique artistic insights to any conversation over a lengthy lunch or dinner.

Staying on the artistic theme, Salvador Dalí was another visitor to the Villa. The surrealist artist found inspiration in the tranquil surroundings of the villa and engaged in discussions with Coco Chanel, fostering a cross-pollination of ideas.

Chanel & guests – Coco can be seen nearest the window

The acclaimed Russian composer Igor Stravinsky: and conductor was known to be a regular visitor to La Pausa. Their meetings lead to a collaboration between him and Chanel in the design of costumes for his ballet "Le Baiser de la Fée" (The Fairy's Kiss).

Jean Cocteau: The French writer, filmmaker, and visual artist loved Chanel's villa and found the conversations on art, literature, and philosophy stimulating and enlightening.

The prominent French author and Nobel laureate André Gide, visited the villa. Someone who was always willing to add his intellectual insights to any discussions.

Marcel Proust, the acclaimed French novelist and essayist found solace and inspiration in the serene environment of the villa, engaging in conversations with Chanel and other guests.

Winston Churchill, the British Prime Minister sought refuge at the villa during World War II, forming a unique bond with Coco Chanel and benefiting from the villa's tranquil setting.

Following the death of Hugh Grosvenor in 1953, Chanel sold La Pausa to the Hungarian publisher Emery Reeves. In the years 1956 – 1958, The former British Prime Minister Winston Churchill, spent roughly a third of each year at La Pausa, as a guest of Reeves and his wife, Wendy. The tranquil surrounding proved the perfect location for him to write and edit a huge part of his acclaimed work, 'History of the English Speaking Peoples'.

World War II

At the outbreak of the second World War, Coco Chanel was at the height of her fame. Sadly, the Second World War would drastically change the course of her life and career.

As the war began to escalate in Europe, many of Chanel's wealthy clients fled to safer areas, leaving her fashion business in a state of decline. In 1939, she closed her couture house and retired to the Hotel Ritz in Paris, where she lived on and off for the duration of the war. The downside of this arrangement was, The Ritz was one of the headquarters for the German army.

It's here, she became involved with a German military officer, Baron Hans Günther von Dincklage, who introduced her to high-ranking Nazi officials. Chanel was known to have close ties with these officials, and some even claimed that she was a spy for the German intelligence agency, the Abwehr. Others have since suggested, she was in fact, feeding valuable information back to Winston Churchll, the wartime leader.

Despite these rumors, there is little concrete evidence to support the claim that Chanel was actually a spy. However, her association with the Nazi regime during the war led to her being viewed as a collaborator by many in the years following the war.

What's less documented is the fact that she split her time between Paris and Switzerland during the war years. In the immediate aftermath of the war, the populace of France was wreaking revenge on suspected female collaborators were being rounded up, beaten and their heads shaved as a mark of shame. This was never going to happen to Coco. After the war, she lived semi-permanently in Switzerland until around 1954. Spending most of her time in Lausanne, a city in the French-speaking part of Switzerland.

During this time, Coco continued to work in the fashion industry. She created several collections and continued to design clothing and accessories. She also continued to promote her brand and worked on expanding her business. Despite the challenges posed by the war and the limited resources available in Switzerland, Coco Chanel managed to maintain her position as a leading figure in the world of fashion.

In addition to her work in fashion, Coco Chanel also used her time in Switzerland to reflect on her life and her place in the world. She became interested in spirituality and studied subjects such as astrology, numerology, and the cabala. She also read extensively and spent time in meditation and introspection.

Overall, Coco Chanel's time in Switzerland was an important period in her life and career. Despite the difficulties she faced, her time in Switzerland allowed her to develop new perspectives and insights that would shape her work for years to come.

She also lived at her country house in Roquebrune for a time.

Her reputation, however, would prove to be a significant obstacle when she attempted to revive her fashion business after the war ended. Not until the 1950s did she fully shake of this tag.

In early 1954, at the age of 70 Chanel made a triumphant return to the fashion world. She first received scathing reviews from French critics, in England, the fashion industry and critics were no kinder. Her redemption came from the most unexpected place – The USA. The higher echelons of American society couldn't get enough of Chanel. Her feminine and easy-fitting designs soon won over the American female and the old practice of visiting Paris for the 'new season' returned.

Reopening her couture house and presenting her first collection in over a decade. Coco was still haunted by the accusations of wartime collaboration. Nevertheless, she continued to design and run her business until her death in 1971.

In conclusion, Coco Chanel's life and career were deeply impacted by the events of the Second World War. Despite her initial retirement, she managed to revive her fashion business and cement her place as one of the most influential designers of the 20th century.

The 1950s

The 1950s were a time of great change and innovation in fashion. The Second World War had just ended, and women were starting to break free from the constraints of the past. They were looking for more practical, comfortable, and stylish clothing that reflected the new spirit of the times. Coco Chanel was perfectly positioned to meet these needs, and she continued to innovate and push the boundaries of what was considered fashionable.

House of Chanel Paris

One of the most notable things about Coco Chanel's designs in the 1950s was her use of luxurious materials and simple, elegant lines. She favored materials such as cashmere, silk, and tweed, and her designs were often accented with pearls, chains, and other elegant details. This simple, sophisticated look was a stark contrast to the elaborate, ornate styles of the past, and it was a major influence on fashion in the 1950s.

Another important aspect of Coco Chanel's work in the 1950s was her focus on comfort and practicality. She was one of the first designers to incorporate comfortable, stretchy materials into her designs, and she was also one of the first to introduce pants as a fashionable item for women.

This focus on comfort and practicality was a major factor in the popularity of her designs, and it helped to usher in a new era of fashion that was more focused on the needs and desires of women.

Finally, Coco Chanel was also known for her pioneering work in fragrance and beauty products. In the 1950s, she extended her fragrances, while Chanel No. 5 remained her most popular and recognizable fragrance. Her beauty products were similarly innovative and luxurious, and they helped to cement her reputation as a leader in the fashion and beauty industries.

The number 5 had a special significance for Chanel. From her earliest days as an orphan at the Abbey, the number five had potent associations for her. For Chanel, the number five was especially esteemed as signifying the pure embodiment of a thing, its spirit, its mystic meaning. The paths that led Chanel to the cathedral for daily prayers were laid out in circular patterns repeating the number five.

Her affinity for the number five co-mingled with the abbey gardens, and by extension the lush surrounding hillsides.

So, it's hardly surprising, that, when in 1920, she was presented with several small glass vials containing sample scents numbered 1 to 5 and 20 to 24 for her assessment, she chose the fifth vial. Chanel told her master perfumer, Ernest Beaux, whom she had commissioned to develop a new fragrance, "I present my dress collections on the fifth of May, the fifth month of the year and so we will let this sample number five keep the name it has already, it will bring good luck." If ever there was an understatement – this has to be it.

In typical Chanel style, less was more. She envisioned a design that would be a world away from the overelaborate fussiness of the crystal fragrance bottles available. These were in her view, totally alien to the purity of the product. She was selling the content, not the bottle. Her bottle would be "pure transparency, an invisible bottle". It's thought that the bottle design was inspired by the rectangular beveled lines of the Charvet toiletry bottles, which came complete with a smart leather travelling case, as favoured by one of her earlier lovers, Arthur Capel. Others say it was a whisky bottle, with its clean cut, angular appearance that sparked her imagination. Whatever the inspiration, it worked.

No 5 was an instant success and over the years has brought many comments from her rich and famous clients - like this one from the screen icon Marilyn Monroe – who famously said in an interview that she wore -

"five drops of Chanel No. 5" and nothing else in bed. "I don't want to say nude," she said, "but it's the truth."

Quotes like this cemented Chanel's place in the hearts and minds of perfume buyers for decades to come. Even the most hapless male knew that he couldn't go wrong with a bottle of No 5 for his favourite lady.

A Chanel Portrait

Another 50s favourite, was the Chanel quilted little black bag, also known as the Chanel 2.55. first introduced by Coco Chanel in February 1955. This iconic bag quickly became a staple in the fashion world and has since remained one of the most popular and recognizable handbags of all time. The quilted leather design, interlocking "CC" logo, and versatile style of the Chanel 2.55 have made it a timeless classic that continues to be in high demand today.

In conclusion, Coco Chanel was a major force in the fashion world in the 1950s. Her innovative designs, focus on comfort and practicality, and luxurious materials and beauty products were a major influence on fashion during this decade, and she remains one of the most famous and respected fashion designers of all time.

Her gift to the world of fashion was – Simplicity. Whether it was the plain black dress (TLBD), the black shiny cosmetic containers, the simple No5 she used for her signature perfume or the slimmed down tailoring - Chanel really did epitomize the quote - Less is More.

Chanel In The 1960s

The 1950s had seen a gradual shift in fashion, a nudge here, a push there but in essence, it was still the French who dictated style and taste.

All that changed in the 1960s. America had a bright new President and his glamourous wife. They were the star couple on a rather dull world stage. Jaqueline Kennedy set the style, others followed. The first lady was not averse to a bit of Chanel and wore it like nobody else could. Despite the tragic assignation of JFK and the subsequent shock waves felt across the globe, the world did recover and some form of normality resumed.

All that changed around 1965 when Paris lost its mantle as the fashion centre of the world. There was a new kid on the block – London.

The advent of the Mini Skirt and many other innovations by the hugely talented Mary Quant, put London squarely on the fashion map. The whole fashion scene exploded with people such a Zandra Rhodes, Biba and countless others now showcasing their talents via Carnaby Street and the Kings Road. The Beatles went hippy and

Twiggy was on every magazine cover. London, not Paris, was the epicentre of all things cool.

Chanel was quoted at the time as hating Mary Quant, saying 'All anybody asks me is what I think of Mary Quant?' For someone of Chanel's stature within the fashion industry, this must have been somewhat irksome. I suspect the word hate is a little strong. She would certainly have felt challenged, it has been well documented that Chanel never praised any other designer.

While their styles and approaches differed greatly, both played influential roles in shaping the fashion landscape of their respective eras. Coco Chanel, known for her timeless elegance and sophisticated designs, and Mary Quant, recognized as a pioneer of the Swinging Sixties and the miniskirt. They may have held contrasting views on fashion and femininity but in a strange sort of way, they were within their respective periods, actually singing from the same hymn sheet. So, what did Coco Chanel actually think of Mary Quant and her impact on fashion?

Coco, like Mary, had been a revolutionary figure in the fashion world. Her philosophy focused on simplicity, comfort, and elegance. Chanel's designs aimed to liberate women from restrictive corsets and embrace a more practical and modern aesthetic. She believed in clean lines, tailored silhouettes, and the use of luxurious fabrics. This could have come from the Mary Quant textbook of fashion.

Their similarities were, on closer inspection, far greater than one would first assume. Quant's designs were characterized by their playful, youthful, and avant-garde nature but she too, was an advocate of clothes that allowed freedom of movement for her clients. She introduced daring cuts, bold colours, and eye-catching patterns, often challenging societal norms and conventions. Quant's most notable contribution was obviously the popularization of the miniskirt, which revolutionized women's fashion.

Given Coco Chanel's strong convictions about elegance and timeless style, it's likely that she at first, had mixed opinions about Mary Quant's aesthetic choices. Chanel valued refinement and a certain timelessness in her designs, which stood in stark contrast to Quant's embrace of the rapidly changing trends of the Swinging Sixties. Chanel's belief in classic elegance may have made her skeptical of Quant's unconventional and bold designs.

Moreover, Chanel was a firm believer in the idea that fashion should reflect the times and adapt to the needs of modern women. While she championed liberation from traditional constraints, Chanel emphasized that comfort should never be sacrificed for style. In this regard, she might have appreciated Quant's emphasis on comfort and practicality in her designs. Quant's rejection of the corseted and structured clothing of previous eras aligned with Chanel's vision of freedom in fashion.

Chanel was nothing if not perceptive. Following the initial shock of the new, Chanel quickly realized that this young lady wasn't going away any day soon. She was sharp enough to adapt to the unstoppable force that Mary had become. Chanel was also a businesswoman who clearly understood the importance of branding and exclusivity. Her fashion house, Chanel, was synonymous with luxury and sophistication.

Quant, on the other hand, embraced a more democratic approach to fashion. She aimed to make her designs accessible to a wider audience through affordable mass production. This contrast in branding strategies might have made Chanel view Quant's approach as diluting the exclusivity associated with high fashion.

Obviously not above adopting the Mini to promote the Chanel brand – a nod to Quant.

Coco was above all, a realist, she soon realized something had to be done and quickly. She created subtle changes, almost as a nod to Quant and also as a direct response to the requests of her clients. Women who rather liked what was happening in London and were looking for a slightly more chic version of the Quant look.

Among those changes, the principle one was the skirt length, Chanel's skirts became shorter but not too short. The question of colour was addressed by creating pinks, blues and greens of varying hues into her range. In addition, the two-piece outfit also became a staple of Coco's offering.

In terms of the French fashion houses adaptation of the London look, Chanel was first off the blocks. Some of the other main players in Paris took a little too long to grasp the concept and the opportunities it offered.

Another aspect to consider is the generational and cultural divide between Chanel and Quant. Chanel was a figure who came to prominence in the early 20th century, while Quant made her mark in the rapidly changing and youth-oriented 1960s. Chanel's designs resonated with the post-World War I era, reflecting the desire for simplicity and elegance after a period of upheaval. Quant, on the other hand, captured the spirit of the Swinging Sixties, a time of rebellion, social change, and youth empowerment. These differences might have contributed to a divergence in their views on fashion and style.

Chanel portrait - She was her own best advert

In conclusion, it is challenging to definitively ascertain Coco Chanel's thoughts on Mary Quant, as there is limited evidence of direct statements or interactions between the two designers. However, based on Chanel's design philosophy and the contrasting nature of their styles, it can be inferred that she might have held reservations about Quant's avant-garde and trend-driven approach. While Chanel valued elegance, timelessness, and exclusivity, Quant embraced experimentation, youthfulness, and accessibility. Nonetheless, both designers left an indelible mark on the fashion industry, shaping the course of fashion for generations to come.

So, on reflection, they probably had more in common than they realized. Both understood the essence of design, they both started their respective careers and early retail in millinery, both created free-style clothing – clothing with women in mind.

While as stated, many fashion houses struggled to adapt to these new styles, Chanel was quick to embrace the changes taking place.

It has to be said that Mary quant's view of Chanel was a little more charitable. She firmly believed that few designers, including herself, would have been as successful as they were, without the ground-breaking vision of Coco Chanel.

Now that's nicer isn't it ?

The ultimate Chanel Look

The fashion house, which had long been known for its classic and timeless designs, saw the opportunity to update its image and appeal to a new generation of customers.

In the early 1960s, Chanel introduced a line of tweed suits with shorter hemlines and boxy jackets, which quickly became a hit among young women. These suits were a departure from the traditional Chanel look and helped to establish the brand as one that was willing to take risks and evolve with the times.

Another key moment for Chanel during this time was the launch of its iconic "Moon Bag," which was inspired by the space race and featured a distinctive crescent-shaped handle. This new design was in stark contrast to the traditional Chanel handbags, and its bold look helped to position the brand as a leader in contemporary fashion.

Overall, Chanel's ability to adapt to the changing fashions of the 1960s and embrace the new styles of London helped to cement its position as one of the world's most prestigious and influential fashion houses. The brand's ability to stay relevant and contemporary, while also maintaining its classic roots, is one of the key reasons it survived this upheaval in fashion.

Chanel had been quick to shift focus but while adapting swiftly to the new, she continued to produce her signature pieces, such as the tweed suit and the quilted handbag and introduced new designs, such as the Chanel logo-emblazoned buttons on her clothing and the famous C on other items. The essence of her clothing took on a more trendy look. She experimented with brighter colours and shorter skirts etc.

Chanel also expanded her brand into new areas, including the introduction of ready-to-wear clothing and accessories. She began to cater to a younger, more modern customer who sought effortless style and versatility in their wardrobe. This shift was reflected in her designs, which became less formal and more relaxed, with a focus on simple, clean lines.

In addition to her fashion work, Chanel continued to be a prominent figure in the social and cultural scene of the 1960s. She was known for her independent spirit and her refusal to follow the traditional rules of society, which made her a role model for many women of the time.

Despite her advanced age, Chanel remained an active and influential force in the fashion world throughout the 1960s. Her legacy continues to this day, with her designs and brand still influencing fashion trends and shaping the way women dress. In the 1960s, Chanel cemented her status as a true icon of the fashion world and one of the most important designers of any era.

Her clothing was worn by a wide range of women, from famous movie stars and socialites to the everyday working woman. Some of the most notable figures who wore Chanel during this decade include:

Jacqueline Kennedy Onassis - The former First Lady was a style icon and a fan of Chanel, often wearing the brand's suits and dresses.

Marilyn Monroe - The Hollywood star was known for her love of Chanel No. 5, and she also wore Chanel clothing on and off screen.

Grace Kelly - The actress turned Princess of Monaco was a fan of Chanel's timeless and elegant designs, and she was often seen wearing the brand's suits and dresses. As was her daughter Princess Caroline.

Catherine Deneuve - The French actress was a muse for Chanel in the 1960s and was often seen wearing the brand's iconic two-piece suits.

Edie Sedgwick - The American actress and socialite was part of Andy Warhol's inner circle and was known for her eclectic style. She was often seen wearing Chanel suits and dresses.

Elizabeth Taylor – The Hollywood legend and twice wife of Richard Burton.

Romy Schneider – The beautiful German actress/movie star and long-time companion of the French heart throb Alain Delon. She had a very close relationship with Romy, one can only guess that they shared losing the loves of their life – Coco with Capel and Romy with Delon.

These women, along with many others, helped to popularize Chanel's designs and make the brand a staple in the wardrobes of women everywhere.

Her famous pink suit, first shown in her 1961 spring collection, took on a life of its own when it was purchased by Jackie Kennedy. The two piece suit entered the status of legend, when her husband John Kennedy was assassinated in Dallas Texas – Jackie was wearing the Pink Suit.

This was the ultimate publicity for all the wrong reasons.

One of Coco's most treasured relationships was the one she shared with Romy Schneider the Austrian-German actress, one of the most popular stars of her generation.

Despite the fact, that Coco Chanel was over 30 years older than Romy Schneider, the two women developed a close and meaningful friendship. They first met in the 1950s when Romy Schneider was just starting her career as an actress, and Coco Chanel took the young actress under her wing. The two women bonded over their shared love of fashion and their mutual appreciation for the finer things in life.

Coco Chanel's influence on Romy Schneider's fashion sense was significant. The actress was known for her timeless, chic style, and many of her looks were inspired by Chanel's designs. In return, Romy Schneider helped to promote Chanel's brand and was often seen wearing her iconic designs on the red carpet and in her films.

Despite the age difference, Coco Chanel and Romy Schneider had a strong, reciprocal friendship that lasted for many years. They travelled and vacationed together, and their friendship was known for its warmth and playfulness. Coco Chanel once said of Romy Schneider, "She was a woman of exceptional grace and charm."

The friendship between Coco Chanel and Romy Schneider is an example of how two women of different generations and backgrounds can come together to form a meaningful and lasting bond. Their relationship continues to be celebrated and remembered as one of the most iconic of the 20th century.

Chanel In The 1970s

The House of Chanel in the 1970s

The 1970s marked a time of change and evolution for the iconic fashion house of Chanel. During this decade, the brand faced several challenges and faced new directions, but managed to maintain its position as a leading fashion brand in the industry.

The introduction of these new styles and materials helped Chanel to appeal to a younger, more modern consumer, and helped to establish the brand as a leader in fashion.

This was a significant change for Chanel, which had previously been known for its conservative and traditional styles.

In addition to its clothing and fragrance lines, Chanel continued to expand into other areas of luxury goods, such as jewelry and accessories. The brand's iconic "CC" logo became synonymous with luxury and exclusivity and was widely recognized around the world.

Despite the challenges and changes that the House of Chanel faced in the 1970s, it managed to maintain its position as a leading fashion brand.

A rare glimpse of Chanel's Parisian apartment

The brand's commitment to quality and its timeless, classic designs helped it to continue to appeal to consumers and establish itself as a symbol of luxury and sophistication.

In conclusion, the 1970s was a decade of change and evolution for the House of Chanel, but it managed to remain at the forefront of the fashion industry and solidify its reputation as one of the most iconic and successful fashion brands in the world.

Coco Chanel, the French fashion designer and businesswoman, died on January 10, 1971, at the age of 87. She passed away in her apartment in Paris, France.

The cause of Coco Chanel's death was not widely reported, but it is believed that she died of natural causes.

See the later chapter -

Chanel In The 80s

The biggest change since the death of the legendary Coco Chanel occurred in early 1983 when Karl Lagerfeld took over as creative director at Chanel.

On entering the hallowed offices at Chanel, he was immediately aware that change had to happen and happen fast. Chanel was frozen in a Coco time warp. So familiar with the ways of Coco, was everybody, that fresh ideas appeared non-existent.

Like the great lady herself, Lagerfeld instantly recognized that the clientele base was also ageing. They needed to attract new, younger clients. He set about studying the core items within the catalogue and pondered on how to attract his target audience.

There was no point in throwing the 'baby out with the bath water.' The secret lay in how to re-dress the baby, so to speak.

He organized his team and together they set about the task of taking the core items such as the Twin Set and The Little Black Dress along with a dozen or so of their classic range and totally reworking

Oh So Clever Lagerfeld

them. Their mission – to create and update based on these proven sellers.

They trimmed and cut, they added fur and piping, they played with colours and cloth galore. The master stroke came though, when Lagerfeld studied the double C logo. He realised, that here was a range of clothing all on its own. He enlarged the C and made it an emblem, placing it on a plain background. Then he reduced the logo, until it became perfect for an all-over pattern, which could then be altered either in its colour or its application.

One of Lagerfeld's most notable contributions to Chanel was his revival of the brand's signature tweed suits. He updated the classic design with modern details, such as leather accents and oversized buttons, and made it relevant for a new generation of fashion-conscious women. He also introduced new product categories, such as handbags, shoes, and sunglasses, that helped to broaden the brand's appeal and cement its position as a leader in the luxury market.

Lagerfeld was known for his unique vision and his ability to blend classic elements of the Chanel aesthetic with a modern, edgy twist. He created collections that were both timeless and current,

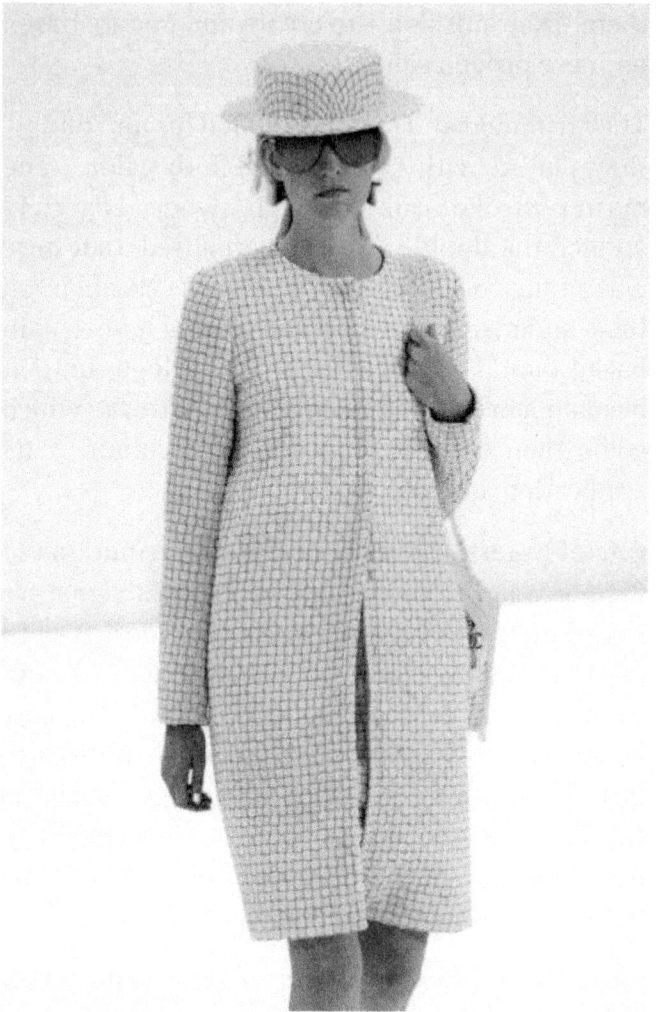

The Lagerfeld Influence – Milan Show

and his designs were sought after by fashion lovers around the world. He was also a master of branding, and he helped to establish Chanel as a global luxury brand with a strong and distinct image.

The new offerings were a sensation at the Paris Show. Lagerfeld knew full well the power of the press and just how important it was to reposition Chanel at the forefront of fashion. His hard work paid off, it became almost a rebirth of this great fashion house and the press loved it.

In addition to his work for Chanel, Lagerfeld was also a prolific photographer and filmmaker. He used his creative skills to produce memorable advertising campaigns and fashion shows that were always thought-provoking and often provocative. He was also known for his sharp wit and his controversial statements, which often made headlines.

Karl Lagerfeld was one of the most iconic and influential fashion designers of our time, and his impact on Chanel was immense. He served as the Creative Director of the brand from 1983 until his death in 2019. During his tenure, he transformed Chanel from a semi- dormant brand into, once

A new Twist on An Old Theme

again, one of the most important and recognizable fashion houses in the world.

Overall, Karl Lagerfeld was an exceptional talent who left an indelible mark on the fashion world. He was a visionary who transformed Chanel into a global brand and set the standard for luxury and style. He will always be remembered as one of the greatest fashion designers of all time.

He is said to have significantly increased the brand's turnover. However, specific numbers on the exact improvement of Chanel's turnover due to Lagerfeld's contributions are not publicly disclosed. The brand is privately owned and its financial information is not publicly available.

Familiar but Not

Chanel In The 90s

The 1990s brought a fresh set of challenges to the House of Chanel. Some that would threaten to undermine its reputation and success. Lagerfeld had been at the helm of Chanel for a considerable period and was responsible for revitalizing the brand and making it relevant to a new generation of customers.

Another challenge facing Chanel in the 1990s was the changing fashion landscape. The rise of minimalism, led by designers such as Calvin Klein and Donna Karan, challenged the traditionally opulent and elaborate styles that Chanel was known for. The brand was seen as outdated and out of touch with the times, and there was a risk that it would lose its relevance and appeal to consumers.

Additionally, the luxury goods market was becoming increasingly competitive, with new brands entering the market and established brands expanding their offerings. Chanel was

The re-working of the past continues

facing more and more competition, and there was a risk that it would be left behind.

Despite these challenges, Chanel managed to overcome them and maintain its position as one of the most prestigious and successful luxury fashion brands in the world, Chanel continued to innovate and evolve, introducing new lines and collections that blended traditional Chanel styles with contemporary fashion trends. It also continued to expand its presence globally, opening new boutiques and stores in major cities around the world.

Overall, the 1990s was a challenging time for Chanel, but the brand proved its resilience and adaptability, and emerged stronger and more successful than ever. Today, it continues to be a leader in the luxury fashion industry, known for its timeless and sophisticated designs, and its commitment to quality and craftsmanship.

2000 & Karl

Karl Lagerfeld, was without doubt, a creative genius and fashion visionary. He made an indelible mark on the world of fashion throughout his career. From the year 2000 onwards, Lagerfeld's design direction and influence on Chanel and the fashion industry in general were unparalleled. It's easy to look at Lagerfeld's work and dismiss him as totally over the top, all show and no substance.

Look a little closer and we see just how clever he was. With his distinctive aesthetic, relentless work ethic, and ability to blend tradition with modernity, Lagerfeld transformed Chanel into a global powerhouse and solidified his status as an icon.

Design Direction at Chanel:

When Lagerfeld took over as creative director of Chanel in 1983, he faced the daunting task of revitalizing a brand that had lost so much of its allure. Lagerfeld infused new life into Chanel by honouring its rich heritage, while at the same time, injecting a fresh perspective. From the year 2000 onwards, Lagerfeld continued to evolve the brand's design direction, pushing boundaries and redefining luxury.

A clever re-work of the classic Chanel jacket

Under Lagerfeld's leadership, Chanel embraced a modern sensibility, incorporating contemporary styling.

Influence on Chanel:

Lagerfeld's influence on Chanel extended far beyond design. He transformed Chanel into a global phenomenon, making it one of the most coveted luxury brands in the world. Karl understood the power of branding and elevated Chanel's image through innovative marketing strategies, high-profile collaborations, and captivating fashion shows.

One of Lagerfeld's most significant contributions to Chanel was his ability to attract a younger demographic without alienating the brand's loyal clientele. He recognized the importance of connecting with the millennial generation and tapped into their desires for individuality and self-expression. Lagerfeld introduced street style influences, casual-chic designs, and accessories that appealed to a younger audience, while maintaining Chanel's essence of sophistication and elegance.

Lagerfeld's take on Coco's country look

Moreover, Lagerfeld's attention to detail and dedication to craftsmanship set new standards for luxury fashion. Like the lady that gave her name to the brand, he insisted on impeccable tailoring, exquisite fabrics, and meticulous finishes, ensuring that each Chanel piece was a work of art (sound familiar?) His perfectionism and pursuit of excellence resonated with consumers, who sought out Chanel for its impeccable quality and attention to detail.

Lagerfeld's influence extended beyond Chanel, as he served as a mentor and inspiration to countless emerging designers. His distinct personal style, characterized by his signature high-collared shirts, fingerless gloves, and powdered white hair, became an iconic fashion statement in its own right. Lagerfeld's persona and unique aesthetic continue to inspire designers and fashion enthusiasts worldwide.

Impact on the Fashion Industry:

His impact on the fashion industry cannot be overstated. His ability to transform and modernize heritage brands like Chanel paved the way for a new era of luxury fashion. Lagerfeld's approach of blending tradition with innovation set a precedent for other designers, encouraging them to reinterpret classic styles for contemporary audiences.

Furthermore, Lagerfeld's forward-thinking mindset embraced technology and the digital age. He recognized the importance of digital platforms and social media in shaping the fashion industry and actively engaged with his audience through various digital channels. Lagerfeld's embrace of technology was instrumental in keeping Chanel relevant and accessible to a global audience.

Pure Chanel – Pure Lagerfeld

In February 2019, the fashion world was met with the news of Karl Lagerfeld's passing at the age of 85. Lagerfeld's death marked the end of an era and left a void in the industry that would be difficult to fill. However, his legacy continues to resonate, and his impact on fashion and popular culture remains enduring.

Lagerfeld's passing was mourned by fashion enthusiasts, designers, and celebrities worldwide. Tributes poured in, recognizing his immense contributions and the mark he left on the industry. Lagerfeld's death sparked a reflection on his extraordinary career, his unique design aesthetic, and his larger-than-life personality.

Lagerfeld's most significant contribution to fashion was his revitalization of Chanel. Throughout his long tenure as creative director, he transformed the brand into a global powerhouse. Lagerfeld's ability to balance tradition with innovation, his meticulous attention to detail, and his unwavering commitment to quality elevated Chanel to unprecedented heights. His legacy at Chanel is evident in the brand's continued success and influence in the fashion world.

Furthermore, Lagerfeld's impact extended beyond fashion. His contributions to the creative world encompassed photography, art, and literature. Lagerfeld was an accomplished photographer, capturing striking images that graced the pages of prestigious magazines and exhibited in galleries. He was also known for his sharp wit and insightful quotes, which showcased his intellect and cultural knowledge.

Lagerfeld's legacy is also defined by his role as a mentor and supporter of emerging talent. Throughout his career, he nurtured and mentored young designers, providing them with opportunities to showcase their work and offering guidance and support.

Goodbye Coco

Coco Chanel, the French fashion designer and businesswoman, died on January 10, 1971, at the age of 87. She passed away in her apartment in Paris, France.

The cause of Coco Chanel's death was not widely reported, but it is believed that she died of natural causes.

The greatest fashion designer of the 20th century, Gabrielle "Coco" Chanel, died suddenly in her suite. Despite it being a Sunday, the 87-year-old was busy working on a new collection, which was shown two weeks after her death.

A perfectionist to the very end, the designer was seen by staff at her fashion house on the rue Cambon the day before her death, checking the slightest details, choosing cloth and inspecting all the buttons.

Associated French Press (AFP) broke the news in the middle of the night:

"Mademoiselle Coco Chanel died on Sunday evening in Paris."

When she returned to Paris in 1954, it was to her suite in the Ritz. She rented a 188-square-metre (2,023-square-foot) suite, on the second floor with a view over Paris's Place Vendome.

Black and white dominated the suite -- where she received few visitors -- in line with her belief that "black is timeless". She furnished it with a suede sofa from her fashion house and Chinese screens with lion talisman, something that later appeared on her tomb -- Chanel was always known as being rather superstitious.

It fell to her close friends at the luxury hotel to announce her passing.

"Her end was very gentle. We are dismayed because nothing in the days running up to it led us to believe this would happen," one said. In keeping with Coco's final wishes, no one was allowed into the suite after her death other than two nieces and a nephew – who were allowed to pay their respects.

This slightest of women, who's silhouette had graced so many magazines and journals, wearing her trademark pearl necklace, a jaunty straw boater and a cigarette, that hung almost magically from her lips, she was a familiar sight at the hotel, which she had called "home" since 1937. She would never again grace the avenues and boulevards of Paris.

On Wednesday, January 13, a crowd of several thousand people gathered in front of the Madeleine church in Paris for the funeral. Most of fashion's big names were there.

Fashion journalists, customers, models and the 250 staff of the Chanel fashion house were out in force. All paid homage to Coco, the orphan made good.

The coffin disappeared after the absolution under an abundance of white flowers, including an immense wreath of camelias -- her favourite flower -- from producers of the Broadway operetta about her life, "Coco".

She was then taken to Switzerland where a small service took place at the Lausanne Chapel in Switzerland, where Chanel had lived on and off in her later years. The chapel was adorned with large arrangements of white camellias.

Chanel's close friends, including the famous couturier, Yves Saint Laurent, and the actress, Susanne Valdon, were in attendance. The service was said to be simple and elegant, reflecting Chanel's timeless sense of style.

After the funeral, Chanel's ashes were interred at the Bois-de-Vaux Cemetery in Lausanne, Switzerland. Her gravesite is marked with a simple plaque that reads "Gabrielle Chanel, 1883-1971."

Her tomb there with its ever-changing floral arrangements has become a place of pilgrimage for fashionistas ever since.

The slight, some would say, severe looking creature, had single-handedly changed fashion forever. She was the creator of what has been dubbed the "perfume of the century" -- Chanel No 5. The label that carried her name would eventually be turned into a $100 billion business by the flamboyant designer Karl Lagerfeld.

The creator of the 'little Black Dress', was no more!

Final Quotes of Coco Chanel

"A fashion that does not reach the streets is not a fashion."

"A style does not go out of style as long as it adapts itself to its period. When there is an incompatibility between the style and a certain state of mind, it is never the style that triumphs."

"In order to be irreplaceable, one must always be different."

"Guilt is perhaps the most painful companion of death."

"How many cares one loses when one decides not to be something but to be someone."

"Those who create are rare; those who cannot are numerous. Therefore, the latter are stronger".

"Great loves too must be endured."

Elegance is not the prerogative of those who have just escaped from adolescence, but of those who have already taken possession of their future."

"Elegance is refusal."

"Elegance does not consist in putting on a new dress." -

"Luxury must be comfortable, otherwise it is not luxury."

"Some people think luxury is the opposite of poverty. It is not. It is the opposite of vulgarity."

"As long as you know men are like children, you know everything!"

"Jump out the window if you are the object of passion. Flee it if you feel it. Passion goes, boredom remains."

"Nature gives you the face you have at twenty; it is up to you to merit the face you have at fifty."

"Since everything is in our heads, we had better not lose them."

"Success is often achieved by those who don't know that failure is inevitable."

Conclusion

Having read countless articles notes and general detail about this fascinating woman, I have come to the conclusion that, she was probably the most influential fashion designer of the 20th century.

Her ingenuity, clarity of vision and sheer work ethic, surpass any of her peers.

While Edwardian women were drowning under ever more elaborate hats, creations that featured mock fruit, feathers and heaven only know what else - Coco opened her hat shop and offered the women of Paris, simple straw boaters decorated with striped bands or petite decoration. She took the market by storm.

She applied the same innate taste and forward thinking to the dress. Out went the multi-layered silks and satins, out too the restrictive corset tops and fitted sleeves. In came loose fitting dresses with minimal undergarments, stylishly cut and above all, comfortable to wear. Here at last, was a woman designing for women. Her dressmaking skills taught her that you could weight the hems of coats and dresses to keep the line of most, soft materials. Once again, the end wearers (women) lapped it up.

Coco was a regular visitor to Deauville, the summer playground of the rich and famous. While enjoying the sailing, the sun or the casino, her sponge-like imagination was taking in all around her. This seaside resort was the inspiration for one of her most iconic garments – the Breton top. Traditionally worn by the fishermen of the area, Coco envisaged the distinctive blue & white, striped top in a softer fabric, perfect for her collection. Once again, her instincts were spot on. This design was used to great effect time and again throughout her seasonal offerings. Sometimes with wide palazzo pants, others, worn under a box jacket or blazer.

Coco had this wonderful knack of looking at everything in a new light. The wool jersey cloth, traditionally the preserve of male underwear, was perfect for her Softline dresses and tops, weighted hems were once again used, along with stiffeners for the collars or cuffs. Perfect style, perfect comfort. No wonder women of the day loved her – she had set them Free!

Other fashion houses had no choice but to emulate her ideas but Coco was always one step ahead.

Other designers had dabbled in perfume, most of them had elaborate names and bottles to match. Not Coco, she stripped the elements back, created the iconic bottle and more importantly, used just her name and a single No5 to introduce the world's most famous fragrance.

She applied the same techniques to jewellery. 'Better to wear a string of fashionable imitation pearls, than rely on a single strand original. Now every shop girl and woman about town could dazzle in pearls.

The list of innovations is endless, the box jacket, the blazer, the two-piece, cut offs, the multi colour shoes, the pill box hats etc, etc.

There is barely a facet of modern clothes design that cannot be attributed directly to this human dynamo.

It's often said that we are all products of our parents and our upbringing. – nature and nurture.

This must have been doubly true for Coco. Losing a mother at such a young age is life changing and bad enough, to then be abandoned by your father is beyond tragic. The sheer tenacity of this young woman in going from life in an orphanage to the very pinnacle of French and world fashion, truly remarkable and testament to her sheer determination.

There are those who say without certain men in her early life, she would have been nothing. That's unkind and is also something we will never know. what we do know however, is, there was no way she was ever going back to an 'ordinary existence'.

Here are just a few of the men who helped Coco in those early years. They all have two things in common, they were either very wealthy or very clever. This is meant in no way to detract from Cocos obvious talents and business acumen.

It's worth remembering that at this time, these individuals would have had the pick of most women within society. There was no end of beautiful women to walk out with but everyone, to a man – chose Coco. That's not to say that young Coco wasn't a beauty in her own right, she certainly was. They obviously saw something more, perhaps, the challenge that this spirited young lady presented.

1908-1909: Étienne de Balsan: a wealthy playboy who discovered Chanel singing in a cabaret café in Moulins.

1909-1919: Boy Capel: Wealthy English aristocrat, a good friend of Balsan and the love of Chanel's life who died in a tragic car accident at 38.

1920: Grand Duke Dmitry Pavlovič: nephew of Tsar Nicholas II and cousin to Prince Philip, Duke of Edinburgh (the husband of Queen Elizabeth II)

1921: Igor Stravinsky's: Chanel supported a Russian-born composer when he was destitute. He moved in with Chanel to work unencumbered and is rumoured to have had an affair with Chanel.

1923-1929: The 2nd Duke of Westminster: Hugh "Bendor "Grosvenor was one of Britain's (and the world's) richest men and friend of Winston Churchill. Bender's fishing and hunting outfits inspired Chanel's iconic tweed suits.

Coco was someone often described as abrasive and difficult. Strange then, that most of her relationships were long-lasting and on more than one occasion she was asked for her hand in marriage.

One of her most famous quotes touched upon this very subject, when the Duke of Westminster asked her to marry him. She refused him, her retort being, there are many Duchesses in the world, there is only one Coco Chanel.

I think that pretty much sums up her attitude to life, no man was ever going to control her – when the one man, who should have loved you unconditionally, your father - abandons you !

That's not to say that she didn't have a great life, she did.

It is therefore my opinion that here was the greatest fashion designer of the 20th Century !

In writing this biography one mental image stayed with me. This concerned her approach to her actual dress designs. Coco was known to pay scant attention to detailed drawings, instead, relying on brief sketches, then simply getting to work with scissors, needle, cotton and pins. A young model was made to bend and stretch in all directions, to show just how the fabric would react to everyday situations – walking up and down stairs, sitting, walking etc.

There are images of Chanel doing just this. A pair of scissors in one hand and the obligatory cigarette in the other.

It struck me that no matter what obstacles she had overcome to reach her unique position in life, her achievements were nothing less than remarkable.

But beneath the glamour and sophistication, there would always be – "The Little Dressmaker".

A Brief Update

Life is curious and the Chanel story is no exception to this rule.

The Mediterranean newspaper featured this advert - A splendid villa overlooking both the Mediterranean and Cap-Martin, uninhabited since 2007, La Pausa has recently been acquired by the House of Chanel.

88 years after Gabrielle Coco Chanel first purchased the land to build her dream vacation home, La Pausa, the House of Chanel has bought the property.

They intend to carry out a full and extensive renovation programme, to restore the villa to its original glory. The famed fashion house is planning to dedicate the place to the brand and its values. The villa is the only house that Mademoiselle Chanel had specially designed, built and decorated for her.

NIGHTMARE ISLAND

AN EXILED SECTOR NOVEL

MILA YOUNG

NIGHTMARE
ISLAND

CONTENTS

Soundtrack   vii
Before You Enter   ix
Welcome to Exiled Sector   x

Prologue   1
Chapter 1   13
Chapter 2   31
Chapter 3   44
Chapter 4   59
Chapter 5   75
Chapter 6   87
Chapter 7   104
Chapter 8   114
Chapter 9   135
Chapter 10   146
Chapter 11   161
Chapter 12   184
Chapter 13   201
Chapter 14   214
Chapter 15   225
Chapter 16   231
Chapter 17   245
Chapter 18   260
BONUS SCENE   277

Banana Claw Crunch Muffins   291
Venom Island   295
Outcast Island   297
About Mila Young   299

DEDICATION

*To those who prefer their love stories with claws, their kisses
with fangs, and their happy endings just a little bloody.*

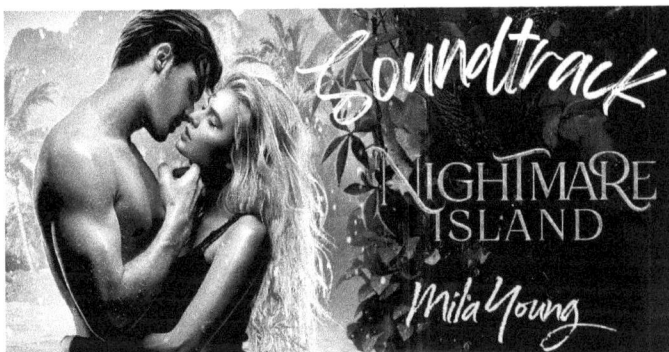

Black Hole Sun

Nouela

Nightmare

Halsey

Damage

Lights

Be My Angel

Mazzy Star

Devil's Worst Nightmare

Fjøra

Burn Your Village

Kiki Rockwell

LOVELOST

margø

Nightmares

Ellise

Dying Star

Ashnikko, Ethel Cain

Never Say Die

Neoni

Twisted

AViVA

Narcissist

Henri Werner, Shivers

Spiracle

Flower Face

Horns

Bryce Fox

Pure Devils

OsMan

Listen to the Soundtrack on Spotify - Nightmare Island playlist by Mila Young

BEFORE YOU ENTER

Nightmare Island is a standalone paranormal romance, and while not a dark story, it contains violence, death, and disturbing elements including ritualistic gifts, along with horror elements.

WELCOME TO EXILED SECTOR

Welcome to the Exiled Sector, home to the most lethal Alphas on the planet.

These beings don't play nice with others. They've been banished.

And a plane full of Omegas just crash-landed on their isles.

This world isn't kind. It's futuristic and dystopian, and over 90 percent of the human population no longer exists. Supernaturals are in charge here, their territories often referred to as "sectors," where Alphas make the rules and everyone else obeys. Those who don't are either killed or sent to Exiled Sector.

Venom Island.

Nightmare Island.

Outcast Island.

All of these islands are part of the notorious Exiled Sector. They're all governed and ruled in entirely different ways. The supernatural species and their dynamics may vary. And they manage themselves.

There's only one rule that applies to all of Exiled Sector:
Once you've been marked for exile, there's no going back.
Exiled Sector is your home now. Embrace it. Survive it.
Or die.

Alpha Ghost and Omega Hel are the main characters of
Nightmare Island. It's a wild land divided in two by two
fierce wolf packs, battling for power.

Below are some themes you may find in *Nightmare Island*:

✓ Masked Alpha

✓ Forced Proximity

✓ Strong, sassy Omega Female

✓ Knotting and Purring

✓ Primal Energy and Chase Scene

✓ Obsessive Alpha Male

✓ Touch Her and Die Vibes

✓ Praise kink

Have fun reading Nightmare Island.

Author's Note: The Exiled Sector series features three fast-paced, action-packed, standalone romance books. Each story guarantees a happily-ever-after ending and can be read in any order.

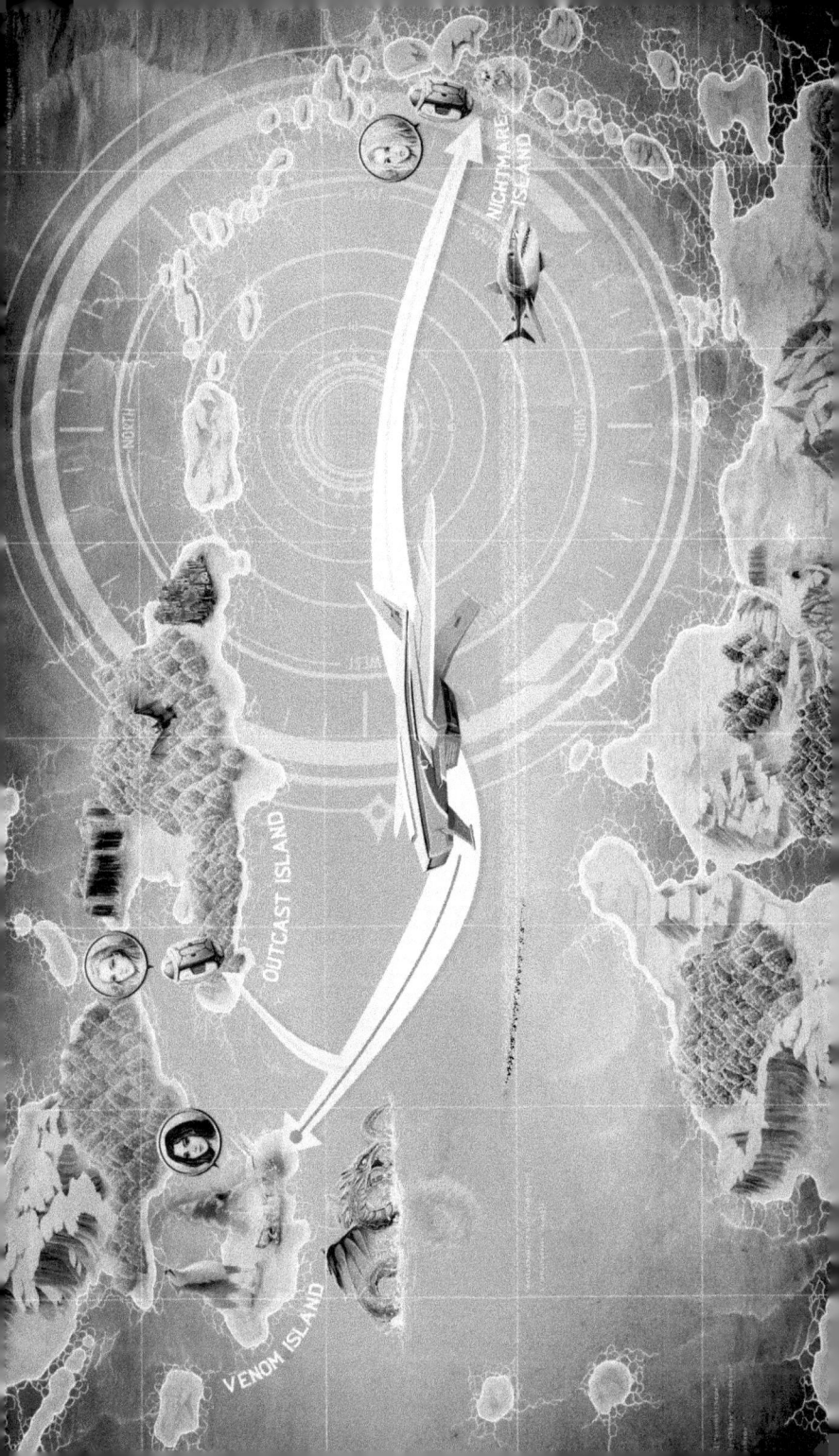

PROLOGUE

GHOST

etter to fight and fall than live without hope.

Fuck that noise. My bastard father can take his sayings and shove them up his ass. I'm not here to fall. I'm here to fucking conquer.

I stand at the edge of the Gravewater pool, my eyes fixed on its inky black water. Spirits writhe just beneath the surface, flashes of white here and there, hungry for their next meal. Well, they can keep waiting. I'm not on the menu today.

The magic that once bled into the land from those who lived here before us still lingers like a sickness. It belongs to the few fae who were sent to this place initially before the wolf shifters arrived and slaughtered them all. And now the water at my feet is where the dead souls of this island end up.

With the balmy breeze blowing through my hair, I

lift my gaze to the sky bleeding crimson, like Nightmare Island itself is anticipating the bloodshed to come. We're on a lofty stone ledge, halfway up one of the two Shadow Piton mountains that dominate the coastline.

Before us rises a solid rock face—the side of the mountain—the lower half twisted into a massive skull. Water pours from its empty eye sockets, raging into the pond with a fury that steals the silence.

I tear my gaze away from the scene to face Sten, the soon-to-be former Alpha of this godforsaken island. He's standing at least twenty feet from my location by the Gravewater pool, smirking in my direction—cocky bastard. His dark blond hair sits in a mess around his round face. Those dead gray eyes of his are smiling at the corners, but there's only the promise of violence behind them.

Good. I'm in the mood for fucking brutal violence.

"You dared to challenge me," he growls gravelly, his tone filled with dark amusement. "Then show me what you're made of."

Squaring my shoulders, I lift my chin higher. Around us, at least two dozen shifters in their wolf forms surround the water, their eyes gleaming with hunger. These fuckers are always hungry for something—food, women, or death. Today, they'll get at least one of those things.

"It'll be over soon enough," I reply steadily. I'm not

putting on a show for these animals. "You still have a choice, Sten. Yield the position of Alpha of your pack to me, and we don't need to do this. Save yourself the humiliation."

Sten barks out a vicious laugh. "You need a lesson, boy, to remember your place."

I grimace, anger flaring hot in my chest. I'm barely two years younger than this prick, and he has the audacity to call me *boy*?

"I saved you when you first arrived," Sten continues, his voice dripping with contempt. "Protected you like a brother. And this is the fucking reward you offer me?" His face twists into a mask of hatred. "I'm going to cover the mountain with your blood." His eyes narrow, a cruel smile warping his lips. "We're doing this officially, with our ritual to show everyone I'm a man of my word who makes anyone who challenges me pay the price with their life. Then, when I win, I will gut you from groin to throat."

Something stings in my chest, a traitorous pang of... what? Guilt? Regret? I push it down ruthlessly. Yes, Sten had helped me when I first washed up on these shores less than six months ago, but the fucker has a demented notion of what protection means. He'd also broken my ribs, chained me like a dog to a tree, and thrown me scraps to drive fear into me.

He had no idea who he was dealing with then. He's about to find out now.

"We doing this, or are you getting emotional?" I snap, tired of the bullshit. Sentiment gets you killed in this world. I saw it happen often enough back in Denmark, where I grew up with the Balor wolf pack, and again here on Nightmare Island.

Sten nods sternly, and we make our way around the pool to the black rocky wall in front of us, keeping a distance between us of around five feet.

I glance back at Aiquen—one man amid the wolves—the oldest on the island, fifty-two, if I remember correctly. He steps forward, his weathered face solemn as he calls out.

"Rules are simple. Challenge for Alpha has been accepted. The first one to make it to the top gets the first strike for the death match. Last man standing becomes the Alpha of Nightmare Island."

The surrounding wolves howl in response, sounding impatient for the challenges to commence rather than the formalities.

Part of me wishes it were as easy as straight combat. I'd take Sten out in a heartbeat. But since arriving in this hellhole, I've discovered there are many feral rules in this place that make no fucking sense to me. I'll abide by them. For now.

As I stare up at the treacherous climb before us, my mind wanders back to how I ended up here.

Exiled.

Dumped on this island to rot by those bastards

back in Denmark. The Balor wolves, my fucking father, always treated me like an outcast. They thought they were sentencing me to death by sending me to the Exiled Sector, but they underestimated me. They always have. I'll make this island mine!

I can't keep living under someone's thumb. Not again. So, this is my chance—my only chance—to create a new path. Not just to survive but to thrive in this place of nightmares.

Aiquen's voice cuts through my thoughts.

"Are you two ready?"

Sten and I lock eyes across the gap between us. There's a flicker of something in his gaze—respect, maybe? Or just bloodlust. It doesn't matter. I give a curt nod, and Sten does the same.

"Then begin!" the old man shouts, his voice carrying over the constant rush of water.

I don't hesitate. The moment the word leaves his mouth, I'm moving. My hands find purchase on the rough stone, muscles bunching as I haul myself upward. The rock face is fucking slick with spray from the waterfall.

Jagged edges dig into my palms, drawing blood, but I barely notice. Pain is temporary. Victory is forever. My bare feet scramble to find my footing on the ruthless surface, toes curling around the smallest of ledges. Each step is a battle against the mountain itself.

Sten is moving, too, his larger frame giving him an advantage as he reaches for handholds farther up, but I'm quicker, more agile. I scramble up the initial incline, ignoring the burning in my muscles.

The wolves below us howl and snarl. To them, this is entertainment—the best kind. Blood sport. I tune them out, focusing on the climb and on Sten's progress beside me.

We're neck and neck as we reach the first major obstacle—a sheer rock with barely any handholds. Sten grins at me, feral and wild, before launching himself at the wall. His fingers dig into tiny crevices, his boots scraping against the stone as he hauls himself upward.

I grit my teeth and follow suit, finding fingerholds to pull myself up. The muscles in my arms scream in protest, but I push through it, heaving for breath.

Pain is just weakness leaving the body, and there's no room for weakness here.

As we near the halfway point, I chance a look up. The summit seems impossibly far, a jagged spire thrust up against the blood-red sky. Doubt creeps in. Can I really do this?

I snarl at my own shortcomings. *Fuck yes, I can do this.* I'm going to own this damn mountain, this insane island, and every lunatic shifter on it.

My heart pounds in my chest. Sweat stings my eyes, blurring my vision. I blink rapidly, trying to clear it. One wrong move, one misplaced hand, and it's all over.

Sten is just to my left, his breathing heavy and labored. I can smell the bitter fear on him, my inner wolf stirring inside me, eager to battle.

The wolves' howls down below grow louder, more frenzied, stirring my own.

My fingers slip on the slick stone, and my pulse charges. I'm convinced I'm going to fall, but I dig deep, drawing on my strength, and pull myself up.

A sharp edge catches my forearm, slicing deep. Blood wells up, hot and sticky.

"Fuck," I hiss through clenched teeth. The cut throbs.

Sten notices my slip and grins. Fucker! He pushes harder, gaining ground. I can't let him win. I won't.

I force myself to go faster, ignoring the stinging of my wounds. Each movement is agony, but I embrace it. Pain means I'm still alive, still fighting.

Three-quarters of the way up, each breath is a struggle. My lungs burn, desperate for oxygen, but I can't slow down. Can't stop.

Sten's breathing grows ragged, too. Our gazes meet for a brief moment. There's a wild desperation in his gaze that sends a chill down my spine.

Suddenly, Sten's hand darts out. He's holding something—a loose rock, jagged and deadly. Before I can react, he hurls it at me with a snarl of rage.

Time seems to slow. I watch the rock spinning toward me, but it misses my head by inches, clattering down the mountainside.

I snarl in response, anger busting within me.

The force of the throw must have pushed him off-balance because as I glare back at him, I watch as his foot suddenly slips, and he's scrabbling for purchase on the smooth stone. He hangs there by one hand.

I grin, watching fear crowd in his eyes as his brow furrows and his lips tighten.

His grip slips.

He falls.

His snarls tear through the air, raw and primal. He plummets, arms flailing wildly as if he could somehow catch the air and stop his descent.

I watch, heart in my throat, as he hits the Gravewater pool with a sickening splash.

The spirits waste no time. They surge toward Sten, a writhing mass of ghostly forms, eager for his death, so he can join them. He thrashes in the water, fighting against the spectral hands that grab at him. Falling in is survivable if you don't let them drag you under to drown you...

Sten frantically claws his way toward the edge.

I can't watch anymore. Can't afford to because he'll be back up the mountain the moment he gets out of the pool. This is my chance. Victory is within my grasp. I turn back to the climb, pushing myself harder than ever.

The summit is just there. Just a few more feet. My muscles ache in protest, but I ignore them. I keep going, my blood smearing the stone.

Then, the rock beneath my foot crumbles, disintegrating under my weight. For a heart-stopping moment, I'm falling, the world spinning around me. My hand shoots out, grabbing desperately for anything to stop my descent.

Panic strangles me.

My fingers catch on a tiny ledge, halting my fall. Pain lances through my arm as my full weight yanks on the joint. The screaming pain is agonizing, and I bite down a bellow. I hang there, heart pounding, breath coming in ragged gasps.

I can feel my grip starting to give way, tiny pieces of rock showering down as the ledge crumbles beneath my grip.

Goddammit.

The ledge gives way, and I fall.

"Fuck!"

Seconds is all it takes.

I plunge into the icy touch of the water, dunked deep under. Instantly, I'm swimming to reach the surface.

Fighting against the current of grabbing arms, I desperately kick and push myself up, my head breaking free as I gasp for air. I catch Sten's glare across the pool. Idiot.

Freezing touches of the dead souls are all over my body, as if they're trying to burrow under my skin. Their moaning echoes in my head, and my skin crawls.

"Having fun over there?" I call out sarcastically to Sten, who only snarls in response.

Fear claws at my gut, but I shove it down. I refuse to let it control me. Instead, I channel it into determination. I push harder through the water, kicking and swinging my arms. The edge is close, and I can almost taste freedom. A smirk tugs at my lips as I near the edge. That's when a shadow looms over me from behind.

Stiffening in response, I whip around, my body protesting in aches from the sudden movement. The glint of a blade catches my attention, and I'm stunned. Sten's expression screams desperation and rage as he slashes the knife at me.

I jerk back, but the blade catches me, slicing from my forehead down over my eye.

Pain explodes through my head, white-hot and blinding. A scream of agony tears from my throat as I instinctively cover my face.

"Fuck!" I shout, blood pouring between my fingers. My vision dances in my good eye, the other completely useless now.

Sten's vicious laugh cuts through the haze of pain.

"That's your payment, you piece of shit. For daring to think you could be an Alpha."

"Is that all you've got?" I snap back, my voice heavy with a thunderous growl, even as the spirits tug harder at me, more frantic than before. My skin pinches at their touch, but I force down the revulsion. I'm already drowning in agony, my skull pulsing.

"I'm just getting started," Sten growls, raising the blade again from the water.

Rage fuels me as I lunge at him in the pool, but he moves faster and drives the blade into my chest, right over my heart. I feel it sink in, a cold shock that quickly blazes into searing agony.

Pain. Fuck, so much pain. It steals my breath, making the world spin. Is this how it ends? Rejected by my family for being different, for my mistakes, only to die in this shithole? This isn't how it was supposed to go.

As darkness creeps at the edges of my vision, a last burst of fury surges through me. With a roar, I shove Sten with all my remaining strength, driving my hands against his shoulders that bob out of the water.

His gaze widens in surprise as he's shoved, and his head flings backward, slamming into the sharp stone edge of the pool with a horrid crack. Blood pours from the back of his head as his body convulses, then goes limp. The spirits swarm over his body like fucking insects going to town on a corpse.

My gut turns.

The howls of the wolves around us fall silent.

As Sten slips beneath the surface, the spirits start swarming toward me. My last coherent thought is a grim satisfaction that if I'm going down, at least I'm taking that bastard with me.

The taste of copper floods my mouth. My lungs ache, each breath a struggle.

Around me, the wolves and the old man stare in shock. But I don't have time to worry about them when my strength fades fast, the sharp ache rattling through my head and my chest.

I feel myself slipping away, yet I keep fighting to get out of the pool. Still, I ponder about why I have no regrets, even on my dying breaths. Only hatred, only anger.

Faces flash before me—my so-called family back in Denmark. The sneers, the disgust, the final look of contempt as they exiled me out of our home. They never saw me as a son, only as a mistake.

I have no regrets because there was nothing to regret. No love lost, no bonds broken. They threw away a wolf who could've been loyal, who could've been strong for them.

Instead, they'll live with the knowledge that they created the very monster they feared.

CHAPTER
ONE

My husband, Jarl, is dead.

Those words echo through my head, but I feel nothing. No grief. No heartache. Just confusion and a bubbling anger about everything he put me through.

I shift in my seat on the jet as the lights flicker. Around me are other Omegas, all of us lost and being taken to freedom. I'm finally going to Savage Sector in Romania to meet up with my brother, Ragnar. I'm ready to put the past behind me, yet my husband's sudden death doesn't leave me.

One minute, Jarl and I had arrived in Bariloche Sector because he decided he'd had enough of my smart mouth. Enough of me. Evidently, being raised to stand up for yourself and speak your mind doesn't make for a submissive little Omega wife. So the asshole brought me to the sector to trade me in for a more tolerable Omega.

I clench my teeth because, as much as I hated him, the ache of rejection by such a monster still stings. Four years of hell, and he was ready to get rid of me. Then chaos erupted at Bariloche Sector—explosions, panicked voices, screams—and suddenly, these new Alphas appeared, telling me that Jarl was dead, and they were taking me away. Offering me a safe passage to wherever I wanted to go.

Too good to be true, right? Yet here we are on the plane, and I'm praying it's not some big hoax.

An explosive boom of thunder sends the entire plane into a shudder, and I grasp the seat in front of me. Someone whimpers nearby, and I quickly glance out my window just in time to witness lightning split the night sky, way too close for comfort.

Is it me? Did I do this?

I try to slow my breathing, counting backward from ten. Thing is, I'm probably a little broken. Okay, a lot broken. And I have an ability where my emotions can influence and sometimes straight up ignite storms.

When we took off, the sky was clear of clouds. Now look at it. It's hell out there.

Great job, Hel. Get angry while you're thousands of feet in the air, and you can plummet to your death.

The plane drops suddenly, and my heart launches

into my throat. More gasps and cries echo through the cabin. Then things are calm again, yet my knees are bouncing wildly.

Another lightning strike illuminates the sky, brighter this time, and images of my past flash back to a stormy night in Denmark.

I'd baked for Jarl once, early on in our forced marriage. When I still thought I could make it work, like some stupid fairy tale. He came home in one of his moods, face thunderous. The cake hit the wall first, then me. I woke up hours later with a splitting headache and found him waiting for me with his belt in hand. It seems that rather than living a fairy tale, I'd ended up marrying the devil.

My hands curl into fists when the plane bucks again.

At the front of the cabin, Enrique, one of the Alphas who rescued us, emerges from the cockpit, looking decidedly unhappy. Great. That's exactly what you want to see on one of your pilot's faces.

"I-I hate storms," the honey blonde across the aisle whispers, her knuckles white on the armrest.

I reach across, barely able to touch her in this tiny jet, placing my hand over hers to comfort her. "It's going to be all right, I'm sure."

"You don't sound too confident yourself."

I shrug, drawing my hand back, and stare at the rain hitting the window sideways.

Another massive crack of thunder drowns out my thoughts. The plane shakes so violently that my teeth rattle. Enrique's voice carries from the front, something about a storm appearing out of nowhere.

That earlier guilt that it might be my fault twists in my stomach.

The plane dips sharply, and my insides try to relocate somewhere around my ears. I gasp aloud while others cry out.

"Everyone, secure your safety belts!" Enrique's voice cuts through the chaos.

I fumble with the buckle, finally getting it latched just as another violent tremor rocks the cabin. He's talking to one of the girls at the front of the plane while I'm being jostled about, trying to calm my breathing.

All right, storm, you've had your fun. You can leave now. Look how calm I am.

My muscles strain to a breaking point as the lie threatens to strangle me.

Enrique moves down the aisle, all powerful grace and barely contained urgency. Under different circumstances, I might appreciate how the emergency lights catch the sharp angles of his face and how incredibly handsome he is. Right now, the grim set of his jaw just sends ice through my veins.

"You take pod A," he tells the Omega in front of me,

then turns those intense eyes my way. "You go to pod B. No time for detailed instructions; follow the automated guidance. The pods weren't affected by the strike."

Strike? Oh, double fuck.

"I'm so sorry," I blurt out as he passes. "I... I don't know what happened..."

He pauses, turning back. "What do you mean?"

I lower my head slightly, shame burning in my chest. "I have some issues. When I get stressed or scared, when my emotions go haywire, I... I influence the weather. I call storms. I've been thinking about my husband and..." I glance at the window where rain pounds, then back at him.

His face goes slack for a moment, processing. I brace for anger, for blame.

"Can you control it?" he asks in a low voice.

"N-no. I've been trying, but it's not working." It never works, in truth. My grip on the belt tightens until my fingers ache.

He straightens his posture, staring at me for a bit too long. "Then you're going in pod A," he says firmly. "We can't risk another bolt to the jet. You need to be far from the others to give them a chance." He leans over to the Omega in front of me, saying, "Change of plan. You're in pod B now."

The guilt hits me hard, but I can't argue. He's right. He waves for me to move now. Every eye is on me, and

MILA YOUNG

my cheeks burn with embarrassment. I want to apologize, but the words never come.

Minutes later, I'm strapped into a tiny pod. It's barely big enough for my seat, with a wraparound window. Screens flash with instructions I have to read three times before my panic-scrambled brain can process them.

"It's all automated. Follow the instructions and leave quickly," Enrique adds, then shuts the door, leaving me alone with my fear and the storm I'm certain I created.

I hit the first black button, and everything hums to life, lights zipping across the dashboard. The second one, as per the instructions, is just as easy to push, and suddenly, I'm dropping, my stomach left somewhere in the jet above. For a heart-stopping moment, I'm in the pod, hovering in the air, out of the plane, then I'm moving.

The jet continues onward, smoke trailing from one side.

"I'm sorry," I whisper, hoping the others make it to safety.

My pod's navigation system has us going in the opposite direction, and fast. The flashing lights on the flight map on the screen reveal a landmass nearby, but right now, all I see is darkness and lightning outside. My hands grip the curved walls that feel like they're closing in. Just when I think I can't take any more,

18

thunder booms, and a streak of light illuminates the world. Down below, I spot a beach fringed with palm trees and mountains rising behind it.

The pod instantly starts descending, and I scream, seeing my own death at this rate. Something's wrong. Instead of the land, we're heading for the beach. Impact into the water comes with a shock, my whole body rocking in the seat, shaking all over. Water crashes against the windows as the pod bobs.

"Fuck this. I don't want to drown inside this thing." Frantically, I search for the emergency release. A dim blue light reveals the panel, and I slam my hand on the hatch. The door hisses open.

Low waves crash around me as I tumble out of the escape pod. Aching all over from the rough landing, my legs sink into the cold water, which reaches my waist. I drag myself to the shore, my heart still racing, and collapse onto my back, gasping for air as the rain pelts into me. For a moment, I just lie there, letting the cool water lap at my legs.

Am I dead?

Did I crash-land in some weird heaven?

The deafening crack of thunder answers that question. Nope, definitely still alive. Lucky me.

I push myself up, blinking rain out of my eyes. The dark beach stretches out before me, a strip of white sand between the water and a wall of palm trees swaying in the wind. Their fronds whip back and forth as though they're trying to flee the storm. Can't say I blame them.

"Well, Hel," I mumble to myself. "You wanted a tropical vacation. Wish granted."

My stomach twists with guilt. Did I cause the storm, the plane to lose control? My *ability* has always been more of a curse than a blessing, but I've never brought down a whole plane before.

The smell of salt and rain fills my nose, mingling with the earthy scent of wet sand and vegetation. Waves crash against the shore, drowned out only by the rumbles of thunder. It would be peaceful if it weren't for, you know, the whole *stranded on a mysterious island* thing.

The moon comes out from behind the storming clouds, giving me some light to help my wolf eyes see better.

Movement in the water nearby catches my attention. Two dark fins cut through the waves, really close to shore, chasing something. Great. Sharks. Because this situation wasn't exciting enough already.

"Sorry, boys," I call out to the sharks. "This little Omega isn't going swimming today."

I scramble to my feet, noticing my escape pod being dragged out to sea. There goes any link to the plane... Though I feel as if I've landed right in the fire. As I watch the pod sink, a thread of worry hits me. Did the other Omegas make it out? Or did they end up... I can't finish the thought.

I turn toward the island, taking in the explosion of trees before me. I can't see far beyond that from the night and storm.

Another crack of thunder shakes the ground, and the rain comes down even harder. It streams down my face, plastering my clothes to my skin.

"You want to drown me now? Bit late for that, don't you think?" I shout at the sky.

The storm, predictably, growls.

I take a deep breath, tasting the metallic tang of the rain.

"Okay, Hel. You survived four years of being married to that ass-wipe Alpha. This is just a little unplanned vacay. No big deal." Once I find a way off this place, I can finally track down my brother, Ragnar, in Savage Sector. He'd promised me that once he took that territory as Alpha, he'd find me. That hasn't happened, so I'm going to find him. Hopefully, he's still alive. So, first, work out where exactly I am and how to leave this island.

I trudge toward the tree line, my boots squelching with every step. Sand cakes the sides, making them feel ten pounds heavier, but hey, at least I'm not barefoot.

As I enter the forest, the rain lessens slightly, the canopy providing some cover. I'm on a small, worn path. Animal trail? Or signs of other people? Not sure which option is more terrifying right now.

Dead palm leaves crunch under my shoes. Fallen coconuts, brown and decayed, litter the ground at my feet. Every now and then, I spot a crab scuttling away into the detritus faster than I can blink.

"Don't worry, little guys," I say. "I'm not here to steal your homes. Just... borrowing the neighborhood for a bit."

The path winds through the trees, gradually sloping upward. My thighs ache from the effort, reminding me that since getting married, I'd fallen out of shape and even put on a bit of weight because of my now-dead husband. A memory flashes through my mind.

"W*here do you think you're going?" Jarl's words are cold and sharp, freezing me in place.*

I turn slowly, my hand still on the doorknob. Jarl looms in the hallway, his six-foot-four frame blocking out the light. At forty-seven, he's more than two decades my senior, but age hasn't softened him. If anything, it's made him harder, meaner.

His thinning blond hair is slicked back, emphasizing the harsh angles of his face. Deep-set eyes, the color of mud, glare at me from beneath bushy brows. They've always been cruel, those eyes, never showing a hint of warmth or love.

"I... I was just going for a jog," I stammer, hating how small my voice sounds.

"A jog?" He laughs. "Since when do you jog?" He crosses the space between us in two long strides.

"I just wanted some fresh air to—"

Pain explodes across my scalp as he grabs a fistful of my hair. His bulky arm flexes as he drags me away from the door. I stumble and cry out, but he doesn't stop until we reach the spare room.

"If you can't respect my commands as your husband to never leave the house without me, you can rot in here until you're ready to apologize." He shoves me inside with a strength that sends me sprawling, the door slamming behind me.

I'm on my feet in an instant, fists pounding against the wood.

"You can't do this! I can't be locked up in the house. I just wanted to go out to get fresh air, you asshole!"

The door flies open. I retreat, fear digging into me as Jarl fills the doorway once more. His massive shoulders nearly touch both sides of the frame, a loose belt dangling from one meaty hand. The overhead light casts shadows across his face, making him look more monster than man.

"What?" he says menacingly, each word precise and terrifying. "What did you call me?"

. . .

T shake my head violently, forcing the memory away. My hands are shaking, and I realize I've stopped in front of a huge palm tree.

Breathe, Hel. Just breathe.

The asshole is dead, and you're not there anymore. You're here, on this island, where the only thing trying to kill you is nature itself.

I force my legs to move again, putting one foot in front of the other. Each step takes me further from that memory, from the prison Jarl made of a house that never felt like home. Each step is a victory, small but mine.

"All right, island," I say, injecting as much bravado into my voice as I can muster. "Show me what you've got. Can't be worse than what I've already survived."

As I continue up the slope, I silently pray I haven't just jinxed myself.

Finally, the trees thin out, and I'm on open ground, ascending directly to what I can now make out is a mountain. I pause, wiping rain from my eyes, and just... stare.

Even in the midst of the storm, the island is breathtaking and overwhelming. In the distance, a waterfall thunders down a cliff face, its spray fusing with the rain.

"Wow," I breathe. "If this is how I'm being

punished for not feeling remorse for my husband's death, sign me up for more."

Yet the beauty doesn't quite quell the fear gnawing at my insides. I'm alone. Lost. As the adrenaline from the crash fades, the reality of my situation starts to sink in. I wrap my arms around myself, suddenly colder, hoping those men who took me from Bariloche Sector might return to save me.

"Get it together, Hel," I whisper. "Find shelter first. Freak out later."

Scanning the slopes, I look for a cave or overhang but I'm too far. Somewhere dry where I can catch my breath and figure out my next move. I refuse to die here, not after everything I've been through.

I think of my father, of the cold look in his eyes as he wed me to our enemy—Jarl from the Balor pack.

"It's for the greater good of our Ulv pack," Father had said.

Greater good. The words echo in my mind, bitter and mocking. What about my good? What about my life, my dreams, my future? But those things didn't matter. Not to him. Not when there was a war to be stopped.

I remember the day he told me, his gaze never quite meeting mine. "You'll marry Jarl of the Balor pack. It will end the bloodshed."

At that moment, I realized I had never been a

daughter to him—just a bargaining chip to be played when the stakes were high enough.

And Jarl? The monster I was sold to? He sent his younger brother, Nikos, to serve my family. "A fair exchange," they all said, nodding and smiling as if they hadn't just shattered my world into a million pieces.

Fair. There's nothing fair about being ripped from everything I've ever known and handed over to a man old enough to be my father, a man with cruelty in his eyes and violence in his touch.

Rage burns in my chest, hot and fierce. Fuck them. Fuck all of them. My father, who saw me as nothing more than a means to an end. Jarl, who took sadistic pleasure in breaking me down day after day. The elders of both packs, who nodded and smiled and called it peace while I paid the price in blood and tears.

I clench my fists, nails digging into my palms. The pain helps, gives me something to focus on besides the ugly memories.

Four years of fear and agony, of gritting my teeth and surviving day by day. I've come too far to let a little thing like a plane crash and a deserted island take me out. I'm finally free of him.

With that, I continue my trek, searching for any sign of shelter. The rain continues to pour, and thunder rumbles overhead.

The rain beats down relentlessly, soaking me to the bone. Shelter. I need shelter. The mountains loom ahead, promising the possibility of caves. It's my best bet—there's no way I'm building a palm leaf hut in this downpour.

A bird's harsh cry cuts through the storm, making me glance up.

That's when I see him.

A man is standing at the edge of the tree line, maybe two hundred yards away. He's holding a burning torch in one hand, revealing him easily. And yet he's staring right at me as if he can see in the darkness. I can make out his imposing figure—dark pants, no shirt, and muscles. So. Many. Muscles.

Oh, fuck. So, I'm not alone after all. This really sucks.

My heart rate kicks up a notch. In this fucked up world, where most humans died out after the virus spread across the globe and shifters took control, females—especially Omegas like me—became in short supply. We're like honey to bees for Alphas. And I've had my fair share of that crap.

The way he's staring at me, already starting to make his way over... I can tell exactly what he wants.

Me.

Dread coils in my stomach. This was supposed to be my paradise island, my escape from monsters until I found a way to reach my brother, but it seems the monsters have found me, anyway.

I turn and run for the mountains, praying there's a

cave, a crevice, anything I can hide in. I keep my human form—if I shift to wolf, he'll track me even faster by my scent. My legs burn, my lungs heaving as I push myself harder than I have in years.

Heart pounding wildly in my chest, I know I'm panicking, but I've encountered enough men in my life to know they're all the same. They want to control, to rut, to breed us. So, if I can just hide, I can spy on who else lives on this island, if they're dangerous, and plan my next move.

I risk a look behind me and nearly trip. He's right there, so close, I can see the individual raindrops on his skin. True fear slams into me, stealing my breath.

"Well, well." His voice is a deep growl that sends shivers down my spine. "What do we have here? A little Omega, all alone out at night?"

I try to dodge faster ahead of him, but he's too fast and keeps up. As I stumble and glance over my shoulder once more, he's there, so damn close. His face is round, framed by light hair plastered to his head by the rain. Scars all over his arms and chest, a horrid grin, but it's his eyes that terrify me most—there's a hunger there that tells me everything I need to know. To him, I'm just a meal to sate his savage Alpha desires.

Not bothering to answer him, I sprint away. His mocking laugh follows me.

"Come on, little Omega. Don't you want to play? I promise to keep you safe from the others on the island."

I turn once more, desperate to know how close he is. Then something red catches my attention from the inside of his left arm. It's a tattoo—two half circles pressed close with a gap at the top and bottom, made of red flames, and in the middle, a straight line of more leaping fire.

I know that mark!

I've seen it before.

A cry catches in my throat as the awful truth hits me. Of all the places I could have landed...

Back in Denmark, both my family's pack, the Ulv wolves, and my dead husband's pack, the Balor wolves, use it. It's a mark for the worst of Alpha kind, those cast out of their own packs for crimes too heinous to forgive. They're sent to this prison island, and the magic mark that is burned into their flesh keeps them trapped here.

So, this place... it's filled with feral shifters who once lived in Denmark. The universe is playing a cruel trick on me, isn't it?

I've heard so many rumors about the violent acts they performed, tales told to scare children into behaving. *Be good, or you'll end up on the island with the feral Alphas.*

Fuck me.

Of all places, I had to land on fucking Nightmare Island.

TWO

The realization that I'm on Nightmare Island feels like a punch to the face. Fear floods my system, but with it comes a surge of adrenaline. I have to run, hide, escape. Hell, I'd rather take my chances with the sharks than these Alphas. I know they're Alphas because only crazy strong ones would survive a monstrous island like this.

I duck under a low-hanging branch, the leaves slapping against my face. As I frantically stare back, the man's arm is swinging out toward me, grasping at air as I dart just out of reach. My heart scales up to my throat, and I somehow escape his clutches.

"Where are you going, little Omega?" His words drip with false concern. "You must be so scared. I can make it all better."

"Yeah, sure you will," I remark, though my words are stolen by the howling storm.

I sprint across the open land leading up to the mountain, my boots splashing on the muddy ground, and plunge deeper into the woods, hoping the dense foliage nearby will give me cover. Except, it's dark and I can barely see anything, so I'm going slower, reaching out for the trees to guide me.

The rain intensifies. Lightning cracks across the sky, illuminating the forest in stark flashes. I've always been this way—the weather reflects my emotions. If only I could control it, summon it at will, but it's as unpredictable as my life has been.

Mom's words about my ability echo in my head. *Don't tell a soul, or it'll get you killed.* She drilled into me the dangers of being an Omega with such power. *You won't be a wife*, she'd warned. *You'll be an experiment.*

Another burst of lightning, another crash of thunder, and I use those spurts of light to see where I'm going.

Yeah, Mom. Message received. Secret's safe, but a fat lot of good it's doing me now.

My heart thunders in my chest. The man's calls behind me don't relent, but there's something in his tone that turns my stomach. He's enjoying this, taking his time, savoring the chase. It's too familiar, too much like—

No. Don't think about him. Don't think about Jarl.

A hand suddenly snags my hair, yanking me back. I cry out, my feet skidding on the muddy ground. Water streams down my face as he spins me around, pinning me against a tree with his body while still holding the flaming torch. All while I'm pushing my hands against his chest, but he's moving. His flame is burning hot so close to me. And the bark's digging into my back, but it's nothing compared to the revulsion I feel at his touch.

"Now, where did you come from?" He laughs in my face, a sound that sets my teeth on edge. "Did you ride in on this storm that came out of the blue?"

If only he knew how close to the truth he was.

"Get your hands off me." I spit the words, pushing against him.

His grip tightens on my hair, unmoved by my outburst. He's grinning, and I hate the way he smiles. His eyes are strange, almost glassy, as if they're not quite real. He stares at me like he's trying to read my soul. Fresh scratches mar his shoulders and arms, evidence of recent fights.

"You'll come with me," he commands like he owns me.

"Fuck you," I snap back.

"Such a mouth on you." He clicks his tongue, pressing closer. "We'll have to do something about that."

Fury climbs up my spine, hot and familiar. I feel

myself slipping into that headspace, the one I visited so often with Jarl—where emotions shut down, replaced by dark fantasies of revenge. The weight of the blade at my hip, stolen and hidden before boarding the plane, is a lifeline.

I soften my expression, forcing a smile. "You're right. I'm sorry. This is all just so... overwhelming."

His gaze lights up. Predators always love it when their prey stops fighting.

"You're such a beautiful creature," he purrs. "Men are going to fight to the death to get a chance to fuck you, you know that?"

I bat my eyes, channeling every submissive Omega stereotype I can think of. "And you'll protect me?"

One of his hands is still tangled in my hair, but his hold loosens slightly as he preens at my apparent submission.

"Of course, little one. I'll keep you safe." His grin widens, showing too many teeth. "Now, why don't you tell me how you got here?"

"Oh!" I let my gaze go wide, as if struck by a sudden thought. "I almost forgot. I have something that might help explain everything."

His curiosity piqued, he leans in closer. Perfect.

In one fluid motion, I draw the blade from its hiding place. My brother's words ring in my ears. *Our ancestors, the Vikings, never backed down. They were never afraid.*

I lift my hand to strike.

The Alpha's face whitens, his gaze locking on to the blade. Fuck!

Rapidly, my arm arcs forward, the blade glinting in his flame. He jerks backward, dropping his flame while releasing me slightly, and my intended killing blow swings at him wide. Instead of his throat, the blade rips across his broad chest, opening a long, angry gash from collarbone to sternum.

For a heartbeat, there's silence. Then a guttural growl rumbles from deep in his chest, his eyes glinting dangerously. Blood wells up from the cut, stark red against his tanned skin, mixing with the rain.

"You whore!" he snarls, his hand darting out faster than I can react. The back of his hand connects with my face with a hard crack. Pain explodes across my cheek and nose, bright spots dancing in my vision. The metallic taste of blood fills my mouth, and I feel a warm trickle running down my upper lip.

I stagger back, my free hand instinctively going to my face. When I pull it away, my fingers are smeared with red. My nose and cheek throb, a sharp, insistent pain that makes my eyes water, but I blink back the tears, refusing to show weakness.

My insides are trembling, but I don't back down. I won't give him the satisfaction.

Instead, I straighten, meeting his gaze defiantly. I

can feel my nose swelling, but I ignore the pain. I've endured worse. I'll endure this, too.

"Is that all you've got?" I spit, along with a mouthful of blood.

He lunges for my hand, his meaty fingers grasping for my blade. I twist away, but his hand clamps around my wrist like an iron vise, squeezing until I fear my bones might snap.

I gasp at his aggression while tugging my arm against his hold. His blood smears across my skin, hot and slick.

The storm escalates around us, trees and the wind thrashing wildly.

With a roar of effort, he slams my arm against the tree trunk.

I scream out as fire-hot pain bursts through my wrist and hand. The blade slips from my numb fingers, dropping away into the underbrush. His grip on me loosens, just for a moment, as he glances at his wounded chest, at so much blood. It's all the opening I need.

I drive my knee upward, catching him right between the legs. He wheezes, doubling over, and I seize my chance. I shove him with all my might, sending him staggering backward.

My feet barely touch the ground as I dash deeper into the forest. The storm rages around me, my heart racing just as fast, wishing I still had my knife.

I don't know where I'm going, but anywhere is better than here.

The Alpha's enraged roars fade behind me, but I don't slow down. I can't. On Nightmare Island, stopping means death... or worse.

Rain lashes at my face, the wind whipping through the trees with a banshee's wail. Every sense is on high alert. The metallic tang of blood—his and mine—mingles with the earthy scent of wet soil and the storm.

It's overwhelming, and my wolf's pressing against my insides for release, to fight this monster, but stopping to transform leaves me vulnerable. I scramble over fallen logs and duck under low branches.

A snap of lightning illuminates a steep slope ahead. Without breaking stride, I half run, half slide down it, using the slick mud to my advantage. It's reckless and dangerous—one wrong move and I could break my neck—but the alternative is worse.

At the bottom, I pause for a split second, straining to hear over the storm. Nothing. No sound of pursuit. But that doesn't mean I'm safe.

I press on, my drenched clothes clinging to me like a second skin.

As I run, a hysterical laugh bubbles up in my throat. Of all the places in the world to crash-land, I end up on an island full of exiled Alphas. It's like the universe looked at my life and thought, *You know what this girl needs? More violent men with control issues!*

However, I'm not the same scared girl I was when Jarl first claimed me. I've endured four years of hell, and I'm still standing.

The forest grows denser, the trees pressing in close. I slow my pace, forced to pick my way more carefully. My lungs burn, my legs tremble with exertion, but I push on. Somewhere in this green hell, there has to be a safe place. A cave, a hollow tree, anything.

As I move, my mind races. How many Alphas are on this island? Are there any other Omegas? Is there any way off this rock, or am I trapped here forever?

One problem at a time, Hel. First, survive. Then, escape.

A distant howl cuts through the storm's roar, sending fresh adrenaline coursing through my veins. He's not giving up. Of course he's not. Fucking Alpha. To him, I'm fresh meat in a world where Omegas are scarce.

I burst out of the woods, and I can see a bit clearer now in the night. My lungs scream with each ragged breath. The clearing before me lifts upward even more, and there, in the distance, I notice what looks like cave openings in the mountainside.

I scramble up the incline, my feet slipping on the wet grass. A snarl rips through the air behind me, and I twist my head to look back.

Oh, fuck me sideways.

The Alpha is hot on my heels, blood still oozing from the gash across his chest. His eyes are wild, feral, promising a world of pain if he catches me. Which, given how fast he's gaining, seems increasingly likely.

"Come here, you little bitch!" he roars. "I'm going to teach you what happens to Omegas who don't know how to behave."

"Sorry," I yell back, surprising myself with how steady my voice sounds. "I left my Submissive Omega rule book on the plane. You'll have to reschedule the lesson!"

I push harder, my legs aching. Just a little further. Just a little—

Movement catches my eye, and I nearly trip over my own twisted grass roots.

There's another male with a flaming torch, farther up the mountain, heading in my direction. But something's... off about him. I squint, trying to make out details through the rain.

Is that... is that a skull?

I'm sure I'm looking at a walking corpse, a body built with muscles, powerful and bulging, yet his head is a skull. I blink hard, certain I must be hallucinating. When I look again, I see it's just a man.

I pause, panic clawing at my throat. The Alpha behind me, Skull-face in front—caught between the devil and the deep blue sea.

"Nowhere to run now, sweetheart," the Alpha jeers, closing in. "Why don't you be a good little Omega and come here to me? I promise to keep you safe from him."

Skull-face says nothing, but his silent approach is somehow even more terrifying.

My heart pounds so fast that I'm surprised it hasn't burst out past my rib cage.

The rain is coming down fast and hard.

My head is racing. I'm tired, I'm scared, and I'm so fucking done with constantly running.

Something snaps inside me. A dam breaks, and suddenly, I'm not just afraid—I'm furious.

"You want me?" I scream, my voice raw with emotion. "Then come and fucking get me!"

Mirroring my scream, the sky lights up. For a split second, the world is bathed in brilliant white. Then comes the boom, so loud I feel it in my bones, feel it in the shaking ground beneath me.

The lightning strikes.

It hits the Alpha square in the chest, right where I cut him.

I'm frozen, stunned.

He's outlined in crackling blue-white energy. His mouth opens in a silent scream, his body rigid and shaking. Then he drops, hitting the ground. He twitches and convulses, smoke rising from his singed clothes and hair.

I stare, slack-jawed. Did I do that? Did I actually call down lightning?

"Holy shit," I breathe. "Thanks for the assist, Thor."

There's no time to celebrate. Skull-face is still coming, his pace quickening now that my other pursuer is down for the count.

I spin away, ready to make a break for the caves, but exhaustion and fear have taken their toll. My foot catches on a rock, and suddenly, the world is tilting, and I'm falling, tumbling down the slope. Pain explodes through my skull as it connects with something hard—a rock, a root, who knows? The world spins, darkness creeping in at the edges of my vision.

No. No, I can't pass out. Not here. Not now.

I try to push myself up, but my arms feel like they're made of stone.

The heavy darkness is closing in fast. The last thing I see is that skull-like face peering down at me.

Is this it? Is this how I go out? Concussed on a mountain, at the mercy of whatever nightmare Skull-face has in mind?

I come to slowly, awareness returning in bits and pieces. Damn smells. A croaking bird somewhere in the distance. Then the pain—my head feels like it's been used as a ball. That's when I notice that I'm no longer being rained on.

I crack one eye open, then immediately shut it again as the dim light sends daggers through my skull.

Okay, Hel. Take it slow.

Deep breath in. Deep breath out.

I try again, this time managing to keep my eyes open long enough to take in my surroundings. I'm in... a cave? The rough stone walls are illuminated by flickering firelight, casting dancing shadows that do nothing to calm my nerves.

I'm lying on something soft. Animal furs, maybe? The thought makes my stomach turn. I try to sit up, but dizziness forces me back down.

A grunt from somewhere to my left startles me. I turn my head, wincing at the pain, and freeze. There, crouched by the fire, is a figure that makes my blood run cold. It's him—the skull-faced man. Only now I can see it's not his actual face, but a mask. A very realistic, very terrifying one that covers his entire face, leaving only his eyes visible, which, from my position, are impossible to see.

"W-where..." I try to speak, but my throat is parched, the words coming out as a rasp.

He doesn't move, doesn't offer help. Just keeps staring.

I swallow hard and try again. "Where am I?"

For a long moment, I think he's not going to answer, but then he says, "Safe."

His voice is low, heavy, muffled slightly by the mask. It's not comforting. If anything, it sends a shiver down my spine.

I attempt to push myself up again, desperate not to be lying prone in front of this stranger. The cave spins, and I have to close my eyes to fight off a wave of nausea.

When I open them again, he's moved closer. I flinch involuntarily.

He stops, tilting his head slightly. The firelight catches on the contours of his mask, making the skull seem to grin. "Rest," he states, the word more command than suggestion.

I want to argue, to demand answers, but my body seems to have other ideas. The cave is starting to fade around the edges, and keeping my eyes open is becoming a monstrous task.

As I slip back into unconsciousness, the last thing I see is that skull mask. I can't tell if I'm looking at my savior or my doom.

Knowing my luck, probably both.

CHAPTER
THREE

GHOST

The darkness of the room suits my mood as I sit in an old, creaking chair, my eyes fixed on the girl lying in my bed. I couldn't leave her in the cave all night, but once she warmed up, I brought her home.

She's a mystery, this one. I found her running for her life from fuckwit Sten in the silent zone—that strip of my territory where I keep the guard presence light. It's a calculated risk, knowing there's no easy way to our part of the island except through tunnels... but one that paid off today as I often find the enemy wolves sniffing around.

At first glance, I thought she was just another of Sten's Omegas, finally making a break for it. I was ready to offer her sanctuary, to bring her over to my side of the island. It wouldn't be the first time I snatched one of his strays from under his nose.

But as I got closer, I realized she was so much more. The power radiating off her, the way the very air seemed to crackle around her—this was no ordinary Omega. And when I saw that lightning strike Sten? Well, there was no way in hell I was going to let him get his hands on her. Since the incident in the Gravewater pool five years ago, the bastard Sten has healed from almost everything I've thrown at him, so I have no doubt he'll survive the lightning, too.

So I interfered directly. Grabbed the Omega and brought her back to my stronghold. And now here she is, in my bed, a potential game changer in the palm of my hand.

I lean back in the chair, letting out a heavy breath. My hand unconsciously moves to my left forearm, fingers tracing the raised scar there. The mark that brands me, that brands all of us exiled here. A constant reminder of why we're on Nightmare Island, of the challenge that brought me to where I am now.

Five years ago, I should have remained dead in that battle against Sten. But somehow I came back. We both did. The memory of that day is still vivid, the taste of defeat bitter on my tongue...

"You both lost your lives temporarily," Aiquen, our elder, said. "Now that you both survived it's the time to make peace."

I laughed. Sten attacked and killed Aiquen. So much for peace.

We ended up splitting the island in half—his territory and mine. The men of the Balor pack joined me, while the Ulv went with him, the number almost equal. In the years since, we've carved out a sort of existence. Well, I have, at least. Sten and his lot still live like barbarians.

Me? I've salvaged what I can from the old civilizations that once called this rock home. The fae left behind buildings, ruins no one knew about until wolves were sent here. It's why I have my territory guarded, why I live in what passes for a mansion on this godforsaken island.

And it's why this mysterious girl is currently occupying my king-size bed, sleeping off the cut on her head from her fall.

I lean forward, elbows on my thighs, studying her in the moonlight that spills through the window. The storm passed as quickly as she lost consciousness, leaving behind this ethereal glow that bathes her in silver.

She's... captivating, her sweet scent still in my nostrils. Her long blonde hair is braided like a warrior's, the front strands woven tight while the rest spills across the pillow. Her face is perfection—strong cheekbones, a petite nose, a mouth with full lips that makes me imagine her naked. She's curvy, more so than others on this island, and in all the right places. The kind of Omega that sets my blood on fire.

I've had my share of the Omegas on this island, but none of them have affected me like this one. Just looking at her makes my wolf stir, makes hunger gnaw at my insides. It's more than physical attraction, though. Her wolf calls to mine in a way I've never experienced before.

Could she be... No. I shut down that line of thinking before it can take root. Hope is a dangerous thing here, especially hope for a true mate. The Omegas here were all exiled for their crimes—killing their Alphas, rejecting them, that sort of thing. We welcomed them, of course. Under my protection, they're safe. Everyone plays their part in our little community, fulfilling desires as they choose.

But a true mate? That's a fucking fairy tale. Every new arrival goes through the process of checking whether they're matched to any of my men. So far, we've come up empty.

Still, the hunger is there. The need to bury my cock deep in an Omega, to knot her, to release the need that builds up day after day on this hellhole of an island. Some days, it's all I can think about. That brings out something raw and animalistic in me, and I fucking crave it.

And this girl... she's special. The power she holds, the leverage it could give me to finally unite both sides of the island... well, after fucking Sten's six feet under, of course.

Her scent is like heaven, doing things to me I can't even begin to describe. Every inch of her calls to my wolf. My heart races, my palms sweat. She's a wolf, obviously, but there's something else there—a hint of humanity and the metallic tang of electricity.

Most wolves don't carry magic, except for a few from Denmark that I'm aware of. So where did this little firecracker come from?

I inhale deeply, letting her scent wash over me. Pine and wild roses, with an undercurrent of ripe berries—it screams Omega, something that tightens my balls. It takes me a moment to place it, but when I do, a growl rumbles in my chest.

Heat. The faint beginning stages of an Omega's heat.

Fuck me.

I rub a hand across my mouth, my mind racing. This complicates things. Makes them infinitely more interesting but also dangerous.

Silence.

I can't take my attention off her, but I try, staring around the room to distract my obsession.

The room is sparse. Wooden floorboards are weathered but solid. A sturdy wardrobe against one wall. There's even a door leading to a bathroom with running water, one of the perks left behind by the fae, their magic keeping the old plumbing functional long after they were gone.

A soft sound draws my attention back to the bed. She's stirring, making little noises that go straight to my cock. I sit back in my seat, forcing myself to remain still as she slowly opens her eyes.

She glances around, confusion evident on her face. Sitting up, she touches the back of her head where I bandaged her wound, then looks down at her now-dry clothes. When she goes to scramble out of bed, I clear my throat.

Her head snaps up, gaze wide as she peers into the shadows where I sit. The moonlight washes over her face, and fuck if she isn't captivating.

She's all legs, this one. Probably hits about five foot eight, which means she'd fit just right under my chin. Her hair's a mess, tangled and wild, as if she's been through hell. It's the color of wheat fields back in Denmark, all golden and shit, with darker streaks running through it. Makes me want to grab a fistful and see if it's as soft as it looks.

Her face? Odin! It's the kind that could start wars. A mouth made for sin and eyes that could freeze me in my tracks. It's too dark to see their color, but they're sharp. Always moving, always watching. She's got the look of someone who's been through shit, who's always waiting for the other shoe to drop.

Her tits strain against her shirt, and her hips flare

out just enough to give me something to hold on to. She moves like a predator, all coiled energy and grace, and I'm fucking intrigued. It has my wolf pacing, itching to chase, to claim.

But it's more than just her looks. There's something about her, some kind of raw power that sets my teeth on edge. My cock twitches, and I have to shift in my seat. Fuck, I haven't reacted like this to a woman in years.

Her shoulders slump slightly, and the jerky movement of her gaze darts around the room, landing on the exit door.

"Well," she says, breaking the silence. "This is cozy. Do you make a habit of kidnapping women, or am I just special?"

I can't help the chuckle that escapes me. "Trust me, sweetheart, if I was in the habit of kidnapping women, I'd have a much fuller house."

She stares at me, squinting into the shadows. "Oh, it's you. Skull-face. You know, watching people sleep is generally considered creepy in civil society."

"Good thing we're not in civil society, then, isn't it?" I lean forward, letting the moonlight illuminate my mask. "Besides, I had to make sure you didn't die on me. That would be inconvenient."

"Gods forbid I inconvenience you with my death," she retorts. "I'll try to schedule any future near-death experiences at more suitable times."

I laugh again. I like this girl. She's got fire.

"Since we're exchanging pleasantries," I say with a low tone, "mind telling me who you are and how you ended up on my island?"

"Your island?" Her gaze narrows. "Funny, I don't remember seeing your name on the *Welcome to Paradise* sign. Must have missed it while I was running for my life."

I stand, moving closer to the bed. She tenses but doesn't retreat. Brave little thing.

"Let me rephrase," I growl, letting a hint of Alpha command seep into my voice. "Who are you?"

She meets my gaze, holding my stare. "I'm the girl who's wondering why she's in a stranger's bed instead of dead in a ditch. Your turn. Who are you, Skull-face?"

I can't help but chuckle. "The man who saved your ass from becoming Sten's new chew toy. You're welcome, by the way."

"My hero," she deadpans. "I'll be sure to send a thank-you note. Now, if you'll excuse me..."

She starts to get out of bed, but I'm not done with her yet.

"Not so fast, sweetheart. You still haven't answered my question. Where did you come from?"

She sighs dramatically. "Would you believe me if I said I fell from the sky?"

"Cute," I growl. "Almost as cute as that little lightning trick you pulled out there. Want to tell me how you managed that?"

She laughs, but it sounds forced even to my ears. "You think if I controlled the weather, I'd let myself get captured by Alphas like you?"

I take another step closer. "I said *lightning*, but you can do the whole weather thing, can't you?"

She glares up at me, her jaw set. "You're delusional."

"And you're a terrible liar," I counter.

"Well, thanks for not leaving me in the woods." She stands up from the bed. "I'd better go."

I'm blocking her path in seconds. She has to crane her neck to look up at me, and I hear her swallow hard. *Yeah, sweetheart, I'm not some runt you can push around.*

"Where will you go?" I ask, my voice deceptively calm. "Is someone waiting to pick you up from the island?"

That has me intrigued if it's the case.

She scoffs but reins it in quickly. It tells me everything I need to know. She's stuck here, just like the rest of us poor bastards.

"So," I continue. "What did you do that was so bad you got thrown onto Nightmare Island?"

She shrugs, aiming for nonchalant but missing by a mile. "Wouldn't you like to know?"

She tries to sidestep me, making her way across

the room. I take a few long strides backward, easily cutting her off again.

"You never answered my question," I state in a darker tone. Deep in my chest, my wolf rumbles, curious about the new toy in front of us.

She stares at my mask, her gaze tracing the contours of it. "Why do you wear that?"

"Why are you avoiding my questions?"

We stand there for a long, silent pause. Finally, she breaks the silence.

"Look, I appreciate the save, really... but I don't know you, and you don't know me. Let's keep it that way."

I lean in close, close enough to catch the faint scent of her impending heat. It takes every ounce of self-control not to bury my face in her neck right then and there, to lick her, taste her, bite her.

"Here's the thing, sweetheart," I growl. "On this island, there are no secrets. Not from me. So you can either start talking, or you can get comfortable because you're not leaving this room until I get some answers."

Her vibrant blue eyes flash with anger, and for a second, I swear I see a spark of electricity dance across her skin. Interesting.

"Do you have a name?"

"Hel," she answers. "And you can't keep me here," she hisses.

I grin behind my mask. "Watch me."

With that, I turn and stride out of the room. I hear her rush forward, but I'm already closing the door. The lock clicks into place.

"You asshole!" she yells through the wood. "You can't do this!"

I laugh, the sound echoing down the hallway, knowing she won't find a way out the window as it has bars on it. Can never be too safe.

"Welcome to Nightmare Island, sweetheart. You might want to get used to disappointment."

Her muffled curses follow me as I make my way down the long hall. We're on the third floor of the old mansion the fae built long ago, and with each step down to the next level, I find my mind caught on her. Who is she? Where did she come from? And most importantly, what the fuck is she capable of?

I can't get her scent out of my head.

I enter my office, blinking against the sunlight pouring through the windows. The room is bright—the opposite of the storm that was silenced the moment our newcomer passed out.

The furniture is worn and old, like everything else on this island, but it serves its purpose. We're lucky we found and restored them, or we'd be living like fucking animals in the woods.

Axel and Knut, my second-in-command and head of guards, respectively, look up as I enter. Axel's leaning against the desk, his massive arms crossed over his chest. The scars on his face twist as he raises an eyebrow at me. Knut's pacing by the window, restless as always. His dark skin gleams in the sunlight, and his eyes are sharp as he turns to me.

"So," Axel rumbles. "Who's the girl? New Omega on the island?"

"Not quite." I shake my head, dropping into the chair behind my desk. "She's not talking, but I'll get her to open up. For now, she doesn't leave the mansion. Watch her if she does manage to get out. I get the impression a locked door won't keep her contained for long."

"Understood." Knut nods, his hand unconsciously moving to the knife at his hip. "But, Ghost, there's something else. We've spotted Sten's men on the north perimeter, near our foraging woods."

I growl under my breath. "Did you catch the fuckers?"

They both shake their heads. Damn it.

"Not even in the traps?"

No response. My gut tightens as I refuse to share our provisions with those fuckers unless they pledge loyalty to me.

"Double the guards," I order, knowing Sten will be on our doorstep to take the girl the moment he heals from his lighting strike because that bastard doesn't stay dead. He'll come to claim that she's his.

Axel shifts, his face serious. "And tomorrow night? The Blood Moon Hunt... is the new girl attending?"

I lean back in my chair, considering. The Blood Moon Hunt is a celebration, giving everyone something to look forward to. It's a time when we let our wolves run free, hunting and howling under the red moon, tracking and killing anything they find.

"She won't be ready," I decide aloud. "Keep her in the mansion."

Knut and Axel exchange a look. I can practically hear the unasked questions hanging in the air.

"Something you want to say?" I challenge.

Knut clears his throat. "It's just... she must be special if you're keeping her under wraps like this. Is she—"

I stand abruptly, cutting him off.

"She's a wild card. And in our game, wild cards can either win you the pot or blow up in your face. Until I know which one she is, we play this close to the chest. Understood?"

They both nod yet stare at me, waiting for me to open up. I trust them with my life. Since the battle with Sten five years ago, they've been loyally by my side, so I give them a short rendition of what just happened out in the field—about the storm, her potential ability.

Eyes bulging, they gape at me before speaking.

"She could change everything for us on the island.

Take out Sten's pack, maybe help us find a way off this fucking island, once we work out how to get these fucking marks off our arms," Axel states my exact thoughts. He's always been canny like that.

"Or we sell her to the right buyer," Knut comments. "Someone as powerful as her would easily be in demand and buy us freedom from our marks."

My teeth grind, and I want to shove him through a wall for his suggestion Except I school my features because she means nothing to me—but I chuckle internally at me trying to delude myself. I already feel my growing obsession with her, unable to stop picturing her beauty. I'm not sure I can give her away.

As the pair turn to leave, a thought strikes me.

"It stays between us," I bark as they head out the door. "Boys," I call out, stopping them at the door. "Tell the pack to get ready. Tomorrow, we're not just hunting deer."

Axel's gaze lights up with understanding. "Sten's men?"

I nod, feeling my wolf stir with anticipation. "If they want to trespass on our land, they'd better be prepared to become prey. Tomorrow, we will remind them why they call this Nightmare Island."

As Axel and Knut break into excited chatter and leave, I turn to look out the window. The forest looms in the distance, promising blood and violence tomorrow, but my mind's still upstairs, fixed on the blonde wildcat who jokes about falling out of the fucking sky.

She's the key. I can feel it in my bones. That lightning, her scent, the way she carries herself—she's not like any Omega I've ever met. And if she can control the weather... Well, that changes everything.

I grip the windowsill, my knuckles turning white. For years, we've been scratching in the dirt, fighting over scraps. But her? She could be our ticket out of this hellhole.

I feel feral on the inside and hungry to discover her secrets. Oh, yes, little storm-bringer, you and I are going to have a long chat. By the time we're done, you'll give me everything I want.

After all, there's more than one way to break an Omega. I'm going to have fun trying them all.

CHAPTER
FOUR
HEL

I jolt awake, my heart pounding like crazy in my chest. For a terrifying moment, I swear I see Jarl standing by the bed, his hulking frame silhouetted against the dim light. He's glaring at me with that familiar mix of contempt and anger, his eyes cold. I flinch back instinctively.

"I'm sorry, I didn't mean to—"

I hate how quickly those words pour from my mouth.

But he's gone, nothing more than a ghost conjured by my sleep-addled brain. I rub my eyes furiously, willing the remnants of the nightmare away. My hands are shaking, and I can feel a chilling sweat on my skin.

Just breathe, Hel.

As my heartbeat slowly returns to normal, I take in

my surroundings. Right. Skull-face's room. I must have dozed off after he left. *Smart move, Hel. Fall asleep in the lair of the beast. Real survival instincts you've got there.*

But honestly, can you blame me? This bed is ridiculously comfortable, a far cry from the hard, lumpy mattress Jarl forced me to sleep on. And the sheets... gods, the sheets. They smell incredible. Like a forest after a thunderstorm, with hints of cocoa and something uniquely... Alpha. It's intoxicating, and I hate how much I love it. I'm practically rolling around in his scent like a pig in mud.

Pathetic, Hel. Real pathetic. But after everything I've been through, don't I deserve a little indulgence? Even if it's just burying my face in some admittedly delicious-smelling sheets?

I glance at the window, trying to gauge the time. The light filtering through the curtains is dimming, casting long shadows across the room. Early morning, maybe?

I yawn, feeling as though I've slept for a week. When was the last time I was allowed to just... rest? Without fear of Jarl barging in, without the constant tension of waiting for the next blow to fall?

Right. Enough lazing about. Time to get my bearings.

Swinging my legs over the side of the bed, I grimace at my clothes. They're dry now but stiff and uncomfortable, clinging to my skin in all the wrong places. A quick scan of the room reveals another door, probably leading to a bathroom.

When I push the door open, the place surprises me. It's like a rougher version of back home in Denmark. Everything's a bit older, more worn, but still... civilized. The dark wood paneling gives the room a cozy feel, despite the faint musty scent that lingers in the air. Since when do feral Alphas have interior decorating skills? I snort at the mental image of Skull-face fussing over throw pillows and color schemes.

The bathroom is all dark wood and faded tiles, with a large window covered by blinds. Faint sunlight streams in at the edges, catching dust motes in its beams. A small wooden rack holds towels and on top... clothes? I unfold them curiously. A navy-colored T-shirt and patched jeans, about my size. The fabric is soft and well-worn but clean. There is also a pair of sneakers.

"Looks like Skull-face has a heart after all." I move my fingers over the clothes. "Or at least a basic understanding of hospitality."

I begin to unbraid my messy hair, then I head into the shower.

If you can call it that. It's a hose-like contraption hanging from the wall. I eye it skeptically, memories of ice-cold baths at Jarl's command flashing through my mind. However, beggars can't be choosers, and I feel grimy from yesterday's ordeal. I strip down, shivering in the cool air, and turn on the tap.

"Shi—" I leap back as ice-cold water sprays out, a startled laugh escaping me. Teeth chattering, I glare at the shower. "One temperature, huh? Sadists, the lot of you."

Gritting my teeth, I dive in for the world's fastest shower. The cold is shocking at first, but as I scrub away the dirt and sweat of yesterday, it becomes almost invigorating. I grab a brand-new soap that smells like coconut, with little flakes in it that gently exfoliate my skin. Probably homemade, like Mom used to do back home with animal fat and fire ashes. The familiar scent brings a lump to my throat. I push the homesickness away, focusing instead on getting clean.

Fresh, freezing, and slightly impressed by their soap-making skills, I towel off vigorously, trying to bring some warmth back into my limbs. I pull on the new clothes, relishing the feeling of soft fabric against my skin, and step into the black sneakers. No mirror, but I feel like a new person.

Back in the main room, I peer out the window. The light's different now—dimmer, with a golden quality that speaks of late afternoon rather than morning. Wait a second. That's not morning light. That's evening. Did I sleep the whole damn day?

My stomach growls in response, loud enough that I half expect Skull-face to come bursting in, thinking it's some kind of monster. I press a hand to my belly, realizing I can't remember the last time I ate. Right. Food. That's the next order of business.

I mean, if they wanted me dead, I'd be long gone into the afterworld, so I think I'm safe to investigate where I am... for now.

The door's locked, of course, but that's never stopped me before. I retrieve the small pick I always keep in my pocket—a habit born from too many time-outs in locked rooms. The lock is old but well maintained. It takes a bit more effort than I'm used to, but finally, I hear that satisfying click.

I ease the door open, wincing at the creak of hinges. The hallway beyond is empty, lit by the warm glow of oil lamps. No guards. Either Skull-face is over-confident, or this is a trap. Knowing my luck, probably both.

The smell of freshly baked bread hits me as I creep down the hall, making my stomach growl even louder. The scent is mouthwatering, reminding me of Sunday mornings back home when Jarl would go hunting, and I was left alone... before everything went to hell. I follow my nose, padding quietly down the carpeted hallway. Old paintings line the walls, landscapes mostly faded and slightly crooked. It's all so... normal, like a run-down country manor, not the lair of dangerous Alpha wolves.

I round a corner and—

"Oof!" I collide with something soft and decidedly human-shaped. Stumbling back, I find myself face-to-face with another woman. She's about my height, maybe a few years older, with huge violet eyes and a mass of brown curls that seem to have a life of their own. She's absolutely beautiful.

"Oh!" she exclaims, looking as startled as I feel. Her eyes widen as she takes me in, a smile spreading across her face. "You're out of the room. We were told you might be and that we're to give you anything you need."

"We?" I blink, thrown off guard. "Why?" The questions tumble out before I can stop them. "I mean, who are you? Where am I exactly?"

She giggles, and I notice how her curls bounce with the motion. It's annoyingly adorable.

"Oh, honey. You really are new here, aren't you? It's not just men on the island, silly!"

"It's not?" I blurt out, feeling like an idiot. Of course it's not. *Get it together, Hel.*

"I mean, clearly it's not. You think only men commit crimes?" She laughs again. "Especially when just going against an Alpha can have an Omega committed to Nightmare Island. At least, that's what my husband did to me." She shrugs as if being exiled is no big deal. "But that's in the past."

My mind is reeling. Other women. Other Omegas. This changes everything.

"So, how many Omegas are here?" I ask, trying to keep the excitement out of my voice. Allies, maybe. Or at least, not everyone here wants to eat me. Probably.

"With you, it's now seventeen," she replies with a tight grin, as though there's more to that answer than she's willing to share. "I'm Eve, by the way. And you look like you could use a meal. Come on, I'll show you to the kitchen."

"Thought you'd never ask," I say, falling into step beside her. My stomach gives another loud growl, and she laughs. "I'm Hel. And maybe on the way, you can tell me more about Skull-face?"

Eve's eyebrows shoot up, her violet eyes sparkling with amusement. "Skull-face? Oh, you mean Ghost! Girl, you've got a lot to learn about this place."

I guess his name makes sense, though I have so many questions about him and that mask.

"So, we had just over one-hundred Alphas on count last month. Ghost," Eve says, her tone taking on a dreamy quality. "He's our leader. Dangerous as hell, but fair if you don't cross him. He's the reason we Omegas have any kind of decent life here."

"Decent life? On a prison island?"

Eve shrugs. "It's better than what we left behind. Trust me." There's darkness in her eyes that I recognize all too well. I decide not to push. We all have our demons.

We turn a corner, and the smell of baked food intensifies.

"So, what's Ghost's deal?" I ask, trying to sound casual. "Why the skull mask? Seems a bit... theatrical for a prison island."

Eve's laugh echoes down the hallway. "That's a long story. Let's just say it's part of what makes him... him. You'll understand when you get to know him better."

I snort. "Hard pass, I'm good. I'm more interested in getting off this island."

Eve stops, turning to face me with a serious expression. "Hel, listen to me. This place... it's not what you think. Things aren't exactly as they seem here. It's dangerous, and bad things happen all the time, even in our pack."

Her voice drops to a whisper, and I have to lean in to hear her.

"These shifters are feral. They lose control often. Never, ever let your guard down."

A shiver runs down my spine as Eve's words sink in. She's trembling slightly, her eyes darting around as if checking for eavesdroppers.

"But I thought you said—" I start, confused by her sudden change in demeanor.

She cuts me off with a sharp shake of her head.

"I know what I said earlier. We have to keep up appearances. You never know who's listening." Her fingers dig into my arm, her nails biting into my skin. "Ghost might seem fair, but he's still an Alpha. And Alphas here... they're not like the ones back home. They're worse."

All things I already knew, but to hear it from her makes it worse, turning my stomach.

"They've been here too long. Cut off from civilization, from any kind of restraint. Some of them... they're more beast than man now."

Before I can respond, I hear footsteps approaching. Eve's expression changes in an instant, a bright smile plastered on her face as she turns toward the sound.

"Let's move," she says, her voice cheerful but her eyes pleading.

Eve leads me down a winding staircase, the wood creaking beneath our feet. The farther we descend, the stronger the aromas of spices, freshly baked bread, and something earthy and wild. My stomach grumbles embarrassingly loud, and Eve shoots me an amused glance.

We round a corner, and I'm covered by a wave of warmth and light. The kitchen is nothing like I expected. It's all worn wood and gleaming copper, bathed in the golden glow of a massive fireplace. A cauldron hangs over the flames, something fragrant bubbling inside. To the side, there's an oven with a sturdy wooden door, and I watch, transfixed, as an older woman pulls out a loaf of bread so perfectly golden it looks like it belongs in a painting. The smell hits me like a physical force, and my mouth waters.

"This is..." I trail off, struggling to find the words. It's like stepping into a fairy-tale kitchen, not a prison-island galley. I wonder if I had it all wrong. Maybe it's just being out there with the men that's the issue. But then I remember Eve's warning. Beauty can hide danger, after all.

A large wooden table dominates the center of the room, covered in a basket overflowing with fruits I've never seen before, their skins a mix of colors. Loaves of bread, some still steaming, are piled high. There are pots of what looks like jam or preserves, their contents glowing like jewels in the firelight.

"This is not what I expected," I admit, taking it all in.

Eve grins. "Wait till you taste it. Mara's baking is legendary."

The older woman only smiles at us as Eve cuts two thick slices of bread.

"You bake incredibly," I say, but Mara nods at me.

"She doesn't talk," Eve explains. She leans in closer, her words barely above a whisper. "Her husband... he cut out her tongue before dumping her here. But her baking skills are exceptional."

The blood drains from my face for her suffering. "That's horrific," I whisper back, fighting the urge to reach out to Mara to offer some comfort. But what comfort could I possibly give?

Eve slathers the bread with what looks like butter, but when I take a bite, a strong taste of coconut fills my mouth. It's delicious, creamy and slightly sweet. I finish it faster than I'd like to admit, licking my fingers without thinking.

As I eat, I can't help but notice fresh scratch marks on Eve's arm, partially hidden by her sleeve, along with faint bruises on her neck. She catches me looking and tugs her sleeve down. All Alphas are the same at the end of the day, aren't they?

Eve places a bowl of stew in front of me. Steam rises from the thick, rich-looking broth, carrying with it a scent that makes me almost drool. Chunks of meat float alongside vegetables. I take a cautious bite, and the flavors explode on my tongue. It's savory, with a hint of something wild and gamy. It tastes like...

"Chicken?" I guess, though I know it can't be. Where would they get chickens on an island like this?

Eve laughs. "Crocodile, actually. Do you like it?"

I almost choke but manage to swallow. The meat is tender, falling apart in my mouth, but knowing what it is makes me hesitate before taking another bite.

"It's delicious."

After the meal, Eve stands. "Let me show you a great view of the island. I'm guessing you'll be here with us now."

I shrug, trying to seem nonchalant. "Well, until I can find a way off this place."

"Yeah, wouldn't that be nice?" she says. She pulls up her sleeve, showing me a burned mark on her arm. "Not unless a miracle happens."

I instinctively pull down my own sleeve, not wanting her to know I'm here by accident and bear no mark. Right now, I want to blend in, then find my own way out without anyone hating me for having a chance they don't.

Eve guides me out of the kitchen, up steps to the third floor to a balcony, not far from my room. Even with the descending sun, the view steals my breath away. The island spreads out before us—vibrant, lush forest and flowing mountains cradled by the bluest sea. It's paradise, or it would be if it weren't a prison with wild Alphas.

"This is our side of the island," Eve explains. "Sten rules the other half."

"Sounds like a charming neighborhood," I murmur sarcastically.

"You just have to abide by a few simple rules, and you should survive," she says, emphasizing the last word in a way that sends chills down my spine.

"Well, that sounds ominous. What's next? Don't feed the Alphas after midnight?"

"Never go into the woods alone late at night. If you must go, don't travel alone. If you're about to come into heat, for gods' sake, tell us and stay away from the men."

I swallow hard. "Anything else?" I ask.

Eve's gaze meets mine, deadly serious. "Never, ever challenge Ghost's authority. The last Omega who did... well, let's just say the crocodiles ate well that week."

A chill runs down my spine, and in a flash, I'm back with Jarl, feeling small and powerless and so, so afraid. But I'm not that girl anymore. I force a smirk, even as my heart races.

"Got it. Don't poke the bear. Or the wolf, in this case. Any other fun island activities I should know about? Volleyball with severed heads, maybe?"

Eve doesn't smile at my joke. Instead, she tugs at my arm, her grip just shy of painful.

"Come on," she says, her voice urgent. "I need to get back to my chores, and you're expected to attend the celebrations tonight. You can help them set up the tables down behind the mansion. I will join you as soon as I finish helping Mara."

She grins, and I join her down a hallway leading away from my room until we reach the end, where there's a dark descending staircase.

"At the bottom and down a long corridor, head out the door. Then you'll be outside. I'll be in the yard."

With a small shove in the back, she rushes back to the way we came from the kitchen. Strange girl.

I turn and take my first steps down when a faint

murmur of voices reaches me from behind. Turning back around, I catch a glimpse of Eve pressed up against Ghost.

Her hands are all over his chest.

He tilts his head to the side, staring at her, that damn skull mask making it impossible to read his expression. Eve's saying something I can't hear, but when Ghost drags his hand down her hair, bunching it at the back of her head, a pang of... something... strikes my chest.

I feel like I'm witnessing a private moment, yet I can't look away. I have no feelings for this man. Sure, he saved me, but Eve has scars. Did he do that to her? He leans in, whispering in her ear, and as Eve gasps, I quickly pull back.

A wave of... is that jealousy? No, it can't be. Who the hell cares what Ghost does or who he does it with?

As the voices die away, followed by footsteps coming my way, I slip into the shadows and rush down the stairs, not wanting Ghost to think I'm spying on him. My heart pounds in my ears as I dart down the dark staircase, Eve's urgent instructions echoing in my mind. Louder footsteps in the hallway above spur me on.

The stairs seem endless, spiraling down into darkness. My hand trails along the cold stone wall. I tell myself I'm just going to help outside, to get to know some people. It's not because I can't shake the image of Eve in Ghost's arms. It's not because I care. It's not.

At the bottom, a long, dimly lit corridor stretches before me to my right. Shadows dance on the walls, cast by flickering torches. It's like something out of a gothic novel, and I expect to see a monster lurking in the corners.

"None of those here," I mumble to myself. "Just bloodthirsty werewolves. Much better."

Hurrying down the corridor, my steps sound around me. Finally, I reach a massive door made of thick wood and iron. I grasp the handle, cool metal against my sweaty palm, and wrench it open with all my strength.

The last rays of sunlight of the day hit my face as I step outside. I'm blinded. Then my eyes adjust, and I'm faced with a wall of dense forest. The trees loom over me, their branches reaching out like gnarled fingers.

The door slams shut behind me with a resounding boom, and I jump, my heart leaping into my throat.

"It's just a door. A very loud, very ominous door."

As I step back, something feels... off. The woodland presses up against what should be the back of the mansion. But what I'm seeing isn't the elegant, if run-down, building I was in moments ago. It's a wall of stone stretching up into the darkening sky, and on either side of me, it curls around, forcing me to go one way only... into the woods.

My stomach drops, a cold weight settling in my gut. This isn't right. This isn't where I'm supposed to be. Did I take a wrong turn? Or did Eve mislead me?

That sickening feeling in my chest tells me I've just been played.

Panic rising, I rush back to the door. The metal handle is unyielding under my grip. Locked.

"No, no, no," I say, yanking at the handle with increasing desperation, remembering all of Eve's rules, and while she could have lied about those, too, I can't convince myself otherwise she did. "Don't do this to me. Open, damn you!"

The forest seems to press closer, the shadows deepening as the sun sinks lower. Then, from somewhere in the depths of the woods, a single howl rises. It's long, mournful, and terrifyingly close. The hairs on the back of my neck stand on end.

Another howl joins the first, then another. I'm pretty sure I know what or who is on the menu.

CHAPTER
FIVE
GHOST

The corridor stretches before me, shadows dancing on the stone walls. I can almost taste the excitement of the upcoming hunt in the air. But something's off. A nagging feeling in my gut that I can't shake.

Suddenly, Eve emerges from the shadows, as if she's been lying in wait. Her hands are on my chest before I can react, fingers splaying across my muscles. A growl rumbles inside me, low and warning.

Eve. The Omega I've spent more time with than I care to admit, but that's all it's ever been—ruts, a physical release, nothing more. She's a distraction, a way to kill time on this godforsaken island. There are only so many hunts a man can go on before he starts to lose his mind.

I'm no fool. I see the crazy in her eyes when she looks at me, the obsession that was endearing at first but now grates on my nerves.

"Ghost," she purrs, batting her eyelashes in a way that's meant to be seductive but just comes off as desperate. "If you're in the mood, we can go back to my room."

I groan, partly in frustration, partly in disgust at my own weakness.

"Is everything ready for the hunt?" I ask, ignoring her comment.

"Of course." She nods, not moving an inch from where she's pressed against me. "But are you sure you don't want to... warm up first?"

My patience snaps. I run my hands down her hair, grasping it aggressively and tugging her head back. "Don't push me today, Eve," I growl in her ear, my voice low and dangerous.

She whimpers, and I hate how much I love that sound. She's prey, helpless and afraid. And I consider it, then shove the idea away.

"I'm sorry," she whispers, her voice trembling, but she doesn't move away. Instead, her chin quivers, and she looks up at me with those big, manipulative eyes. "Ghost, there's something you should know. About the new Omega."

I stiffen, my mind instantly going to the blonde spitfire I rescued. "What about her?"

Eve's voice drops to a whisper, as if she's sharing some dark secret. "She's dangerous, Ghost. She controls the weather. What happens if she gets really angry at us or if someone hurts her? Will she bring a hurricane down on us, killing us all?"

I blink, anger bubbling in my chest like lava ready to erupt. "Who told you she has abilities?" I growl, feeling Eve tremble against me.

"She did," Eve squeaks. "She was proud of it, almost bragging. Or no, more like a threat. I don't think she belongs with us. Maybe we should feed her to the Alphas in the hunt. There are worse ways to go." She shrugs nonchalantly.

Her brutality shouldn't surprise me. Eve has always had this dark anger in her, a residue from her past. Most days, I don't give a shit about it, but today, that side of her infuriates me. The thought of Hel being torn apart by feral Alphas... it does something to me. Something I'm not ready to examine too closely.

My hands fall to Eve's shoulders, and I shove her off me, harder than necessary.

"Listen to me," I snarl. "You don't breathe a word of this to anyone. Not a single fucking soul. Or I'll feed you to the others myself. Understand?"

Fear blanches her face, and she nods frantically before slipping away, disappearing back into the shadows she came from.

The hunt suddenly seems less important.

"Ghost! Need your help," Knut's voice echoes down the hallway, interrupting my thoughts. He waves a hand for me to join him, an expression of urgency on his face.

I sigh, pinching the bridge of my nose under my mask.

"What the fuck now?" I state more to myself than to him.

fter helping Knut with a brawl that broke out between four Alphas, I've been in my study. Instead of joining the hunt, I'm here, trapped within these walls by my own racing thoughts. My fingers trace the edge of my mask, the bone-white skull smooth under my touch. It's a reminder of who I am, what I've become.

Howls pierce the night as the hunt has started in the woods.

But fuck, I'm distracted. The new Omega hasn't left my mind. I've kept my distance since yesterday to give her time. But hell if she doesn't invade my thoughts every second of the damn day and night. And the constant hard-on isn't helping matters, either.

Finally, I can't take it anymore. I stride out of the room and head toward my room—her room now. My pulse thumps in my veins as I approach the door. The need to get her out of my thoughts wars with the memory of her impending heat. That sweet scent... it's making me damn near obsessed.

I knock, the sound sharp and demanding in the quiet hallway. The door swings open with a slight creak at my knock. I shove it the rest of the way, only to find the room empty. The bed is untouched, the sheets still messy. Her scent lingers in the air, teasing me, mocking me.

"Hel?" I call out, my voice gruff with frustration. I cross to the bathroom, my steps quick and agitated. Empty. Fuck!

I make a beeline for the kitchen, hoping she's there for a meal. Eve and Mara are often there together. Though Eve doesn't get along well with the other fifteen Omegas in the pack, preferring the company of Alphas. I've seen her flirting with them, her hands lingering a bit too long, her laugh a bit too breathy. But with over one hundred men in my pack needing attention, I don't give a fuck what she does.

Right now, though, I'm fuming. I march down the corridors, my footsteps echoing off the stone walls. The mansion is a maze of hallways and rooms, a relic of the island's past inhabitants. Tapestries, faded and worn, line the walls, depicting hunts and battles long forgotten. The air is thick with the scent of old wood,

MILA YOUNG

dust, and the faint metallic tang of blood that never quite fades.

I burst into the kitchen, the heavy oak door slamming against the wall. The girls lounging around the large wooden table jump, startled by my sudden entrance. Mara stands by the old stone oven, her weathered hands kneading dough. She doesn't even flinch at my arrival, her eyes downcast as always.

My gaze locks on Eve, who scrambles to her feet. Her eyes are wide with worry or maybe fear. Good.

"Ghost?" she mumbles, her voice small.

I stride up to her, barely containing my anger. The other two Omegas in the kitchen shrink back, their gazes are darting between us.

"Where did you last see Hel?" I demand with a growl. "She's not in her room or here with you."

Eve blinks rapidly, looking like a lost puppy. It's an act she's perfected over the years, one that usually works on the other Alphas. Not on me. Not today.

"Last I saw her, she was headed back to your room, but she was acting weird."

"How so?" I press, looming over her. I can smell the fear rolling off her in waves.

"Like... glancing at every staircase, door. Like she was searching for a way out or something." Eve's words tremble slightly. "She seemed... I don't know, nervous? Distracted?"

One of the other Omegas, a petite redhead whose

80

name I can never remember, pipes up, "I haven't seen her at all today." She shrinks back when I turn my gaze to her, nearly knocking over her chair in her haste to put distance between us.

Frustration gnaws at me, hot and insistent.

I stare at Eve. "Did she say anything to you? Mention any plans?"

"No, nothing." She shakes her head, her brown curls bouncing with the movement. "She just seemed... off. I didn't think much of it at the time. I mean, she's new here, right? I figured she was just adjusting."

"And you didn't think to mention this earlier?" My patience wears thin.

"I... I didn't think it was important," Eve stammers, taking a step back. Her hip bumps against the table, rattling the plates and cups.

I take a deep breath, trying to calm myself. It doesn't work.

"The moment you see her, take her to her room and stay with her until I return. Understood?"

"Of course." Eve nods, a hand to her chest in a show of sincerity that doesn't quite reach her eyes.

I march out, my mind racing. Where could she have gone? The mansion is huge, but it's not infinite. There are only so many places she could hide. Her scent had been strong in the bedroom, but I can't pick it up here at all. I check all the stairways leading from my room, questioning the guards posted at each entry point. They all give the same answer—no one has passed through or seen her.

She's bound to have used one if she tried to escape. All entries are guarded, and the underground way out is locked from the inside. She has to be in the mansion. She has to be.

I search frantically, moving from room to room. The Omega quarters are on the second floor, a series of rooms with shared common areas. I throw open doors, ignoring the startled cries of the Omegas inside. Some are alone, some in pairs or small groups. None of them are Hel.

The few Alphas who report directly to me have rooms on the third floor. I burst into their quarters without warning, met with growls and challenging stares. But one look at my face, at the fury barely contained behind my mask, and they back down.

The rest of my pack lives outside in huts scattered around the mansion grounds, but she couldn't have made it past the guards. Could she?

As I round a corner, I nearly collide with Knut. He's dressed for the hunt—shirtless, with intricate war paint covering his muscled torso and face. He's one to go completely wild on hunt nights. When he sees me, his eyes widen.

"What's going on?"

"She's gone," I growl, the words tasting bitter in my mouth. "I can't fucking find her."

"Hel?" Knut asks, his brow furrowing.

"Yes, fucking Hel!" I snap, my control slipping. "Who else would I be talking about?"

"Easy, Ghost." Knut holds up his hands, palms out. "We'll find her. Where have you looked?"

"Everywhere," I spit out, running a hand through my hair in frustration. "Her room, the kitchen, the common areas. It's like she fucking vanished into thin air."

"Could she have used the underground passage?" he suggests, an eyebrow arching upward.

I shake my head, the movement sharp and angry. "I locked those myself last night. There's no way..." But even as I say it, a nagging doubt creeps in. What if I missed something? What if she found a way? "Go search for her in the mansion once more," I command. "Take whoever you need. I want every inch of this place turned upside down."

"You got it, boss." Knut nods, already turning to go. "We'll find her."

As he marches off, barking orders to the nearest Alpha since most are in the hunt, I stand there, indecision gnawing at me. Then, on an impulse, I head for the staircase leading to the underground passage.

The stairs are narrow and steep, carved directly into the bedrock. At the bottom, a heavy iron door blocks the way. It's always locked from the outside, preventing unauthorized entry, but it has a separate lock that can be controlled from the inside, allowing me to decide whether anyone can leave the mansion. I keep the master key back in the study.

I reach for the handle, my heart pounding.

It turns easily, the door swinging open with a groan of protest.

"What the fuck?" I mutter, examining the lock. I know I locked it from the inside. It doesn't look tampered with.

I step outside, the door shutting behind me, the cool night air hitting me like a slap. The soil is still soft from yesterday's rain, and fresh footprints lead away from the door. They're small, delicate... definitely hers. Smart girl didn't shift—she knows she'd be harder to scent in human form. But of all the times to escape, she chooses now, with the ferals out hunting.

"Fuck," I growl, plunging into the woods.

The forest is alive with sounds—rustling leaves, distant howls, and the scurrying of small animals. The Blood Moon casts a red glow through the canopy, turning familiar shapes into twisted shadows. I sniff the air, trying to catch her scent, but there's nothing. Just the earthy smell of damp soil and vegetation, the sharp tang of pine, and something else... something old and musty, which is mostly this island.

I push deeper into the woods, my eyes scanning

the ground for signs of her passage. Every now and then, I spot another footprint, half hidden under fallen leaves or partially washed away by lingering puddles. Each one spurs me on, a breadcrumb trail.

The farther I go, the denser the forest becomes. Ancient trees loom overhead, their gnarled branches reaching out like grasping fingers. Roots snake across the forest floor, threatening to trip me with every step, but I press on.

The sun has almost set, the last streaks of orange and pink fading from the sky. Soon, it will be fully dark, and even my enhanced vision will struggle in the gloom. Howls echo from all directions, sending a chill down my spine. My pack is out there, hunting, their bloodlust fueled by the Blood Moon. And Hel is out here, alone and in danger.

I push myself faster, worry and anger warring inside me. I should have watched her myself. I should have known she'd find a way out, but something still feels off about that lock... about this whole situation.

Branches whip at my face and arms as I run.

Finally, I burst into a small clearing. The Blood Moon hangs low in the sky, huge and ominous. Its red light bathes everything in a surreal glow. I pause, chest heaving, and scan the ground.

There—a footprint leading to the right. Away from the mansion and the hunting grounds. My gut tightens as I realize where she's heading. Wreckage—

the old ghost town where humans once lived, back when humanity still existed in this world. It's a place so haunted by the past that none of my pack will set foot in it. But for me, it's always been a sanctuary, a place to find peace and solitude.

With a guttural growl, I swing right and bullet toward Wreckage.

CHAPTER
SIX

HEL

My lungs sting as I tear through the dark woods out of pure panic from the numerous howls, the damn branches whipping at my face and arms.

I'd started my trek by following the mountain of stone carved into the woods, hoping it would bring me back around to the mansion, but with the darkness and the fact that I'm moving fast, I've lost track of the wall. And now I swear I'm lost.

The sound of my ragged breathing fills my ears while the distant howls of wolves have me moving faster. And all I can think about is how much I really hate Eve, how I don't think she sent me down the stairs by accident. She doesn't even know me, yet she pulled this stunt?

But I'm tenacious, and I'll return to the mansion for the simple act of confronting her.

The forest is a blur of shadows and moonlight, each tree looking like a potential predator ready to pounce. Roots seem to reach up from the ground, trying to snag my feet. I stumble, catching myself against the rough bark of a massive oak, using that second of rest to catch my breath. I really need to take up jogging and improve my fitness.

Just keep moving. Don't stop. Don't look back.

I push off from the tree, leaves crunching under my sneakers as I resume my frantic pace. The air is thick with the scent of earth and pine trees. Something rustles in the underbrush to my left, and I instinctively veer right, not wanting to find out if it's a harmless rabbit or something with far sharper teeth.

Suddenly, the woods spit me out as if I'm an unwanted morsel. I stumble, momentum carrying me forward onto a stone path that appears out of nowhere. My hands scrape against rough stone as I catch myself, preventing a face-first meeting with the ground. As I regain my balance, I realize I'm standing between two decayed stone walls, their jagged edges reaching toward the sky like broken teeth.

"Well, this isn't ominous at all," I murmur. The constant background noise of the forest, buzzing insects and rustling leaves, has disappeared, leaving behind a stillness that has my skin crawling.

I take a tentative step forward. The path stretches out before me, winding between what appear to be the ruins of an old settlement. Most of the buildings are little more than piles of rubble, but I can almost imagine what this place might have looked like when it was alive—people bustling about, children playing in the streets, the air filled with the sounds of life and laughter. It makes me wonder if it's back from the time of humans living here.

And now, it's a ghost town.

The Blood Moon might light up the darkness to a degree, but thank the gods for enhanced werewolf vision, or I'd be stumbling around like a drunk. As it is, I can see every crack in the stones, every blade of grass pushing its way through the ancient path.

I step farther into the town, my attention darting from side to side. It's a single long road, seeming to wind ahead into the gloom. The hair on my arms stands up. I've never been one to believe in ghosts, but if they exist, this place is definitely prime real estate for them.

"Okay, Hel," I whisper, needing to hear a human voice, even if it's my own. "This could be a good place to hide out until sunrise." Just find a cozy little ruin and settle in for the night. Easy-peasy.

As I start to wander down the curved road, I catch movement from the corner of my eye. I whip my head around, heart pounding, but there's nothing there. Just shadows. Right? Bats, perhaps?

"Get it together," I whisper under my breath, running a shaky hand through my hair. "Next thing you know, you'll be jumping at dust bunnies." I try to tell myself to stop talking, but hearing my voice calms me in the dark, and I've always talked to myself. Something Jarl hated about me... well, that and a hundred other things.

I continue on, trying to ignore the way the shadows seem to move when I'm not looking directly at them. The ruins loom on either side of me, some barely more than foundations, others still reaching the sky with broken walls and gaping windows.

Rubbing the chill out of my arms, I listen for any sounds, for anything to indicate that someone followed me here.

A sudden snap echoes from the woods behind me, and I nearly jump out of my skin. My heart, which had just started to slow down, kicks into overdrive again. Without thinking, I break into a run, pelting down the curving road. The wind picks up, whistling through the ruins and carrying with it the musty scent of decay.

Finally, I spot a building that's mostly intact, which is surprising given the state of everything else. It's a two-story structure, though the upper floor is partially missing, open to the sky. The forest has begun to claim this one, too, with small trees growing through cracks in the walls and grass threading its way along the path leading to the door.

Another snap from the woods has me moving closer to the house. I pause at the open doorway that yawns with darkness, my stomach churning with dread. Part of me screams that this is exactly the kind of place in which people die in horror stories I've heard, but it's a shelter, and right now, that's what I need most.

I step inside cautiously, the floorboards creaking faintly under my weight. The darkness is almost absolute at first. I freeze, letting my eyes adjust. The musty smell of old wood fills my nostrils, and I can taste dust on my tongue.

Silence.

Slowly, shapes begin to emerge from the gloom as my vision improves. Moonlight filters through the windows and the hole in the roof, casting long shadows across from the broken furniture that remains in what must have been the main room. The building is larger than it looked from the outside, with three doorways at the back leading to who knows where.

"Eeny, meeny, miny, moe," I whisper, eyeing the doorways. "Catch a wolf by his toe. If he hollers, run like hell and hope you don't die." Not my best rhyme, but I'll cut myself some slack. I'm under a lot of stress here.

I take a cautious step forward, wincing at the loud creak of the floorboard. Another step and I choose the far-left doorway, passing through it. It's dark, but the holes in the ceiling and walls let enough moonlight in to help me see that I'm alone in another smaller room... maybe a kitchen once upon a time?

Creak.

My gaze darts around the room, trying to take in everything at once in case I missed someone standing in a corner. Was that movement? Just a shadow, surely.

Get a grip, Hel.

Something rolls under my foot on my next step, nearly sending me sprawling, my stomach lurching. I stare down to see what looks like an old bottle, its glass cloudy with age. I bend down to examine the bottle, more out of a need to do something than actual curiosity. As I straighten up, my blood runs cold.

I'm being watched. I can feel it in the shiver that zips up my spine.

"Who's there?" I say softly, immediately regretting it. *Way to announce your presence to any psycho were-wolves who might be around, genius.*

Silence is my only answer, but it feels... expectant. Like the whole house is holding its breath, waiting for something to happen.

I take a deep inhale, needing to calm my racing heart. Okay, maybe this wasn't such a great idea. Time to find somewhere else to—

A loud groan of wood cuts me off, the sound of heavy footsteps coming from the main room. I freeze, my throat constricting. The darkness seems to press in around me, and after a long moment, I swear I can hear something breathing in the house.

Slowly, carefully, I creep back toward the main room. The slight creak of wood under my feet has me cringing. I reach the doorway and peer out.

Nothing.

The room remains empty, moonlight streaming in through the broken roof. The wind has picked up outside, though, thrashing the trees and whistling through the broken windows and door. That must have been what I heard. Just the wind. Just the house settling.

I let out a shaky breath, relief flooding through me.

A door slams somewhere in the house, the sound like a gunshot in the silence. I yelp, spinning around so fast I almost give myself whiplash.

"Hello?" I call out. "Look, if this is someone's idea of a joke, it's not funny. I've had a really long day, and I'm not in the mood for—"

A hot breath rushes across the back of my neck suddenly.

I freeze.

Shaking.

Struggling to take in air.

Every muscle in my body tenses.

I'm about to pass out, my body shuddering in terror. Slowly, so slowly, I turn around.

But there's nothing there, only darkness. Yet I swear that's where I felt someone or something...

I turn back around, ready to leave this building, when I come face-to-face with a skull, almost glowing in the dim light.

"Boo!" he shouts.

I scream.

All logic flies out the window. It doesn't matter that my brain is telling me it's Ghost—my lizard brain has taken over, and it's screaming one thing: RUN!

I bolt, nearly tripping over my own feet in my haste to get out of the building. Terror leaches into my legs, spurring me on faster than I thought possible. I run blindly, not caring where I'm going as long as it's away from here.

Outside, the wind is blowing a blizzard, and the town blurs around me, ruins looming out of the darkness like grasping hands. The weather howls.

Fucking Ghost... Of course he'd pursue and scare me.

I chance a look behind me, trying to see if he followed me. In that moment of distraction, I nearly miss the intact building ahead of me.

Without thinking, I dart inside, drawing the door behind me without a sound. My chest heaves as I try to gasp for air, ears straining for any sound of pursuit. My hands are shaking hard, my teeth chattering.

I turn to the room, which is dark, but as my eyes adjust, I can make out the shapes of old furniture, covered in sheets that look like pale ghosts in the dim light.

Rushing forward, I leave behind the main room and try once more to find a place to hide. As the initial panic begins to fade, embarrassment and anger take its place.

Ghost. What a dick move!

"When I get my hands on him," I murmur, fists clenching at my sides. "I'm going to shove that mask so far up his—"

A floorboard creaks behind me from deeper in the house.

I whirl around, fists raised, ready to give Ghost a piece of my mind. But the words die in my throat as I take in the scene before me.

This isn't Ghost.

A figure stands in the shadows, its form shifting and twisting in ways that defy reality. It's as if the darkness itself has come alive, taking on the vaguely humanoid shape of my dead husband.

Jarl.

I blink hard, certain my mind is playing tricks on

me, but when I open my eyes, he's still there. Jarl, or something wearing his face, stands before me. He's translucent, edges blurring and shifting like smoke in the wind. His eyes, still cold and cruel like before.

He opens his mouth. No sound comes out, but I can almost hear the echoes of his voice in my head, the cutting words that used to tear me down day after day. His hand reaches out toward me, fingers elongating unnaturally, grasping at the air between us.

"Get away from me, you asshole," I manage to choke out. "You treated me like crap enough when you were alive. No way you get to come haunt me now. Don't you have some other poor Omega to torment in the afterlife?"

As he takes a step forward, I recoil, my heels hitting the wall behind me. A scream builds in my lungs. This can't be real. It can't be happening.

And then, nothing.

He's gone just like that.

I feel lightheaded and dizzy, and I'm darting into another room, still confused as to whether I actually saw a fucking apparition of my husband or if I had imagined it.

"What are you doing out here, sweetheart?"

I flinch hard at Ghost's deep, raspy voice coming from somewhere in the house... though he sounds like he's in the new room with me. I frantically search the darkness.

"Going somewhere?" he continues, yet it's as though his voice is coming from all around me. Must be weird acoustics and I assume he's somewhere else in the house. "You don't think I'm going to let you leave, do you?"

Biting my lip, unsure if he's spotted me yet, I slide sideways into the shadows.

The floorboards creak somewhere to my left, directly where I moved to.

Pulse racing, I lift my gaze to where I thought the darkness would conceal me. Instead, I find myself staring directly into the deep eyes of Ghost's skull mask.

Seeing him there, just hiding and watching me has my blood running cold. Stalker.

I go to move, to slip away, but his hand shoots out, fingers wrapping around my arm with an iron grip. Before I can react, he spins me, my back hitting the wall with a soft thud that knocks the air from my lungs.

Ghost looms over me, his body a solid wall of heat and muscle. One hand is planted on the wall beside my head, effectively caging me in. The other suddenly on my throat, not tight, but enough to hold me in place.

The warmth of his breath feathers over my face.

"You know, most Alphas buy an Omega dinner before they pin her to a wall. Just saying."

His laughter is loud and leaves me covered in goose bumps, the kind that excite me more than scare me. Which is so wrong.

And he's so close, the skull mask filling my vision, one of his eyes seeming to glow faintly blue, the other hidden by shadows.

"You should know by now... on this island, there's no escaping me."

I swallow hard. "And if I don't intend to stay on this island?"

"You're not going anywhere," he continues, and there's something different in his voice now. Darker. Excited. A predator who's caught the scent of his prey. "This is my domain, sweetheart. Every shadow, every creaking board... they all answer to me." He reaches down from his hand on the wall and curls a lock of my hair around his finger, his body pressed closer to mine, so close I feel his hard cock. "Unless you know a secret way of leaving Nightmare Island you want to share?"

He's enjoying this, the sick bastard, but what terrifies me most is that part of me kind of likes it. The thrill of him against me, the intoxicating masculine and woodsy scent, the way my wolf is awake in his presence, as if she's demanding to come out and play with him. Not to mention the way his voice makes heat pool in my belly, despite my fear.

Gods, what's wrong with me?

"Wish I had a crystal ball for you, but I don't," I

say, aiming for sarcasm but hearing the tremor in my voice. "I'm just a desperate Omega trying to escape a dangerous island, doing my best not to fall victim to a tempting Alpha."

Ghost chuckles, the sound low and rich. His grip on my arm and neck loosens slightly, but he doesn't step back.

"You find me tempting?"

"It's called sarcasm."

"You're quick with those quips, aren't you? I admire that—a sharp mind to match that fiery spirit."

I shrug, smirking. "I try my best."

His hand leaves my hair and traces a feathery touch down my jawline. I suppress an excited shiver at his fingertips.

"Watch what you say," he murmurs. "It's been a long time since such a delicious Omega caught my attention. And I'm a possessive bastard. You might not like what you're inviting."

The deepness in his voice makes my breath catch. Fire burns off him, his scent drowning me. He leans in closer, his mask nearly touching my cheek.

"I'm the darkness, sweetheart. And you? You're the flame. Bright, beautiful, and oh so tempting to extinguish." When he speaks in my ear, his voice rumbles through me, vibrating in my very bones.

A gasp escapes my lips before I can stop it. *Damn him.* His words are doing things to me, having me imagine myself beneath him as he makes me scream. As I squeeze my thighs together, the intensity of the tingling escalates through me. I'm going to lose control at this stage. I picture his hands on me while I'm surrendering to the darkness he offers. I want it so badly it hurts.

I shake my head, needing to come to my senses. The image of him with Eve flashes through my mind, steeling my resolve. I'm just another Omega to him. I'm not here to stay.

"I don't need you, so you can leave," I state.

"I'm going to make you mine," Ghost confesses, pulling back. "And anything that's mine stays with me, doesn't run off. Anyone who touches you will die."

The possessiveness in his voice should repulse me. Instead, it sends a thrill through my body, my traitorous Omega instincts responding to his Alpha dominance.

"You're crazy," I shoot back.

He chuckles, the sound curling shivers between my thighs. "Of course I am, little flame. Sanity is overrated, especially on an island full of monsters. But I'm the monster you want, sweetheart. The one you need."

I glance around, noticing that behind him is a door that heads into another room where I can directly see the missing back door leading outside. My way out...

"I don't need any monsters, thanks. I've had my fill."

"Oh, but you've only just met me," Ghost purrs, and I swear my wolf is whining in response, desperate for him. What is wrong with me?

"What makes you so special?" I ask, proud of how steady my voice sounds. "You're just another Alpha with delusions of grandeur. I've dealt with plenty of those."

"I'm not like the others, little flame. I'm the thing they fear in the dark. The monster under the bed. The shadow that swallows the light."

His words should terrify me, and they do, but not in the way they should. Instead of wanting to run, I want to step closer to the danger he represents.

I fight the desire and glance at the doorway behind him once more, at the open back door. Hope surges through me.

"Sorry to disappoint, but I'm not interested in being anyone's chew toy. Even a big bad Alpha's."

He buries his face in my neck, inhaling deeply. A growl rumbles through his chest, the vibrations traveling through my body and settling deep in my stomach.

"You're going to destroy me," he breathes against my skin from under his mask.

I tremble, my nipples hardening against his chest, and a growing ache spreads through me. What is he doing to me? I try to ignore the way my body reacts to him, the heat gathering in my core, the way my breath speeds up.

"Funny, I was about to say the same thing about you," I respond.

Ghost pulls back slightly, his grip on me loosening. Even through the mask, I can feel the intensity of his gaze, leaving me curious as to what he really looks like.

He's laughing again, so I use that moment. I throw myself from under him and bolt to the back exit door while he just laughs.

"You'd better run now, little flame. I'll give you a head start, and you'd better use it." There's a hunger in his voice that makes my skin prickle. "Because when I catch you—and I will catch you—all bets are off."

Something in his tone, in the predatory stance of his body, tells me he means it. So I turn and run, hating how I respond to his voice, how this macabre game he's playing awakens a hunger inside me. I'm terrified, I'm turned on, and I'm so fucking confused.

Outside, the wind hits me like a physical force, nearly knocking me off my feet, seeming to push against me as if it's trying to force me back in Ghost's direction. "Are you insane?" I call up to the sky. In response, the wind howls, the trees swaying violently, branches reaching for me like grasping fingers.

I race around the back of the house, curving down its side. I scan the surrounding area for an escape route, then spot an old metal basement door near the house, the kind that leads down to an underground shelter. There's even a rusted lock on it, glinting in the moonlight, which I find strange.

Ghost's words echo in my head. *I'm the darkness.* Going underground seems like playing right into his hands. Besides, the idea of being trapped down there, in the dark, with him hunting me... it's not going to work.

So I keep going.

On my next hurried step, the earth suddenly gives way beneath me.

A scream tears from my throat as I fall, and I'm plunging into darkness.

CHAPTER
SEVEN
HEL

One moment, I'm running for my life, and the next, I'm falling.

The world tilts and spins, my stomach lurching as gravity takes hold. I claw at the air, desperate for purchase, panic biting into my skin, but there's nothing to grab on to. Just empty space and the rushing air.

I hit the ground hard, the impact knocking the wind out of me. Sharp pain spreads through my body, centered on my hip where I landed. I can't breathe, can't think, can't do anything but lie here as agony pulses through me in waves.

Dust and broken planks of wood rain down around me, filling the air with a choking cloud. I cough, struggling to catch my breath as I blink away the grit in my eyes. As the dust settles, I find myself in near-total darkness. The air is thick, heavy, with the scent of mold and decay. It presses against me, almost a physical presence, reminding me of old blood and forgotten places.

"What a fucking night." I glance up, squinting in the dim moonlight. The hole I fell through is a good ten feet above me, a jagged mouth of broken wooden beams in the ceiling.

Groaning, I push myself to my feet, wincing at the throb in my hip. Each movement sends a fresh wave of pain through me, reminding me of how close I came to serious injury. Or worse. I take stock of my body— bruised all over, probably some cuts—but nothing seems broken.

A sound comes from deeper in the darkness, something guttural and... wrong.

I'm rooted to the spot.

"Ghost?" I call out, hating the tremor in my voice. "That had better not be you, or I swear I'll—"

The sound comes again, louder this time. Closer. I'm not alone down here.

"Oh, fuck," I whisper, backing away slowly.

Something is shuffling toward me, a dark shape in the gloom.

Ragged breathing and a wet, gurgling sound turn my stomach. The smell hits me next—the stench of rotting flesh, overwhelming and nauseating. The odor is so strong I can almost taste it.

"Ghost!" I scream, panic overtaking me. My word echoes in the confined space, bouncing back at me mockingly. "Ghost, fuck, you'd better help me out of here."

I'm still staring into the dark where the sounds are coming from.

Suddenly, there's a form there, stepping forward out of the shadows and into the moonlight.

Where there should be eyes, there are only black holes, and its mouth—oh gods, its mouth—is a gaping maw, filled with teeth that seem to go on forever.

It staggers toward me, each step accompanied by the sound of bones cracking and flesh tearing. The air grows cold, so cold I can see my breath misting in front of me. The thing reaches out a hand—if you can call it that—toward me, fingers elongated.

Are you kidding me?

A fucking zombie! We have them back home, and we barricaded ourselves into our secured town—a way to deal with them—so what the hell is this thing doing down here when the island doesn't seem to have any... well, as far as I've seen?

A scream builds in my throat.

Suddenly, the thing lunges at me, and I see it clearly for the first time.

Flesh hanging in rotting strips and patches of its skull are visible, with yellowed bone peeking through decayed skin. Its mouth hangs open.

I scream, the sound tearing from my throat as pure terror takes over. My mind goes blank, all thought obliterated by the desperate need to survive.

The zombie slams into me, its weight surprisingly light but its strength terrifying. We crash to the ground, the air rushing out of my lungs. Its face is inches from mine, jaws snapping as it tries to bite. The stench of its breath makes me gag, a rotten-meat smell that clogs my nostrils and makes my eyes water.

I manage to get my arm up, pressing it against its throat, my whole body trembling. My other hand shoves at its bony shoulder, feeling flesh slough off under my fingers. The sensation makes me want to vomit, but I can't afford to give in to the nausea. Its skin is cold and slimy, like touching raw chicken left out too long.

"Get off me, you rotting piece of shit!" I yell, my tone high pitched and panicked.

The zombie's strength is relentless, though. Its teeth snap inches from my face, and I can feel its fetid breath on my skin. My arms tremble with the effort of holding it back. I know I can't keep this up for long. I manage to knee it in the stomach, but the thing doesn't budge or even seem to feel pain.

I can't die in this fucking basement. This can't end here.

In a flash, something yanks the zombie off me.

I gasp, frantically drawing backward and scrambling to my feet.

There's a blur of movement in front of me, and suddenly, Ghost is there, ripping the creature in half with his bare hands, as if it's made of paper.

I'm about to say something when movement behind him catches my attention.

Apparitions, faint but undeniably there, hover in the darkness of the basement. Translucent figures flicker in and out of existence, their faces twisted. And for a moment, Ghost looks like one of them—pale, almost transparent in the moonlight, more spirit than flesh.

A gasp falls from my lips as I back away, trembling. Fear, real fear, floods through me.

What is he?

Ghost tosses the twitching halves aside, dust and bones everywhere, but impossibly, horrifyingly, the thing is still moving. Its upper half drags itself toward me.

"Oh, shit!" I gasp.

With a growl that sounds more animal than human, Ghost pulls a blade from his boot and rams it into the zombie's skull. The crack of bone is sickeningly loud. Finally, it goes still.

There's silence, broken only by my ragged breathing and the hammering of my heart. Then Ghost turns to me, his mask gleaming in the dim light.

Even with his face hidden, I sense the intensity of his gaze on me.

"Did it bite you?" he demands. "I had no idea there were any fucking zombies on this island. Are you hurt?"

I shake my head, unable to form words. My whole body is shaking, adrenaline coursing through me. We live in a broken world where the virus that eliminated civilization resulted in many of the dead rising into zombies. Because living with dominant wolf Alphas isn't challenging enough.

Ghost strides toward me, and I flinch involuntarily, my body reacting before my mind can process that he's not a threat.

"Easy," he says, his voice softer than I've ever heard it. "You're safe. I've got you."

"I don't feel safe." I scan the darkness around us, ready to jump out of my skin.

He reaches for me, and suddenly, I'm clinging to him, my face pressed against his chest. I can feel the solid muscle beneath his shirt and smell his scent— earthy and masculine, with hints of cocoa and something wild. It grounds me, pulling me back from the edge of hysteria.

"I've got you," Ghost repeats, stroking my hair. The gentleness of the words is not what I expect from him. "But we need to get out of here."

Without warning, he lifts me fast toward the

gaping hole in the ceiling, powerful hands gripping my hips like I weigh nothing. The strength in his arms, the power coiled in his body, comes through his touch. Suddenly, I'm at the hole in the ceiling of the basement and frantically scrambling up, pulling myself free into the open air.

He's out in seconds, too, having leapt to grab the edges and hauled himself up. My eyes lock on those flexing, thick biceps, and I'm admiring him way too long. When he glances up and notices me staring, I quickly lift my gaze to the moon.

That's when I feel a difference in the air. Or maybe it's the moon, full and blood-red in the sky. Or the distant howls that echo through the night. Whatever it is, it's awakening something primal in me. Adrenaline courses through my veins, but it's more than that. It's a need, an instinct so powerful it threatens to overwhelm me.

My wolf, usually a quiet presence in the back of my mind, surges forward. She's stronger than I've ever felt her. I stumble, caught off guard by her sudden push to emerge.

My bones start to shift, my skin prickling as fur threatens to sprout. I fall to my knees, hands braced against the ground as convulsions rack my body. Clothes tear off me, falling away in shreds. In seconds, I'm standing on four white paws.

Ghost takes a step closer, his hand outstretched.

"It's okay," he reassures. "You don't need to be afraid. I'll keep you safe."

A growl rips from my throat, surprising even me. My lips pull back, baring teeth that are already sharpening into fangs.

Ghost freezes, his body tense.

The change is faster than I've ever experienced before.

"Hel," Ghost says, his Alpha command in his voice. "Don't run. Listen to me. Do not run. Wait for me to take you back."

My wolf is already backing away from him, not listening. All she knows is the need to escape, to run, to find safety. Before I can stop myself, before I can even think, I'm darting into the woods.

Ghost curses behind me, but I don't glance back. I just run, letting the wolf take control, surrendering to the primal instincts that now guide me.

The forest swallows me up, branches whipping past as I plunge into the woods. Part of me knows this is dangerous, knows I should turn back, but the wolf is in charge now, and she has only one thought—run.

Then there's the sound of tearing fabric behind me. He's shifted, too. I don't look back. I just keep running.

The forest is a blur around me. Branches slap at my face, leaving stinging scratches. Roots threaten to trip me at every step, but I'm faster in this form, more agile. I leap over fallen logs and duck under low-hanging branches. The cool night air rushes through my fur, carrying a thousand earthy scents as small animals scurry out of my path.

Twigs snap behind me, and I know he's gaining ground with every stride. His growls send shivers down my spine, a mixture of fear and something else I don't want to examine too closely. Part of me, the Omega part, wants to submit, to bare my throat and let this powerful Alpha claim me, but I push that feeling down. I never felt this way before, not even with my husband.

My paw catches on something sharp, and I trip as it feels like someone drove a blade into my back leg.

I crumple instantly, collapsing and whimpering from the agonizing pain lancing, stabbing and immediate. I yelp, the sound pitiful, even to my own ears.

In an instant, Ghost is there. He shifts back to human form, naked, kneeling beside me. His hands are gentle as he examines my injured leg. He makes a sighing sound, the kind that tells me the injury is bad.

"Stubborn little flame," he mutters, but there's no real heat in his words. "I told you not to run."

The pain triggers my own shift back, and I lie there, naked and trembling, crying from the worst pain in the world traveling up my leg. I can't even speak, can barely move. Ghost has me in his arms in seconds, cradling me. And I'm holding onto those huge muscles, but my eyes are blurring, every movement sending me into another round of whimpers.

"I've got you," he says, his voice gruff but not unkind. "Let's get you somewhere safe."

As he carries me through the forest, I find myself softening against him. There's something about his strength, his presence, that makes me feel... not safe, exactly, but less afraid. The steady heat of his body covers me, and the smell of his scent comforts me.

We break through the tree line, and I gasp. The sky above is a riot of stars, more than I've ever seen before. And there, hanging low and ominous, is the blood moon, casting its eerie red glow over everything.

"Beautiful, isn't it?" Ghost says, following my gaze. "Terrible, but beautiful. Like so much on this island."

I look at him, *really* look at him, for the first time in the moonlight—with his mask and his strength and the gentleness with which he holds me.

And it makes me realize that I know nothing about this Alpha.

When he moves up a slope, the pain shoots again, and I'm writhing with agony.

"Hang on, you're losing a lot of blood," he tells me.

I hold on just a little tighter, as though he's everything I've ever needed.

EIGHT

I quickly carry Hel to my bedroom, her body too light in my arms, her skin growing paler with each passing moment. Blood trails down her leg where the branch struck, the metallic scent filling my nostrils and setting my wolf on edge.

"You're so damn stubborn," I mutter. "You should have waited for me."

She doesn't seem to hear me, her eyes closed tight, her body shaking. Her hand clutches weakly at my neck.

"Are we there yet? Everything's spinning."

Seeing her this way does something to me, making my chest tighten. I quicken my pace, shouldering through my bedroom door.

"Stay with me, little flame," I murmur as I lay her on my bed.

She hisses in pain, tears leaking from the corners of her eyes.

"Ghost?" Her voice is barely a whisper now. "I can't feel my toes anymore, yet the pain is still there. That's bad, right?"

"You're not dying. Not even Death can take you from me," I tell her firmly, though my heart races at how pale she's become. "And your wolf healing will have you back to your cheerful self in no time."

A weak laugh escapes her. "Didn't know... Death took orders from Alphas." Her eyes flutter, struggling to stay open. A delicate hand reaches for my mask, fingers trembling as they brush the bone-white surface. No one touches the mask—ever—but I find myself leaning into her touch.

"Am I going to die?" The sass is gone from her voice, replaced by raw fear. "Because it feels like it."

"Not happening," I growl, tightening my grip on her. "Stay awake," I command, my voice harsh with a worry I can't hide. I need to get bandages and clean the wound, but the thought of leaving her makes my wolf snarl in protest. He knows there's so much more between Hel and me that I suspect I'll have to confirm with her soon enough. There's only one way to determine if she's my true mate—but now's not the time to bite her.

"I just need to close my eyes for a minute..." she whispers, drawing me from my thoughts.

"Hel!" I bark, using my Alpha voice. Her eyes snap open. "Talk to me. Keep talking."

She tries to focus on my mask. "About what?"

"Anything. Tell me about your favorite food. What about how you got to the island?"

"Muffins and cake. That's easy." She gives me a weak smile, then stares at me. "Why do they call you Ghost?"

"Focus on staying awake, and tell me more about your favorite muffin flavor. Mara makes the best banana muffins. She calls them 'Banana Claw Crunch.'"

Her eyes light up, then she winces. "I will need to taste them if I survive."

I laugh. "Hold two moments." I dart into the bathroom and grab towels. When I return, I begin cleaning the injury carefully, checking for any remaining splinters, but the blood continues flowing, rich and insistent. Without thinking, I lean in, drawn by something deeper than thought. Her eyes meet mine, her brow pinching between her eyes.

Slowly, deliberately, I run my tongue along the gash.

"Ghost, don't... what are you..." Her words trail off, but she remains still, tension thrumming through her body.

I taste copper, salt, life itself, then something

more. Something that makes my entire being howl in recognition. Every cell in my body ignites, my wolf surging forward with fierce and desperate hunger. Mate. The word echoes through my bones like a death knell.

A laugh bubbles from her throat, brittle and nervous. "Should I be worried that you like the way my blood tastes?"

I lift my head, fighting to keep my voice steady, and lick my lips. "My saliva has some healing properties that will help." The words come out rougher than intended.

She attempts a smirk, but I see the tremor in her lips, the way her pupils have dilated, her body writhing once more, her leg shaking.

I need to take away her pain.

I press a clean towel to her leg.

"You have no idea what you are, do you?" I whisper, more to myself than to her. The taste of her lingers on my tongue.

"A girl feeling like I'm at death's door." Then she cries out, her head pressed back into her pillow, her brow glistening in perspiration.

Next thing, she's hugging a pillow to her chest, and it's impossible for me, even with her in agony, not to stare at her naked body. Fuck, I've got nothing on, but that's normal for me. While she... she's fucking stunning—the curves, the tiny line of hair between her thighs, her round breasts. Absolutely captivating.

Back to the job, I apply a second towel as the first one is already red. She cries out again, the sound tearing at something inside me.

Mate.

The word floats in my mind, and I'm unsure what to do with it, having told myself I'd never find mine. And I was damn fine with it. Now look at me.

I position spare pillows under her injured leg, elevating it, trying to slow the bleeding. Her blood is everywhere—on my hands, on the sheets, on her pale skin. It's taking everything in me not to let my wolf take over, not to howl at the sight of her hurt.

"Ghost?" Her voice is smaller now, frightened. "Don't leave me. Please. Everyone always does."

Something in my chest cracks at her words. I lean down, pushing sweat-dampened hair from her face.

"I'm not going to do that, but I need to get help. Our healer can stop the pain and bleeding."

"Promise you'll come back?" Her hand catches my wrist, surprisingly strong for someone losing so much blood.

"I always keep my word, little flame." The endearment slips out again, feeling right on my tongue, despite everything.

"Why do you call me that?" she asks, her blue eyes struggling to focus on me.

"Because you're the flame in my darkness," I find myself saying. "Bright. Dangerous. Beautiful."

"Now I know I must be dying." A faint blush colors her cheeks, the first shade of life I've seen on her face since her fall. "You're almost being nice to me."

I shake my head, smirking. "Stay awake, sweetheart. I'll be right back."

"Ghost?" she calls as I reach the door.

I pause, glancing back at her lying in my bed, covered in blood but still somehow the most captivating thing I've ever seen.

"Thank you. For helping me again."

The words hit me hard. I don't respond, can't respond. Instead, I turn and run, my footsteps echoing through the halls as I race to find Awa. Every second away from Hel feels wrong, my wolf pacing and snarling inside me.

My mind charges with every step. Images of Hel's pale face, her blood-soaked skin, the way she looked at me as though I was her only lifeline—they drive me faster, harder. The wolf in me wants to howl, to tear apart anything that stands between me and getting her help.

Her voice echoes in my head. *Everyone always leaves.*

That resonates a bit too close to home... Maybe we have more in common than I thought.

Making a fast detour to my temporary room, I grab

a pair of black cargo pants and drag them on, then I dart down the halls once more.

I crash through Awa's door without knocking, the wood at her lock splintering under my force. She leaps from her chair, her book tumbling to the floor. The scent of fear spikes in the air.

"Ghost!" Awa's hand flies to her chest. "What in the—"

"She's dying," I cut her off, the words tasting like ash in my mouth. "The new Omega. Hel. Major leg wound, too much blood loss."

Awa's eyes widen as she takes in my state—blood covers my hands, chest. She moves quickly to her shelves, gathering supplies.

"How long has she been bleeding?" she asks, her medic mask sliding into place.

"Too fucking long," I growl. "Hurry."

"Ghost." Her voice is stern despite her obvious nervousness. "I need to know how long."

"Twenty minutes. Maybe more." I pace the small room like a caged animal. "She's getting weaker, but she hasn't passed out yet."

Awa nods, shoving herbs and bandages into a bag. "The milk of rum," she says, nodding to a shelf. "And the clear bottle beside it. For disinfectant."

I snatch both bottles, already turning toward the door. "Move faster."

"I know you're worried—"

"I'm not worried. I'm fucking terrified she'll get an infection, and that her blood loss will lead to something more serious," I snap.

"She's that special?" Awa asks quietly, her knowing tone making my wolf bristle. She and I have always gotten along and respected one another, so I feel more comfortable sharing my emotions with her than with others.

I nod.

We rush back through the corridors, my longer strides forcing Awa to practically run to keep up. The Blood Moon's light streams through the windows, bathing everything in a reddish hue.

"The Blood Moon... it might affect her healing. The magic is different tonight," Awa explains.

I growl in response, pushing faster. We're almost there, not wanting to hear excuses. Just a few more seconds and—

A scream pierces the air. Hel's scream.

I'm through the bedroom door before the sound fades, Awa forgotten behind me. Hel's thrashing on the bed, her back arched in pain.

She's managed to half drag a blanket over herself, yet she's shivering violently despite the warmth of the room. Her skin glistens with sweat, her hair plastered to her forehead, and her breathing comes in short, painful gasps. The towels around her leg are soaked through with blood, the metallic scent thick in the air.

"I'm here." I'm at her side instantly, catching her flailing hands. "I'm back."

Her eyes find mine, glazed with pain and fear. "You came back," she whispers as if she still can't quite believe it.

"I promised, didn't I?" My voice sounds rougher than I intended.

The corner of her mouth twitches. "You surprised me," she mumbles, then her eyes roll back, and she fights to keep them open.

Awa's there in the room in seconds, taking in the scene, her silver-streaked hair escaping its braid as she moves. Setting down her bag with a thud at the side of the bed near Hel's feet, she glances at her with a smile.

"You certainly know how to make an entrance, don't you, dear?"

Hel's eyes flutter open wider at the new voice. "I like to keep things interesting," she croaks.

"I'm Awa. Nice to meet you." Her expression softens. "I can see why he likes you." Then, she thrusts a small wooden bowl into my hands, the liquid inside a milky caramel color. Bits of herbs float on top, and the scent of rum and coconut rises with the steam.

"Make her drink all of it," she orders, already laying out her supplies on the bed. Her weathered hands are then arranging a large needle and thread. "And don't give me that look, Ghost. I don't care if you're the Alpha. In this room, when someone's bleeding, I'm in charge."

The corner of my mouth twitches despite the situation. Awa's the only one who dares speak to me this way, and only when she's healing someone. Any other time, she's as respectful as the rest of the pack, but get her in her element, and she transforms.

"What's in it?" Hel asks me weakly, eyeing the bowl.

"Rum, coconut cream, and herbs," Awa answers, not looking up from where she's starting to peel the towels off her leg. "My own special recipe. Works every time to ease the pain." She pauses her work to wink at Hel, her dark eyes twinkling. "And if it doesn't, well, at least you'll be too drunk to care about my terrible stitching."

A ghost of a smile touches Hel's lips, but it's quickly replaced by a grimace of pain.

I move to the bed, sitting carefully on the edge. The mattress dips under my weight, and Hel's hand clutches at the blanket.

"Easy," I murmur, reaching out slowly as I would with a wounded animal. "Let me help tuck another pillow under your head."

She eyes my hand warily. "I can manage."

"Of course you can," I say, letting a hint of sarcasm

color my voice as she does just that. "Just like you managed that escape attempt so well."

Her gaze flashes with anger—good, anger is better than fear.

"I got pretty far, didn't I? And you can't blame my wolf for going all protective after I was attacked in that basement."

I cradle her head gently, ignoring how right it feels to touch her.

"Here's the part where you drink this and stop arguing with me."

She studies my mask intently.

"I won't hurt you," I murmur, low enough that only she can hear.

"That's what they all say." She tries to smirk, but it comes out more like a grimace. "Every Alpha thinks he knows what's best."

"Oh, honey," Awa chimes in, wiping the blood away. "If Ghost wanted to hurt you, he wouldn't have broken down my door to get me to help you. I've never seen him so worked up over anyone."

I growl at her, but Hel's laugh turns into a pained cough.

"Drink," I order, pressing the bowl to her lips. "Before I change my mind about being nice."

She parts her lips hesitantly, allowing me to tip the liquid into her mouth. The first sip makes her eyes widen.

"That's... not terrible," she admits, taking another swallow.

"Give it time," Awa says cheerfully. "The herbs are an acquired taste."

Hel drinks steadily, finishing the bowl, and I set it on the bedside table. I can feel her relaxing slightly against my hand where I support her head. The rum starts working quickly, her cheeks flushing pink, and her eyes take on a glassy sheen.

After a long pause of her resting, she stares at me strangely.

"You're really strong," she observes suddenly, her free hand reaching out to touch my chest. "Like, really, really strong."

Awa snickers as she prepares her needle. "The rum milk works fast on an empty stomach."

"Don't tell anyone," Hel whispers, leaning closer. "But you're naked." Her gaze dips down my stomach, then she giggles. "Very naked."

Something in my chest tightens at the sound of her laugh. She looks younger like this, softer somehow. Almost innocent.

"I'm wearing pants, little flame," I remind her, trying to keep my voice stern despite my amusement.

"Mm-hmm," she hums, unconvinced. "Very nice pants. But mostly naked." She pokes my chest with one finger. "So many muscles."

Awa's shoulders shake with silent laughter. "I

haven't seen anyone react quite like this to my rum milk in ages."

"I'm not drunk," Hel protests, then frowns. "The room's just... spinny. Did you know your mask glows in the dark?"

"It doesn't," I say, but she's already reaching for it again.

"Pretty skull-face man," she murmurs, her fingers tracing the contours of the mask. "With pretty muscles."

I snatch her hand before she can pull the mask away, but I'm gentle.

"Behave."

"Or what?" she challenges, then winces as Awa begins stitching. But the rum's done its work; the pain seems distant to her now.

"You're good at that," Hel says, her words slightly slurred. "Like a... a needle artist. A stabby seamstress."

"Years of practice, honey," Awa responds, her needle moving swiftly. "Though most of my patients aren't quite so entertaining."

Hel beams at the compliment, then turns that radiant smile on me. It hits me like a physical blow.

"You're still here," she says, sounding surprised and pleased.

"I promised, didn't I?"

"Mm-hmm." Her eyes are getting heavy. "You smell good. Like forest, cocoa, and danger and... something else. Can't put my finger on it." She tries literally putting her finger on it, poking my chest again.

I catch her hand again, holding it still. Her skin is soft against my callused palm.

"All done," Awa announces, tying off the last stitch.

Hel barely notices, too busy studying our joined hands with fascination.

"Thank you," I tell Awa quietly as she packs up her supplies. She gives me a knowing look that I choose to ignore.

"Keep her still for the next day or two at least," she instructs. "I'll come and change the bandages tomorrow."

Then, as Awa slips out the door, Hel's face lights up.

"Oh!" she exclaims. "We're all alone now! Just the big bad Alpha and little ol' me." She attempts to waggle her eyebrows suggestively, but the effect is somewhat ruined by her increasingly unfocused gaze.

"Sleep, little flame," I tell her, trying to sound stern despite the warmth spreading through my chest.

"Don't wanna," she murmurs, even as her eyes drift shut. "Might wake up and you'll be gone."

"I'll be here," I promise.

She smiles faintly, already mostly asleep. "Liar," she whispers. "But you're a pretty liar. With pretty muscles."

I watch her fighting sleep, her eyes fluttering like butterfly wings. Each time they open, she looks at me anew, a soft smile touching her lips as if discovering me all over again. Something about that smile makes my chest tighten.

Her hand keeps reaching for me in the dim light, fingers grasping weakly at the air between us.

The torchlight in my room plays across her skin, and that's when I notice it—or rather, the absence of it. Her inner arms are bare, unmarked by the prisoner's mark that brands every exile on this island. I frown, scanning what I can see of her skin. I hadn't seen it anywhere else when I helped her, unless it's on her back, which I haven't seen, but everyone else's is on the arm.

The truth hits me.

She's not supposed to be here.

"Who are you, sweetheart?" I ask.

"I'm Hel," she answers, her voice dreamy and distant. "Just Hel. Nobody special."

The lie in those words makes my wolf growl. I push hair from her forehead, letting my hand linger longer than necessary. Her skin burns under my touch.

"Tell me why you're really on this island."

It takes her several moments to focus on my mask, her pupils dilated from the rum milk.

"Told you," she slurs, then giggles. "I fell out of the sky. Like a shooting star. Except less graceful. And with more screaming." Her eyes suddenly go wide with alarm. "Oh! You shouldn't know that." She tries to press a finger to my mask where my lips would be, missing completely and poking my chest instead. "Shhhhh. The damaged plane I escaped from is a secret."

I can't help but laugh. "And why's that?"

"Because," she whispers, suddenly serious. "Then you might try to sell me like everyone else has done in my life."

The raw pain in her voice cuts through her drunken haze, making my wolf snarl with the need to hunt down everyone who's ever hurt her.

Many in this fucked-up world are in the business of selling Omegas, trading them. When something is in small supply but huge demand, there's a damn market for it. I've seen it firsthand back in Denmark. Families who had female children would sometimes sell them for wealth, and I fucking hate the practice. Hate it because I know what it's like to be taken from my family, to be treated as a nobody and sent away.

That shit right there, where your family rejects you, fucks you up for life.

"Look at me," I command softly, waiting until her glassy eyes meet mine. "No one is selling you. Not here. Not ever again."

She studies me. "Promise?"

"I put my life behind my vow." The words come

easily, even if promises are dangerous things, especially on this island.

"And where are you from, then?" I ask, trying to distract myself from the way she's looking at me, as if I'm something worth trusting.

"Denmark." She giggles, the sound light and carefree. "Land of Vikings and very grumpy wolves." Her nose scrunches up adorably. "So many grumpy wolves."

I stiffen. Denmark? The coincidence is too great. My mind races through possibilities, through connections I haven't thought about in years.

"Which pack?"

"You ask too many questions, silly Alpha." Her head flops to the side, and suddenly, she's sleeping deeply, making tiny snoring sounds that are impossibly endearing. My fearsome reputation would never recover if anyone knew how those little snores affect me.

I stare down at her, my mind racing. Who is this girl, really? Do I know her? What pack broke her, made her run? And why does the mystery of her pull at something deep inside me, something I thought died years ago?

When I slowly rise to leave, she turns to her side, reaching for me.

"Stay," she whimpers, a plea that goes straight to my gut. "Please."

The need in her voice matches the need clawing at my chest. That's when I spot something red on the back of her forearm—a scratch with dried blood around it.

"You got hurt there, too."

She glances at the cut like she's surprised to find it there. "Ouch," she says simply, making me smile despite myself.

I sit back beside her, leaning over her arm, not thinking twice about needing to clean it for her.

Her gaze locks with mine as I slowly, deliberately, take a long lick of the wound, then another, her blood almost sweet on my tongue. I tell myself it's just to clean it, to prevent infection, but we both know that's a lie.

I'm becoming obsessed with her taste, with everything about her.

"That tickles," she breathes, her chest rising more prominently. The blanket slips lower, revealing her beautiful breasts and small nipples, tight and the color of the darkest pink.

My cock punches hard, thick and ready, and I breathe in the delicious sweetness of her arousal. My gaze is locked on those full tits, and a deep pulse shakes me. My balls tight, the ache to reach over, to touch and taste them, strangles me.

Mate.

The words boom in my head like a reminder that

she's mine to claim, to show her why she belongs to me.

My wolf surges forward, clawing at my control.

She must sense something in my stillness because she says, "Please, Ghost."

I stare at her, fighting every instinct that screams at me to take what she's offering, ignoring my aching cock. My chest heaves with the effort of restraint. She's drunk, injured, and vulnerable—everything that in me craves and needs to protect.

"Don't you want me?" she purrs, and the insecurity beneath her words has my heart clenching.

"You have no idea how much I do," I growl, drinking in her curves, memorizing them before forcing myself to pull the blanket back over them. The action feels like tearing off my own skin. "When I claim you—and I will—I want you fully conscious. I want you to know exactly what you're getting into. Not like this, not when you're hurt."

She blinks, a blush crawling over her cheeks, and pulls her hand back. I catch it, unable to let her retreat completely. Her pulse flutters under my fingers like a trapped bird.

"It takes a damn strong man to resist you right now, sweetheart, and I like to think I am such an Alpha." I trace circles on her inner wrist, feeling her shiver. "But I can only resist so much when you're everything I..." I pause, the weight of unspoken words heavy.

"It's okay," she whispers, then she goes silent, tugging the blanket to her chin.

My chest aches with words I can't say, promises I shouldn't make. My wolf is singing with what I tasted in her blood, with the knowledge that fate or chance or this cursed island has given me what I never thought to find.

She's mine for eternity. My mate. My salvation. My damnation. She just doesn't know it yet, but she'll find out soon enough.

The only issue is her ability to leave the island. If she escapes my clutches, I can't follow. The brand on my arm ensures that. The thought makes my wolf rage, makes the darkness in me rise up with plans and schemes I shouldn't contemplate.

Heart thundering, frustration boiling in my veins, I lean over to whisper, "Sleep, little flame. I'm not going anywhere."

Her eyes are closing, her breathing heavy.

I move to the corner of the room, settling into a chair before shutting off the torch. In the darkness, I watch her breathing even out. She looks peaceful now, unaware of how much she's upended my world.

My thoughts are obsessed with her.

My to-be mate.

All while images of her bare breasts, of her offering her body to me, keenly suffocate me with need.

She shifts in her sleep, mumbling something that might be my name.

As I settle in for my watch over her, I know one thing with bone-deep certainty—whatever game fate is playing with us, I intend to win and not lose my fated mate. No matter the cost.

CHAPTER
NINE
HEL

I wake with a fuzzy head. The morning light streaming through the window is too bright, making me squint as memories from last night start trickling back in fragments—Eve's betrayal, that creepy ghost town, being chased, falling over, my leg...

As if the thought summons it, a dull ache throbs in my shin, not nearly as bad as last night, though. More memories surface hazily, mostly about Ghost being near me, him making me drink something bitter. Something to help with the pain, they'd said. Something to make me forget...

That explains my foggy brain.

When I manage to lift my gaze, my breath catches. Ghost is slumped in a chair by the window, head bent forward, sunlight pouring over him like liquid gold. He's only in black pants, and my gaze shoots to his bare chest, stomach rippled with muscles, at how uncomfortable he looks in that seat, like he's about to spill out. Why does he have to be so damn muscular that all I can think about is running my hands over him? I haven't even seen his face, yet here I am, drooling over him being half naked.

Scars crisscross his torso, some silvery with age, others still pink and angry. The kind of marks you get from war or something worse.

And he's still wearing that ridiculous mask, even while sleeping.

He stretches his arms above his head with a low groan that does things to my insides I refuse to acknowledge.

"Morning, sweetheart. How are you feeling?" He rises from the chair in one fluid motion.

I clutch the blanket to my chest, suddenly very aware of my own vulnerable state, of my nakedness. "I'm feeling better," I answer quickly.

A low chuckle rumbles from behind his mask. "You're suddenly shy, unlike last night?"

My heart stops. "What exactly are you saying? Did we... you know, do something?" Gods, what did I do? And why can't I remember?

"Giggled quite a bit, mostly, and touched my chest. You seemed to enjoy that a lot," he admits with a grin.

Fire burns my cheeks to think that I groped him while high on painkiller medication.

He's just standing there, staring at me, and for the first time, I can properly see his eyes in the clear morning light. They're not the same color—one is a milky, pale green, while the other is a deeper bottle-green. He sits on the edge of the bed next to me, close enough that the heat radiating from his skin pours over me.

I reach for his mask. My fingers brush against his jaw, feather-light, seeking the edge. His hand catches mine, yet he doesn't push me away. Just holds my hand there, his thumb brushing over my knuckles.

"Why do you wear it?" The question comes out barely above a whisper.

"I hate getting attention and people staring at my injury."

I can't help but snort. "Right, because a skull mask is totally inconspicuous. Nobody ever stares at the guy in the creepy mask."

"Better they fear me than pity me." His voice is light, but there's steel underneath.

Something in my chest tightens. "Can I see?"

His thumb stills on my hand. "Be careful. You may not like what you see."

"I doubt that." The words come out softer than I meant them to, more honest.

There's a long pause as he just looks at me, his gaze searching mine for something. Then, slowly, he reaches up with his free hand and pulls the mask to the top of his head.

My breath catches, but I force myself not to react. A brutal scar cuts down across his pale green eye, the skin puckered and raised like a ridge of angry flesh. The eyelashes are missing in a stark line where the scar passes, and that ghostly eye seems to have a diagonal scar, too. It seems to stare right through me.

His jaw is clenched tight. I keep my face carefully neutral, even as my heart aches for the pain he must have endured.

"I'm blind out of that eye," he confesses with a rough voice.

"What happened?"

His good eye darkens. "Remember that fucking dickhead you met when I first found you on the island? Let's just say we had a huge disagreement. After that savage fight, we split the island in half, but I've vowed to destroy the son of a bitch for what he did to me. And, well, he's got the same vendetta against me."

Before I can stop myself, my hand comes up to cup his cheek, fingers gentle against the scarred flesh. "I'm so sorry he did that to you."

"I gave as good as I got." He pulls away slightly. "But I don't want to talk about the bastard or your pity." The mask goes on, and I let my hand fall back to the blanket.

"What about you?" He turns those mismatched

eyes on me again. "Seeing as we're sharing... your turn. I notice you don't have a bonding mark on your arm, so you weren't sent here as a prisoner. You mentioned something about a plane crash?"

"I did?" I squirm internally. Gods, what else did I say last night? But he did save my life, and he's shown me something deeply personal. He deserves at least part of the truth.

"I was on a plane to Romania, going to my brother." The words come slowly. "There was a storm suddenly..."

"Your doing?" His response is casual, too casual.

I fix him with my flattest stare, but my heart is racing. He doesn't even guess but is convinced of my abilities. Or did I reveal that, too, in my drug-induced haze?

"If I could control storms, do you really think I'd still be stuck on this island?"

He leans in, and I have to fight the urge to get closer into him. His presence is like gravity, pulling at something deep in my core.

"So you don't have control of your ability, then?"

I narrow my gaze on him, unsure how much I can trust him yet. "What's with the inquisition?"

He shrugs. "It's important to know who I bring into my home for the safety of my pack. And you're still not being forthcoming."

"And I think you're not exactly an open book yourself." I meet his gaze steadily, even as my pulse thunders in my ears.

A slow smile spreads across his face; I can see it in his eyes, even if the mask hides his mouth. "Touché."

The morning sun catches his good eye, turning it to sapphire, and for a moment, I forget to breathe. There's something magnetic, dangerous, and alluring about him that makes me want to trace every scar on his body and learn their history. But there's also something dark there—whispers of violence and anger. Something that says this man is not meant for happy endings.

I should be trying to get away from him, not trying to resist the desire to touch him again. Then his hand finds mine once more, his thumb resuming that maddening stroke across my knuckles, and I know I'm already in too deep.

"Did your ability to control storms cause the plane to crash?"

His words rattle me, and I press a hand to my chest in mock offense, though my heart is hammering so hard I wonder if he can hear it.

"You make it sound like I crashed the plane on purpose," I accuse.

"Did you?"

There's something in his tone that irritates me. Does he see me as dangerous to his pack? I give him my best deadpan stare.

"Yes, because I absolutely love nearly dying and ending up stranded on Murder Island. It's been my lifelong dream, actually. Really living my best life here."

He shrugs, and if every muscle in my body wasn't screaming in protest, I'd throw all the pillows at his stupidly attractive body. Or his mask. Whatever.

"Hey, asshole, I have no control over my ability," I say finally, the words tasting like dirt in my mouth, telling him the truth. "Trust me, if I did, a lot of things would be different."

The silence that follows is heavy, loaded with all the things I'm not saying. He just... watches me. I resist the urge to pull the blanket higher.

He rises to his feet. "Let me bring you some food."

"I'd appreciate that." As he turns to leave, something compels me to call out, "Ghost?"

He pauses, glancing back, waiting.

"Thanks. For saving me. With the zombie and in the woods."

"Of course. I'd do anything for my fated mate."

I choke on air. "Wait, what?"

His only response is a low chuckle as he strolls out of the room, leaving me gaping after him.

"Is he fucking joking?" I say to the empty room. "When did this... No, he can't be." My responses rise in pitch with each word until I sound like I've been inhaling helium.

I press my hands to my temples, trying to make sense of this bombshell. *Fated mates.* The words echo in my head like a bad song you can't forget. I wasn't even a soul-mate match with my husband, but that hadn't mattered for the forced arrangement. I'd accepted long ago that I would never find my true mate—it wasn't in my future. Only a dream for people who had the luxury of choice.

"Okay, brain," I mumble to myself. "Time to earn your keep. What exactly happened last night that made him think..." I trail off, trying to pierce through the fog of medication-induced memories. "And why didn't anyone tell me the pain medicine came with a side of temporary amnesia? That seems like something that should be on the label."

Even as I try to dismiss his words, I can't ignore the way my body reacts to his presence, how my wolf practically purrs when he's near. I've never felt drawn to anyone like this before, as though there's an invisible thread connecting us, pulling tighter every time he's close.

"No, no, absolutely not." I shake my head violently, then immediately regret it as the room spins. "This is not happening. This cannot be happening. I refuse to let it happen."

A hysterical laugh bubbles up in my throat.

"Being his mate would mean..." The truth scares me because it means I'd be stuck here. Forever. On this island. With him. Where he's imprisoned. Where someone tried to have me killed on day one. Where I'm surrounded by feral Alphas.

I remember seeing Ghost with Eve yesterday, how intimate they looked together, and my stomach turns.

"Great. Fantastic. Because what this situation really needs is some bizarre love triangle." Running my hands through my tangled hair, I try to think rationally.

Okay, let's look at the facts. One. I'm supposedly the mate of a masked man who's basically running a prison island. Two. His girlfriend already hates me. Three. I have absolutely no idea what I did last night while under the influence of whatever they gave me.

Pushing away all those panicked thoughts spiraling in my head, I pull back the blanket carefully, wincing as I examine my bandaged leg. A line of red has seeped through the white bandages right where I remember stitches being mentioned. That memory is clear enough. But then another memory surfaces, and I gasp in mortification.

"Oh, you idiot." I cover my face with my hands from sheer embarrassment. "Please tell me I didn't actually try to seduce him by pulling down the blanket to my waist and offering him my breasts."

The memory becomes clearer—me giggling and Ghost firmly tucking it back around me, rejecting me.

The fuck! I'm not sure if I should be grateful or angry at him.

"Odin, Thor, anybody listening... if you have any mercy at all, please split open the ground and swallow me whole right now." I peek through my fingers at the still-solid floor. "No? Thanks for nothing."

A thought strikes me, and I groan again.

"Oh gods, what if that's why he thinks we're mates? Did I let him bite me?" I quickly run my hands over my body but feel no fresh marks. I pause.

The sound of footsteps in the hallway makes me snap my mouth shut. If Ghost heard any of that... well, maybe he'd be kind enough to just kill me quickly instead of letting me die of embarrassment.

As the footsteps pass by without stopping, I sink back into the pillows with a sigh. The ceiling, unsurprisingly, offers no comfort.

With more footsteps approaching, I close my eyes and pretend to be asleep. Apparently, I've reverted to childhood logic where if I can't see him, he can't see me.

"I can tell you're faking," his amused response reaches me.

Without opening my eyes, I respond, "No, you can't."

His laugh makes my eyes fly open of their own accord. He's standing there with a tray of food, and even with the mask, I can tell he's smirking.

He sets the tray down beside me. "Now eat your breakfast, sweetheart. You'll need your strength for all the catching up we're going to be doing."

I throw a pillow at him. He catches it effortlessly, the bastard.

"I hate you," I inform him primly.

"No, you don't."

The worst part is, he's right. I don't loathe him at all. And that might be the scariest thing about this whole situation.

CHAPTER
TEN
GHOST

She scared the fuck out of me last night.

Not that I'd admit it to anyone, but finding her in Wreckage, seeing that zombie coming after her, watching her struggle with the savage fall— my heart hasn't stopped racing since. If this is what having a fated mate feels like, I won't have to worry about anyone taking me out. My damn heart might do the job.

She's only been with us less than a week, and I'm already growing damn infatuated with her, crazy obsessed.

Here I am, watching her sleep again after she dozed off with a belly full of breakfast. Even now, watching her chest rise and fall with each breath, I can't shake this overwhelming urge to protect her. To keep her close. It's foreign to me—I'm not used to feeling this... vulnerable.

When her eyes finally flutter open, she fixes me with that defiant stare I'm starting to look forward to.

"You're not going to give up, are you?" she croaks.

I shake my head, fighting a smile behind my mask. "Come on. You need some fresh air. I'm taking you outdoors."

I retrieve clothes for her from a chest of drawers— one of the Omega's donated some things. When I turn back, she's sitting up straighter, chin lifted in that stubborn way of hers.

"Turn around," she commands, as if she's the Alpha here.

It's amusing enough that I comply, though I can't resist glancing back when I hear her grunt with effort.

"Don't look!" she snaps.

"It's nothing I didn't see the other night," I remind her. "And with all those sounds, you need my help."

"I don't need anything." She comes back at me fast, but I hear the strain in her voice. "And if you peek again, I'll find a way to make that mask a permanent fixture."

"Such violence," I drawl but keep my eyes forward. "And here I thought we were becoming friends."

"Okay, fine. I'm... decent."

I turn, and my breath catches. She's managed to

slip into a simple cotton dress that falls past her knees. The pale blue fabric makes her eyes look stormy. Her blonde hair is mussed from sleep, falling in soft waves around her face. Something in my chest tightens.

Without warning, I scoop her up into my arms. She lets out a squeak that she'll probably deny later.

"I can walk!"

"Sure you can, sweetheart. Just like you could dress yourself."

She mutters something that sounds suspiciously like "smug bastard" but settles against my chest.

I carry her through the mansion and out onto the grounds. Other pack members are scattered around, trying to look busy while obviously staring. I feel her tense in my arms.

"They've all been talking about you, you know," I tell her, heading for the pond behind the mansion. "The mysterious woman who crashed onto our island."

Her head snaps up. "They have?"

"You're the most interesting thing that's happened here in years." I settle her carefully on a wooden bench overlooking the water. Palm trees surround us, and the sun turns her hair almost white. The way she lifts her head, closes her eyes, and takes in the warmth has me grinning.

Fuck, I don't know what's wrong with me. I

haven't smiled this much in my whole life. Now look at me. I'm a fucking clown.

I grab a partially cut palm tree trunk—heavy son of a bitch but worth it to see her expression when I set it in front of her as a footrest. She lifts her legs to rest them on it.

"My very own throne, complete with palm tree ottoman?" Her lips twitch. "You sure know how to spoil a girl."

"Only the ones who crash-land on my island." I flop down beside her, close enough to feel her warmth. "Speaking of which, what pack in Denmark are you from?"

"Straight to business, then." She hesitates, and I see walls going up behind her eyes. "Why does it matter?"

"You're stuck here. What are you still protecting?"

"Fine." She shrugs, but there's nothing casual about it, her gaze skimming out over the still pond. "You want to know? I'm from Ulv pack, and I fucking hate my father because he sold me to a bastard enemy in Balor pack in a forced marriage." Her voice turns bitter. "I'm nobody. Just an object others sell for profit."

Hate fills me at hearing her story, my hands curling into fists. Fucking bastards, yet I'm not surprised, as I'd witnessed it happening back in Denmark too often.

Children were pawns for parents to use as they deemed fit, and I fucking loathed it. I wanted to hurt them, to make them feel abandoned and betrayed.

I study Hel as she stares at a tiny bird landing at the edge of the water, drinking, her fingers twisting over one another.

Reaching down, I gather a handful of smooth pebbles and place them in her lap. She immediately starts fidgeting with them.

"Sorry to hear that," I say quietly. "And your husband?"

"Fuck him." The words explode out of her like she's been holding them in too long. Anger radiates from her so strongly I can almost taste it. I tilt my head, studying her, wondering what that bastard did to make her this furious. Was he the reason she was on that plane? Did he trigger her abilities? Was he on the plane when it crashed? One can hope. The questions burn in my throat, but I hold them back until she's ready.

"You may hate me," I say instead. "But I'm from the Balor wolf pack."

Her head whips around, studying me. And after a long pause, she just says, "I don't hate you." A pebble she throws splashes into the pond. "How'd you end up here, then?"

I lean back, taking a deep breath as memories darken my thoughts, hatred rising like bile. I'm not ready to show her the ugly truth of my past, why I belong here among the monsters, so I go for a softer option.

"My family. Once I turned eighteen, they offered me the option of either going to this island or dying after my fucker of a father blamed me for every damn thing that went wrong in the village. The man loathed me and beat me daily." I choke on a forced laugh. "So it was easy to select the island if it meant leaving home."

Her lips pinch, and she places her hand on mine, her warmth spreading over me. "That's so fucked up."

"Tell me about it."

Silence.

I find myself enjoying the peace, the heat, the view. Her company. She's easy to be with, which is rare for me. I may lead the pack, but those are different dynamics—fear ensures they follow. It's not my preferred option, but when dealing with monsters who don't know any other way, sometimes it's necessary.

"See? My shit's just as crazy and broken," I admit as she tosses another pebble into the pond.

She reaches down to scratch around her wound, and I remember something from a few nights ago.

"When we were in Wreckage..."

"The ghost town?" She glances at me, her head bending to the side in an adorable look. "Is that what it's called?"

MILA YOUNG

I nod. "I sensed something around you."

She blinks. "Not sure what that means."

"Well," I shift, uncomfortable with sharing this part of myself, but I want her to trust me and not take off again or try to escape. "I can sometimes sense spirits. Wreckage is full of them." I clear my throat, unable to believe I admitted it aloud.

"Wait." Her eyes go wide. "You can see ghosts?" Her shoulders are square, and she's alert and super interested.

"Sometimes," I mutter. "And it's not a big deal."

"Are you kidding me?" She stares at me like I've grown a second head. "Okay, go on. You sensed something on me?"

"Yeah, energy lingering near you."

"Did you see it?"

"Nope, only sensed it."

She studies me for a long pause, her expression unreadable.

"Is that why... after you destroyed the zombie in that basement, I thought I was seeing things, but I swore I spotted white figures behind you in the dark. Even you looked partially ghostlike." She shakes her head. "I figured I'd just hit my head. Or, you know, the normal reaction to being attacked by a zombie."

"Sometimes, I drift into their world. I fucking hate it, as I can see them clearly while our world goes

152

blurry. Doesn't happen often. Thank fuck for that, because it sets me on edge."

She throws her last pebble, watching it sink.

I reach over, resting my hand on her thigh, her warmth leaping up my arm, and my fingers tighten a bit, craving more.

"How's the pain?"

She's gone still under my touch, her breath catching, face flushing pink. I turn to her, enjoying her reaction, the way her pulse jumps in her throat and how her pupils dilate ever so slightly. But I notice wariness in her eyes, too, the way she holds herself back even as her body betrays her attraction. She doesn't trust me. Smart girl.

The truth is, she shouldn't trust me. I'm not the hero. I'm the monster they warn children about, the darkness that swallows the light. And I know better than anyone that there are no happy endings on Nightmare Island.

Yet, part of my brain is confusing me, making me believe it's possible.

I'm clearly in for a fucking rude awakening. Nothing has ever gone well for me.

Watching her flushed face and the rapid rise and fall of her chest, something primal stirs inside me. My hand is still on her thigh. She's trying so hard to appear unaffected, but her body betrays her at every turn.

In my mind, I'm picturing my hand sliding under her cotton dress, spreading her legs, and pushing my fingers between her folds, finding her drenched and ready for me. Fuck, the thought alone has my cock throbbing to life.

"Does my touch make you nervous, sweetheart?" I keep my voice low, knowing the effect it has on her.

She lifts her chin, defiant as ever, and my gaze burns into her. Her beauty is captivating. Those fierce eyes with long lashes, full lips with a hint of pink, the little crease she wears often at the bridge of her nose... I can't get enough of watching her.

A group of pack members walks by, their gazes lingering too long on her. My growl is automatic, territorial, and they hastily look away.

"Look, I appreciate you saving my life," she begins. "Multiple times, actually, which is kind of embarrassing now that I think about it. But I can't... I'm not sure what's happening here, but I'm not ready for anything."

I want to laugh because she thinks she has a choice, and I'm not talking about me making her mine.

"Sweetheart, sometimes none of us have a choice when fate intervenes."

She picks up another pebble I missed, turning it over in her hands.

"Is that why you said earlier that I was your mate?"

A breeze carries the honeyed scent of her across my face, and my wolf stirs restlessly. She smells like rain and lightning, like sex. Like mine.

"I know what I sense in your scent, when I tasted your blood. It's right there, but you'll find out soon enough."

She eyes me as if she's ready to set me on fire. "I'm not ready."

"I doubt anyone is. Are you worried about your husband? I can take care of him if he ever comes here for you."

She half chuckles. "Wow, you just offered to take someone out for me?"

"You seem to be misunderstanding the intense connection between true fated mates. You're under my protection now. Anyone who tries to hurt you will answer to me."

"And what about you?" Her voice is barely a whisper. "Who do you answer to?"

The question hits harder than she probably intended. Images flash through my mind—blood on my hands, screams in the dark, the weight of choices I can never take back.

"I answer to no one."

"Alphas should answer to someone. Even monsters."

"Is that what you think I am? A monster?"

She studies me for a long moment, her gaze tracing the edges of my mask.

"I think you're whatever you needed to become to survive. Just like me."

Her words sink into me like claws, finding truth I'd rather keep buried. Before I can respond, she winces, shifting her injured leg.

"The pain's getting worse." A weak smile takes the sting out of her words. "And I'm really tired of hurting."

"Let me take you back inside." I stand, ready to lift her.

"Wait." She catches my hand, and the simple touch sends electricity through my veins, through my body, and down to my cock. "Just... a few more minutes? It's peaceful here."

"Okay." I settle back beside her, closer this time. She doesn't pull away when our shoulders touch.

"*Peaceful* isn't a word most people would use to describe Nightmare Island."

"Maybe that says more about my life than your island." She leans into me slightly, probably not even aware she's doing it. "Besides, the view isn't bad... when you ignore the whole prison island vibe. And the zombies. And the ghosts. And the scary masked Alpha."

I burst out laughing at her jab. "Yeah, he's not so

bad. When he's not being all mysterious and cryptic about the whole mate thing."

I have no idea how long we've spent outside, but time flew by—and that never happens on the island. The breeze has picked up, and the sun is descending.

"Now?" I stand, scooping her up before she can protest. "Let's head inside."

She wraps her arms around my neck, her side boob against my chest, and it's hard to concentrate on anything but how soft it feels, how desperately I want it in my mouth.

Back in the room, I set her on the bed and brush my fingertips against her cheek. Her skin is soft, and she shivers at my touch. It takes every ounce of control I possess to step back. To not lie on her, spread her legs, and show her she's my damn mate. To eradicate her doubts.

I retreat, and I fucking hate feeling so weak. What has she done to me?

"I'll send Awa to replace the bandages on your leg," I say and close the door behind me, lingering for just a moment to breathe in her scent one last time. My wolf paces restlessly within me, already aching to return to her.

Pushing off the wall, I adjust my mask. I'm two floors down from her room when the sounds of chaos erupt from the courtyard—hooting, shouting, the unmistakable sounds of flesh meeting flesh. Normally, I let these fights play out. My men need outlets for their aggression, especially trapped on this fucking island.

From the balcony, I spot the circle of men below. My blood runs cold when I recognize Knut, one of my seconds, in full berserker mode. His normally controlled movements are wild, savage, as he tears into—I squint—some massive, rather hairy bastard I don't recognize. Who the hell?

My jaw clenches when I spot Axel, my head of guards, lounging against a palm tree, arms crossed, watching the scene like it's today's entertainment.

I don't recognize the huge beast down there, which means we have an intruder from Sten's territory. And Axel, who's supposed to be working with Knut as a team, is doing jack shit to end this and not watch it as a sport.

Fury burns through my veins. I vault over the balcony railing, dropping the full story to land in a crouch on the packed dirt. Men scramble back as I approach them.

As I push through the circle, my wolf surges forward. It takes me two seconds to reach them, then another half second to grab the intruder by the throat and slam him to the ground. My boot replaces my hand on his neck, and he wheezes, clawing at my ankle.

"What the fuck are you doing?" I snarl at Axel, not

bothering to hide my disgust. "You think this is a show? You and Knut work as a damn team, and you're sitting there on the fucking sidelines?"

Axel's face darkens with anger. "He had it under control!"

"That's not the damn point. It's that we have this intruder, and they are taken out fast, not allowed to lay punches into one of our own!"

"Understood," Axel growls under his breath but lowers his gaze and head to me, a show of respect.

"Get out!" I roar at the crowd. They scatter, leaving just the four of us. "Axel, tie this piece of shit up."

I turn to Knut, who's wiping his bloody mouth with the back of his hand, the deep gash across his cheekbone dripping with red.

"Who the fuck is this?"

Knut spits blood onto the ground, his wolf eyes still gleaming with berserker gold.

"Caught him scaling the rock wall on the north side. Had to chase him half a mile before I could pin him down."

"Fuck." The word comes out in a growl. I increase the pressure on the intruder's neck, watching him struggle, ignoring his weak strikes at my leg.

Sten is making his move, sending his pawns to probe our defenses and find our soft spots. I know how that sadistic bastard thinks—this is just the beginning.

He's coming for my Hel.

"Bring him." I lift my boot, letting Axel haul the gasping man to his feet. "We're going to have a little chat about how he got past our guards. And then..." I bare my teeth. "We're going to find out exactly what Sten is planning."

The intruder snarls, tightening against Axel, but I let him handle it. It's the least he can fucking do. I need to figure out how to protect a certain stubborn she-wolf when we have nowhere to run to hide her.

ELEVEN

HEL

T hree days have passed since I injured my leg. Now, the scar's nothing more than a bumpy line, courtesy of Awa's incredible help, along with my fast wolf healing abilities.

Yep, I'm finally standing without wincing. The stitches are gone, and so is most of the pain. I stretch carefully, testing my weight on both legs.

"You've healed so fast." Awa's words carry from the doorway to the bedroom.

"Guess I'm harder to kill than expected." With a grin, I cross the room, feeling steady on my feet and about damn time.

"Hel, don't joke about such things." But there's a glimmer in her eyes that tells me she's fighting a smile, too.

MILA YOUNG

The weather outside my window is disgustingly perfect—blue skies, gentle breeze, not a storm cloud in sight. It's almost offensive how calm everything is now that I'm not running for my life or having emotional meltdowns. My storm-brewing *gift* seems to be taking a vacation.

"My mother never..." I start, then catch myself.

But Awa's already reading between the lines, the way she always does. She enters the room casually, smiling, hands in the pockets of her jeans.

"Never what?"

"She never just checked on me. Never just... talked normally to me." I shrug, aiming for casual but probably missing by a mile. Maybe she knew what was coming—the arranged marriage, everything. Maybe keeping her distance was her way of being kind.

Tightness forms in my throat, and I hate that after her coldness, all I can think about is her tears and pleading with my father not to sell me off on the day I was delivered to Jarl. It was the only time I felt like she truly loved me.

Awa's face softens, watching me. I blink my eyes, frustrated that I should shed a tear for her after everything.

"Or maybe she didn't know how to love properly. Not everyone does."

"Yeah, well, fuck that." I wince at my own

162

language, but Awa just chuckles. "Sorry. I just... distance doesn't make anything hurt less. Trust me, I'm an expert on emotional distance by now."

"Come on," Awa says, throwing an arm around my shoulders and pulling me against her side. "There's a gathering outside. Food, fire, fresh air, and company— all the things you need."

We head outside the room. I adore Awa for being so kind to me, so down to earth. She's in her early to mid-thirties, yet we get along so easily.

"You never told me," I say on our stroll down the hallway. There are a few guards around, something I noticed since the incident with my leg, which would be Ghost not trusting I won't disappear again.

"What's that?" she asks.

"How did you end up in this place?"

Her lips pinch tight. "I killed my new Alpha in self-defense. That was, of course, after he rejected me as his mate and intended to feed me to his pack."

"The fucker!" I growl, pressing closer to her. "I hope you made it really hurt. Like, made him suffer."

She laughs. "I love how evil you sound. I used a screwdriver in all the places it hurt."

We both chuckle, which makes us sadists, considering our topic of discussion, but I never said I was pure and perfect.

The front yard of the enormous mansion is alive

with activity when we step outside. A massive bonfire dominates the center, flames licking at the darkening sky. The smell of woodsmoke mingles with cooking meat, making me salivate.

Around us, the scene is pure chaos... but organized chaos, like a wild family reunion. Two men wrestle in the corner, all snarls and muscles, while others cheer them on. Several wolves in their shifted forms lounge in the grass, their fur catching the golden light of sunset. A group of men practice throwing knives at a tree trunk, the blades thunking into the bark with deadly precision. Others are drinking, eating, chatting.

Then there are a few totally naked men walking around like it's the most natural thing in the world. I roll my eyes but still stare because I'm a hot-blooded woman.

The Omegas cluster together in small groups near the flames, though I notice a few chatting with Alphas. The whole yard thrums with energy, laughter, and the occasional playful growl. I remember Eve telling me how deadly they are, and I'm not saying they aren't dangerous as fuck, but they all get along, too.

Then I spot him. *Ghost.*

He's standing by the fire, deep in conversation with two men I haven't met yet. Even from here, the sight of him makes my insides burn up, butterflies bursting to life in my stomach, and my nipples harden.

Calm down, girl. He hasn't even looked at you yet.

His feet are bare, and he's wearing jeans that hang indecently low on his hips and a white V-neck shirt that's definitely struggling with the task of containing his biceps. His dark hair is longer on top, wild in the breeze, and that mask... that damn mask that should be terrifying but somehow just turns me on.

He twists his head, catching my gaze, and smirks.

My pulse speeds up, heat burns me up, and fire pools between my thighs so fast that I blush. I feel giddy and crazy hot. What in the world is wrong with me?

All three men start walking our way, and I'm struck again by how Ghost moves—with a predatory grace, all shoulders, and raw power. He towers over his companions, who are hardly small men themselves.

Awa nudges into me. "Hey, I'm going to go say hi to some friends. You've got company coming." She gives me the most sinful grin in the world, wiggling her eyebrows, and I playfully push her away.

My body's reaction to him is getting harder to ignore. There's this constant warmth under my skin, a restlessness I can't shake. When he's near, it gets worse—my pulse races, my skin feels too tight, and there's an ache deep inside I don't want to think about. Something's changing in me, and it's equal parts thrilling and terrifying.

The guy with the wild, dark hair and tanned skin drops to all fours in human form and lets out a howl. Several others join in, and I can't help but laugh at them.

One of the men with Ghost has a collection of small scars across his face. His khaki cargo pants and loose top give him a more casual air than Ghost, but his careful assessment of me is anything but casual.

"How is your leg?" Ghost asks first, studying me up and down, his attention the kind that misses nothing.

"Good as new. Well, except for the sexy battle scar." I pause. "That's what we're calling injuries these days, right? Sexy battle scars? You all seem to have them, too."

One of his men howls with laughter. "Oh man, Ghost, she's perfect for you."

Ghost seems to ignore his comment but has eyes only for me before turning to his two companions.

"This here is Axel," he says, nudging the casual-looking guy, who hasn't taken his sights off me. I can't deny that he's cute, but he's nothing compared to Ghost. "And there, we have Knut." He points to the one acting like a damn wolf in human form with others. "My two closest commanders."

"Hey," I say, smiling, unsure what else one says. I'm not exactly practiced at socializing.

"So, this is the infamous new arrival," Knut calls out, finally standing up and joining us. His amber eyes are intense, fixed on me. He's extremely gorgeous, with that chiseled look that would make any girl's legs buckle.

I tilt my head to the side. "Infamous already? I've barely had time to earn my bad reputation here."

Ghost's laugh is heavy and rich. "Give it time. You seem to find trouble easily enough."

"Trouble?" I press a hand to my chest in mock offense.

Axel grins. "Oh, we've heard stories."

"All lies, I'm sure. Unless they're really good stories, in which case they're absolutely true."

Ghost moves closer to me, and there's something different about him today—more intensity in his gaze, more tension in his shoulders. The air between us feels charged, and the moment he lays a hand around my waist, which I realize is his way of declaring to everyone that I'm his, my insides melt. I'm suddenly breathing harder and lean into him because my body seems to be taking over now.

It's been getting worse as I've been healing—this constant thrumming awareness, the way my body seems to know when he's near even before I see him. Sometimes, I wake up burning, sheets damp with sweat, and his name on my lips as I come undone from an orgasm.

I glance over at Awa, who's settled on a nearby log, watching a few Alphas prepare meat for cooking. The excuse to escape this moment where all three are staring at me, and I'm not sure what to say, presents itself.

"I should probably..."

"Of course," Ghost states as though he read my mind, but his gaze doesn't leave me. That mask hides so much, but his eyes... they give everything away if you know how to look.

That's when I spot Eve around the other end of the fire.

My blood runs cold as memories flood back of her tricking me into getting stuck out in the woods at night. I remember the fear.

She spots me, too, and immediately tries to move out of my line of sight.

I hurry away from the men, smile at Awa, and keep going. My healed leg protests the sudden fast motion, but I ignore it.

Eve moves toward the tree line, but I follow. She's wearing a flowing dress that catches on roots and overgrown shrubs, and her brown curls bounce as she walks. When I catch up, she's staring into the shadows like they might offer an escape route.

"Hey there, bestie!" I call out, layering on the fake sweetness. My heart is pounding, but I'll be damned if I let her see how much she rattled me. "Thanks so much for trying to kill me the other day. Really thoughtful of you."

"Are you insane?" She laughs nervously, fingers twisting in her dress as she looks at me. "I heard you got lost and went out of bounds. That's on you for not following instructions."

My mouth falls open for a moment, then I close it up and step closer, anger burning me up.

"Oh, you mean the 'go down these steps and out this door' instructions? Those super helpful, totally not murderous instructions? Because I've got to tell you, your tour guide skills need serious work."

"Look, I don't know what you think happened—"

"Let's break it down, then, shall we?" My voice is trembling now, but with rage rather than uncertainty. "You nudged me down the stairs. And you knew exactly what you were doing. What I can't figure out is why. What did I do to you, Eve? I'd been here five minutes."

She lifts her chin, defiance replacing the nervousness. "You really don't get it, do you? You waltz in here, and suddenly, you're all he sees. Do you have any idea what it's like—"

"To be replaced?" The laugh that escapes me is bitter. "Bestie, I've been unwanted my entire life. My own mother couldn't wait to trade me away. At least you had something to lose."

"It's not that simple."

"Then explain why you thought murder was the answer."

She takes a step forward, then another. "You don't understand what it's like here. What it means to be an Omega, to finally find someone who sees you, really sees you, and then—"

"Ladies." Ghost's voice makes us both jump as he approaches, towering over us. My heart slams against my ribs. "Everything all right here?"

Time seems to slow down. I look at Eve, really look at her—the fear she's trying to hide, the desperation in her eyes, the tremble in her arms. She tried to kill me. The words are right there on my tongue—words that would seal her fate. Ghost doesn't seem like the kind of guy who forgives betrayal. I've seen the darkness in him.

My throat feels tight.

She's staring at me with a tight smile, as if pleading with me.

Images flash through my mind of being naive, scared, and traded away like I meant nothing. The helplessness. The rage. But also the promise I made to myself—that I wouldn't become the monsters who hurt me.

The words shift and die in my throat.

Ghost makes a clearing sound since no one has responded to him.

"Just Omega talk," I say finally, forcing a smile. "You know how it is."

His eyes narrow behind the mask, that penetrating gaze shifting between us. "If you're sure?"

Every instinct screams to tell him the truth. My wolf prowls beneath my skin, wanting justice, wanting blood. The heat that's been building in me flares higher in his presence, making it hard to think. But I suspect Ghost might kill her or at least hurt her gravely, and I didn't want that on my conscience. He'd do it without hesitation, and another Omega would disappear, and everyone would look the other way because that's just how things work in our world.

I refuse to be part of that cycle.

"Totally sure," I affirm, meeting his gaze steadily. "We're good here."

He glances at Eve, who's nodding. "Nothing to worry about."

He leaves, but reluctantly, his suspicion obvious in every line of his body. The silence stretches between Eve and me until he's out of earshot.

She leans in closer. "Why didn't you tell him? What do you want from me?" she demands finally, her voice barely above a whisper.

"Because I'm not a fucking monster," I snap. "And contrary to popular belief, I don't actually want you dead. I know you're involved with him... or were... or whatever. I never planned to come here and disrupt that."

I could have told her there's nothing between

Ghost and me, but the words stick in my throat. It's impossible to ignore the possessive way he is around me.

"Listen carefully," I continue, keeping my voice low. My wolf is still restless, wanting retribution, but I push her down. "If you ever try anything like that again, if you so much as look at me wrong, I will tell him everything. And we both know how that will end. I'm giving you one more chance than you gave me to do better."

Eve's face pales. "You don't understand—"

"I get it; you're hurt. You're angry. Welcome to the club. But trying to kill me was your choice. Using my ignorance of this place against me was your choice. Remember that."

She stares at me for a long moment, something shifting in her expression. "You really mean it, don't you? About not telling him?"

"Yeah, well, don't make me regret it." I run a hand through my hair, suddenly exhausted. "Look, I've had enough people in my life decide I was disposable. I'm not going to do that to someone else, even if they probably deserve it."

She stares at me for another long moment before turning away, her dress catching the last rays of sunlight as she disappears around the other side of the bonfire. I stay there, letting the cool evening air calm my racing pulse. My hands are shaking—from anger, from adrenaline, from this damn heat under my skin that won't go away.

A wolf howls in the distance, and several others answer. The sound echoes through my bones, and my wolf wants to answer, too. It's getting harder to ignore these new instincts, these changes in my body. Everything feels heightened lately—smells are stronger, sounds are clearer, and my emotions... well, they're a mess.

When I finally return to the fire, the sky has deepened to purple and gold. The flames cast dancing shadows across the gathered wolves, some now sprawled on blankets, others perched on logs or standing in small groups. The smell of cooking meat makes my mouth water.

"Here," Ghost says, appearing at my side with a metal plate. Two thick cuts of meat steam on it, barely cooked. The sight of it, pink and juicy, makes my stomach clench with want. "You need to eat."

I take the plate, trying to ignore how my fingers tingle where they brush his. "Thanks." Though I usually prefer my meat a little less... alive.

His eyes crinkle behind the mask—he's smiling—then he moves over to talk to more of his Alphas, all of them eating the meat with their hands, their teeth tearing into it.

I bite into the meat and have to stifle a moan. The

taste explodes on my tongue, rich and primal and perfect. My wolf purrs in satisfaction.

I enjoy the barbecued meat like I haven't eaten in days, which honestly isn't far from the truth. Awa plops down beside me, offering me fresh bread slices slathered in coconut butter.

"Oh, Mara's bread. Yes, please. You're going to make me fatter."

She laughs at me. "You are not fat in the slightest."

The fire crackles and is beautiful to watch. Maybe it's the flames, or maybe it's the three helpings of meat I've devoured, but I'm feeling oddly brave.

"So... any special someone caught your eye in the pack?"

Awa's laugh rings out, rich and full. "I have four."

I choke on my bread. "Four? As in four different men?" My eyes must be huge. "Wow, I like how you think. Share your wisdom, O Great One."

"When you've been around as long as I have on this island, you learn not to limit your options." She winks, tearing off another piece of bread.

As night settles in, we keep chatting and watch couples disappear into the woods. Other Alphas are passing around what I'm pretty sure is rum, their off-key singing making me wonder if werewolves can get alcohol poisoning.

Then there's Ghost.

He's deep in conversation with Knut, but I can't

stop staring. The firelight catches his profile just right, and something in my chest does this annoying flutter thing.

My breathing suddenly thickens, struggles. I place my plate down on the grass at my feet and get up.

"I need some air," I say.

"We're outside," Awa points out because, apparently, she's appointed herself Captain Obvious tonight.

"More air. Different air. Air that's not..." Not making me feel like I'm about to combust. Not filled with his scent that's doing things to my brain I refuse to acknowledge. "Just... different air."

Understanding dawns in her eyes, along with something that looks suspiciously like pity.

"Walk by the woods where the air is clearer and with fewer Alphas scents," she advises. "But not too far. The men are wild on these nights."

I head toward the tree line. The farther I get from the fire, the clearer my head becomes. Or at least that's what I tell myself. Taking a few deep inhales, I stop before the tree line, having no intention of going in there, and with the fire at my back and others beyond that, I close my eyes.

Breathe. In and out.

Why am I sweating so much?

The cool night air carries the scent of pine and burning wood.

"Beautiful night, isn't it?" A deep voice cuts through my thoughts, coming from behind me. I turn to find one of the Alphas; he doesn't look familiar. Tall, broad chest, with dirty-blond hair and a hungry stare in his brown eyes.

"Yeah, great," I reply, deliberately taking a step away. The heat from the bonfire feels too intense suddenly, or maybe it's the way he's looking at me.

I make it about three steps before I glance back at the party and immediately wish I hadn't.

Eve is practically draped over Ghost like she's auditioning for the role of a blanket. Her fingers trace his bicep while she laughs at something that probably isn't even funny. And he... he just stands there, looking amused. Not moving away. Not stopping her.

Something ugly twists in my gut—definitely the barbecued meat. Has to be. Certainly not the way she's looking at him like he's dessert. He doesn't seem to be responding to her, yet my heartbeat is a frenzy right now. On fire.

I mean, it shouldn't matter. It doesn't matter. We're not a thing. I want to heal and most likely look for a way to leave and go track down my brother in Romania.

Except, didn't Ghost just spend the past few days making me feel like I was the only Omega he saw? Or maybe that's his signature move—make each of us feel special until we're all in his little harem like Awa's group of men. For all I know, he's got a whole rotation schedule worked out.

Monday: Brooding stares at me.

Tuesday: Eve gets the smoldering looks.

Wednesday: Probably some other Omega I haven't met yet gets the full Ghost experience.

I wrap my arms around myself, suddenly cold despite the bonfire's heat.

"I'm Nic," the Alpha says.

Turning to him, I mumble, "Oh, you're still here."

His hand brushes my arm, lingering too long, as he moves to stand in my way. The touch makes my skin crawl, and I shove him away.

"I was actually just leaving." I try to move past him, but he doesn't move. The playful facade drops from his face.

"Why so rushed?" His fingers wrap around my wrist. "Night's just getting started."

My stomach lurches. "Fuck you!" I yank my arm back, but he's stronger, much stronger. In a heartbeat, he shoves me against the tree, his mouth crushing against mine, tongue down my throat. I gag, driving my hands against his chest. The taste of alcohol and something bitter floods my mouth. I jerk my knee up instinctively into his groin.

He grunts but doesn't release me. Terror spikes through my body, then freezes as a thunderous growl rips through the night air. The sound isn't human. It isn't even wolf. It's something ancient and terrifying.

Nic is suddenly gone from my space. Through blurred vision, I watch Ghost materialize from the shadows like a vengeful spirit—eyes blazing gold in the firelight, shoulders curled forward, chest puffed. The sound coming from his chest makes the hair on my arms stand up.

Other Alphas are gathering from the party, but my attention is on Ghost and Nic. Ghost is holding him off his feet by his throat. The man is gurgling, clawing at Ghost's grip.

"You dare fucking touch what's mine!" he roars.

Okay, so I'm his, but then he lets Eve drape all over him?

Awa's at my side in seconds, grabbing my arm. "We need to go. Now!" Her voice is urgent, scared.

"But—" I start to protest.

"Trust me," she cuts in, already pulling me away. "You don't want to see what happens next. When Alphas get jealous, it's ugly." She shakes her head, tugging harder.

My feet finally move, and we're running, the sounds of snarls and shouts fading behind us. My stomach churns as a horrible scream fills the night, one of pure torture or fear. My stomach turns. Part of me wants that creep to suffer and wants Ghost to make him pay for touching me, but another part feels sick knowing what's happening back there, knowing it's because of me.

We sprint across the compound, past confused onlookers, until we reach the safety of my room. Awa pushes me inside, her usually calm face tight with worry.

"Lock the door," she orders. "Don't open it for anyone but Ghost or me."

"Awa, what's going to happen back there?"

She shakes her head. "Nothing that wasn't earned. But these things... they can get out of hand. The blood-lust spreads like a disease among Alphas. Stay here."

Then she's gone, leaving me alone with my racing thoughts. I pace the room, unable to sit still. My lips still feel bruised, and I scrub at them frantically with the back of my hand, trying to erase the memory of Nic's touch.

Every sound makes me jump—footsteps in the hall, voices outside, the creaking of the old building. I count my breaths, trying to calm down, but the adrenaline won't fade. Even staring out the window shows me nothing, as it overlooks at a different part of the yard.

Suddenly, the door bursts open.

I flinch hard, backing away until I hit the wall. Ghost fills the doorway, and my breath catches in my throat.

He's transformed from the man I know into something else entirely. His black hair is wild, his chest growling with each breath. Blood spatters his white shirt and smears his knuckles. But it's his eyes that hold me. They're still that molten gold, pupils blown wide with rage and something else, something hungry.

"Did he hurt you?"

I quickly shake my head.

He stalks into the room, his movements fluid and predatory. Power radiates from him in waves. My heart thunders against my ribs—not in fear exactly but in recognition of something primal and ancient.

"Ghost," I whisper.

A growl rumbles from deep in his chest. He stalks closer until I feel the heat rolling off his body. His hand comes up to brace against the wall beside my head, and I catch the scent of blood, pine, smoke, and perspiration.

"You're mine." The words seem to tear from him. "Mine to protect. Mine to defend." His other hand comes up to cup my face, surprisingly gentle despite the violence still thrumming through him. "Anyone who touches you without your permission forfeits their right to breathe."

I should be terrified. Should be running from the barely contained violence in front of me.

He pushes something into my hand, something hot, warm, and sticky, while saying, "Anyone who dares touch you will lose that part of their body because only I get to touch you."

I glance down at the slimy, gross, red tongue in my hand. A scream bursts from my mouth, and I fling the tongue away. It hits the wall with a wet thump, then slides down.

"What the fuck, Ghost!"

He's there in my face, hands on my arms, drawing me against him, and I shake him off, already rushing to the bathroom to wash my hands. He's right there before me, doing the same.

"Do you know how it felt to look over and see that fucking monkey with his tongue down your throat?" he said, glancing over me. "I practically vomited and flew to come for you. It murdered me seeing someone else taste you."

"Oh, that's funny coming from you," I snap, trying to ignore how my body automatically leans against him. "You want to talk about murder? Try watching Eve treat your bicep like her personal stress ball while you just stand there looking amused." I inject as much venom into the word as possible, even as my traitorous body floods with warmth at his proximity.

I march out of the bathroom, and he's on my heels. When I stop, he pauses, looking genuinely startled. "Eve?"

"Don't act dense. It doesn't suit you." My hands

press against his chest—to push him away or pull him closer, I'm not even sure anymore.

"She means nothing to me. I should have pushed her away." His voice drops lower, rougher. "Sometimes I'm so used to her being there, like a bug, that she's invisible to me."

"A bug?" I'm laughing. "Wow, that's actually kind of mean. I like it."

Suddenly, he's on his knees before me, his hands gripping my hips with a possessiveness that makes my breath catch.

"Hel, I'm sorry. Fuck, I'll grovel all night to show you that you're mine and the only one I want."

Something molten unfurls in my chest at his words. My wolf is snarling at me to submit, to let go, to give in to whatever this crackling energy between us is. My rational brain is trying to remind me that I've known him less than a week, but it's fighting a losing battle against the way my body is responding to him.

With trembling fingers, I reach for his skull mask, pulling it up and off. He stays perfectly still as I lift it away, like a predator allowing their prey one last move. The moment I set it aside and look down at him, I see it blazing in his good eye—the hunger, arousal, possession. His hands slide up my dress, leaving fire in their wake.

Then he climbs to his feet, towering over me.

"Maybe we shouldn't," I murmur, even as my body arches into his touch.

He growls and hauls me closer. "If I don't have you right now, I'll burn this whole fucking forest down."

The raw desire in his voice makes me shiver, but then his mouth finds that spot on my neck, and coherent thought becomes a distant memory.

"Ghost..." My voice catches as his teeth graze my skin.

"Say it again," he demands against my throat. "Say my name."

CHAPTER
TWELVE
HEL

"Ghost," I moan his name as his fingers trace my collarbone, his tongue on my neck, leaving me shivering with need. The hunger of his touch melts through me, leaving my knees close to buckling.

"Tell me what you're thinking." His tone is rough, strained with control as he pulls back to stare at me, his face so close that his breath flutters over my cheeks.

I laugh shakily. "Bold of you to assume I can think right now."

"Try." His thumb traces my lower lip, and my whole body shudders. "I want to hear your voice."

"I'm thinking..." I swallow hard. "That this is probably a terrible idea. That this is going to end with me hurt. That I should run."

"But?"

"But I don't want to." I force myself to hold his gaze. "And that terrifies me more than you do. I've only ever been with one other man in my life."

He makes a sound low in his throat, something like a growl. "I wish I'd found you years ago, made you mine, so I was the only man you'd ever feel."

"It's time to start working on a time machine!" I try to smile, but it fails as he continues to run his fingertips along the low neckline of my dress, leaving me breathless.

"You're trembling," he says.

"Really? I hadn't noticed." My voice shakes, too. I'm a complete mess when he stares at me with that sinful look in his eyes when I'm in his hands.

He steps closer, and I swear the temperature in the room spikes.

"Always with your sass," he murmurs, his breath hot against my ear. "Even now."

"It's part of my charm." Despite my words, my nerves are in overdrive.

His hands slide down my arms, leaving trails of fire in their wake. "You're not in trouble here."

"No?" I laugh, but it comes out breathy. "Then why does it feel like I'm about to do something incredibly stupid?"

"Because you think too much." He finds the hem of my dress. "May I?"

No, my brain screams. *Yes*, my body answers. And I nod, not trusting my voice.

The fabric whispers over my skin as he lifts it away, leaving me in just my underwear. The cool air hits my bare back, and I resist the urge to cover myself.

"Absolutely beautiful." His gaze inhales me as it travels down my body, pausing a bit too long on my breasts, his tongue slipping out, dragging across his lower lip. "I've been dreaming of this moment, little flame. Jerked off dozens of times just thinking of claiming you."

"Dozens, you say?"

He chuckles while my nipples tighten as if in command to his reaction, and I catch the grin tugging at the corner of his mouth... He noticed, too.

My heart's fluttering so hard now, and the fire between my thighs is a pool of desire. He moves in closer, leaning in, and his mouth grazes mine. I press against him, needing this, craving it.

His kiss is possessive and dominant, just like him. Fingers tangle in my hair, tugging my head back as his mouth claims mine, and my hands are fisting his shirt. I gasp against him, never having been kissed this way before—tender yet so full of passion that it leaves me dizzy. His other hand grips my waist, drawing me firmly against him.

I'm falling hard for him, so much so that I won't be

able to escape. Maybe I don't want to. Maybe it's my turn to finally find something good for a change.

His tongue presses into my mouth, tangling with mine, and I suck down on it, shuddering at how much I love the sensation of hearing him groan against me with pleasure. His cock is so fucking hard against me, only thin fabrics between us, and I feel him throbbing for me.

He breaks the kiss, only to trail down to my neck once more, taking long licks and mock bites.

"Ghost," I breathe his name.

"Too late," he whispers against my skin, sending me trembling. "I'm not stopping now."

"I want more."

He lifts his gaze, then his body, smirking like the devil.

"My good little flame. That's the right answer."

His mouth captures mine again, more demanding, more dominating, and I surrender to his darkness. With his hands on my shoulders, he pulls away, then turns me to face the wall, sweeping my hair over one shoulder.

His lips find my neck, and the moan that escapes me is beyond needy, my thighs clenching tight. Then he goes still, his body tensing behind me. A low growl builds in his chest.

"Is everything all right?" I ask, glancing over my

shoulder at him, but he's got his gaze lowered on me, brow furrowed deeply.

"What are these scars on your back?"

My heart stops. Those marks are from my bastard husband. I try to turn, but Ghost's hands hold me firmly in place. His fingers trace the raised lines gently, but each touch brings back flashes of memories.

The whistle of leather through the air. The crack of the belt. "This is for your own good, Hel." His voice thick with arousal as I tried to crawl away. The sharp bite of metal when the buckle caught my skin.

"Hel," Ghost's voice pulls me back.

"It's nothing," I say automatically. *Don't complain. Don't let it get back to Jarl. He'll make it worse next time.*

I hate that those thoughts still linger.

"He did this to you." It's not a question. The heat of Ghost's body behind me has turned from arousing to protective, his hands now cradling me.

"Can we skip the part where you pity me?" I sigh, hating this moment. Hating that I told him about my husband in the first place, about the forced marriage. Hating the weakness that crept into my voice when I did. "I've got enough issues without adding that to the mix."

He turns me around, and I stare at his chest, my arms crossed protectively over my breasts.

"Look at me," he says gently.

I peek up through my lashes, expecting sympathy, condescension, disgust—any of the usual reactions. Instead, I find tenderness. His good eye burns with it.

"I'm going to get off this fucking island," he growls. "And when I do, I'm going to—"

"You won't—"

"I'll destroy the motherfucker. I'll take my time, too. Make it last."

"Ghost, it's not that simple..."

"Don't worry, sweetheart. I'll make sure he suffers."

"He's dead." My words pour out. "He's gone. There's nothing left to fix. Just me, with all these shit memories and ugly scars."

His hands cup my face, staring at me intently. "You think that matters to me? You are the most beautiful thing I've seen, gorgeous just as you are, and you're mine to protect now. Don't ever think you're anything but perfect."

The possessiveness in his voice should frighten me. Instead, it makes that heat flare higher. I feel like things have moved so fast, and he's already overly captivated with me. I can't deny that I'm struggling to think of him not being at my side, too.

Ghost doesn't say anything, just holds me tighter as years of pain finally break free. I tremble in his arms, and he strokes me, kissing my brow.

When I pull back, it's only far enough to tilt my

chin up. His tongue traces the tear tracks on my cheeks.

"You taste like electricity," he murmurs. "Like a storm about to break."

"Smooth talker." I half grin as the heat under my skin pulses in time with my heart. My wolf is restless, wanting more of Ghost, wanting everything. For the first time since I arrived on Nightmare Island, I truly feel like maybe I belong here.

Maybe that should scare me more than it does.

"I'm sorry he did that to you, but I promise to make you feel like the queen you should be."

I'm smiling, still struggling to believe that something good might be happening to me for a change.

Ghost lifts my chin with his finger and kisses me again, gently at first, then rising to a crescendo of sucking on my tongue and my lips, coaxing a purr from me... a sound I've never made before.

"You're such a good girl," he whispers, and those words have me purring more.

I lean into his kiss, holding on to him like he's my world, my everything. It's so strange to think that hearing his sweet praise gets me more excited to be with him than anything I've experienced.

"You like it when I call you that?" he asks softly, his hands falling to my hips, his thumbs slipping under the elastic of my panties.

I nod, breathing heavily, knowing I'm completely

drenched for him. Of course, that's when he tugs my underwear down my legs, kneeling in front of me, leaving a trail of kisses on the way—down the valley between my breasts, my stomach—then he has his mouth right where I'm burning up.

I step out of the underwear as he presses his nose against my pussy, deeper still, taking a sharp intake of breath. His fingers slide between the crack of my ass, the sensation overwhelmingly incredible.

Gasping, I weave my hands through his hair while his touch slide up my inner thighs, nudging them wider. He's relentless, pushy, and unstoppable. And I love it.

"You have no idea how long I've been waiting to have your sweet cunt all over my face, to tongue-fuck you, to make you come on me, covering me with your creamy orgasm."

A moan spills past my throat. Grasping his hair, I stare down at him. He glances up, winking.

"Don't tease a girl now."

He abruptly lifts me off my feet, his powerful arms circling around my thighs and carrying me to the bed.

"If I'm going to eat, I need it spread out for me."

I laugh at him as an excited shiver races down my spine, all the way to my core, where my pussy quivers for more.

"I've never had anyone lick me down there before," I admit, feeling stupid for saying anything.

Ghost's eye lights up, and his grin is sinful. "I'll be the first mouth, first tongue, to devour your cunt?"

I nod, laughing at him.

He moves even faster, and in seconds, I'm lying flat on the bed, my ass on the edge of the mattress, while he's spreading my legs.

My face blushes.

He doesn't even notice, as he has eyes only for my offering. He kneels in front of me beside the bed, preparing for his meal.

"Are you ready for me to take care of you?" he drawls.

I nod, holding my breath at how desperately I need him. It's as though I've been ready for him from the first moment I laid eyes on him.

He leans in, and there's no pause... his tongue is on me, traveling between my lips, pushing deeper into my folds. My body arches, a loud purr in my throat. I never expected it to feel so amazing. He wastes no time licking me all over.

I need more. My hips rock with the tightness building inside me while my Alpha lowers his mouth to my entrance, where he goes wild, the tingles driving me crazy. I cry out as his thumb is on my clit, and he's rubbing me like a wild man. It's tingly and so sensitive, that I'm wriggling beneath him.

In moments, I'm fisting the blanket harder, riding

his face, and screaming from the orgasm tearing through me.

He's licking me savagely now, my thighs trembling, my breaths labored. My pussy is swollen and so unbelievably wet. I glance down at Ghost, who's pulling back, staring at me with a grin.

His mouth and chin are glistening with my juices. Yet, his fingers never leave my pussy, one of them pushing into me like he can't let go.

It feels incredible, and I'm floating.

"The prettiest cunt I've ever seen, so greedy, too, sucking down on my fingers. She wants every inch of me, doesn't she?"

"Yes," I breathe, tilting my hips. "It's yours."

"All of you is mine." He moves two fingers to my clit, rubbing it in a clockwise manner, slowly at first, then building.

I may have just exploded all over his face, but the addiction is returning like a storm. The tempo of his strokes quickens, and I shudder all over, the slow build of pleasure inside me taking over.

"Would you like me to stop, sweetheart?"

"Only if you want me to haunt your dreams forever," I answer between ragged breaths, coaxing a laugh out of him.

He's on his feet. "Good, because I'm about to fuck your brains out, little flame. Give you something you'll never forget." He unbuttons his pants and drops them, revealing that he's completely naked underneath.

He steps out of them, and my sight is caught on his huge cock. I didn't know they grew that big, the tip reddish and glistening, a thick vein running down the shaft. I swallow hard at the pulsing length of pleasure that I desperately need inside of me.

"It's fucking big."

Ghost grins as he reaches out and palms himself a few times, his eyes almost rolling back into his head.

"It's all yours, sweetheart."

He leans forward, and I scoot up onto the bed. When he kneels between my legs, his body covers mine, his hands on either side of me.

"You taste even more delicious than I expected, but now I need to be inside you. My balls are so fucking tight. Are you going to be a good girl for me?"

"Yes," I gasp, struggling to form words when I'm floating, and all I can think about is being fucked.

This is what I've missed my whole life—someone to show me what it's like to be adored, a protector, a safe place.

A real Alpha.

He leans in, his tongue dancing up my neck to my earlobe, then he's kissing me, sucking on my tongue. My hands curl around the back of his neck, drawing him closer.

The bulbous tip of his cock slides over my pussy,

pushing into my entrance, and he's huge against me. But he's not going slow. He's shoving into me, and I'm moaning loudly.

"Fuck, sweetheart, you have a tight cunt. Now, be a good girl for me and take a deep breath."

I nod while my breaths are speeding. There's a pulsing from him, and I realize it's his huge vein pulsing as he pushes into me.

"This is where I want to be, cock-deep in your little cunt, telling you how beautiful you are."

My heart flutters at his words. "Who would have thought you'd be such a sweet talker?"

He howls with laughter, then starts to fuck me... like, really fuck me. There's no buildup with Ghost, just him shoving into me, hard and fast, and I scream from the sudden pain but also from the pleasure that doesn't want him to stop.

There's no pause, just his hips jerking violently, rattling me, making the room spin. I've dreamed of being with someone I can cling to, stare into his eyes, knowing that it's something we both want. And I'm living my fantasy.

"Such a good girl, taking all of me." Then he's kissing me. "Is this what you've wanted? For me to fill your belly with my cum, to bring out your true Omega?"

I don't know what he means by the last part, but I'm too consumed by him, my voice raspy from my cries, and I can't focus on anything but him claiming me.

"Don't stop... I need more." There's no sarcasm in my voice for a change, but more dirty arousal.

He's building up, going faster, and I'm screaming now, my second climax crashing through me viciously, my thighs closing tight against his hips.

Head back, I'm shuddering and rocking with Ghost as he unleashes a thunderous growl, and hot cum starts to spurt out inside of me. I feel the warmth, the sensation, along with his cock's knot expanding inside me.

"Such a good girl," he growls, his brow glistening.

My heart's pounding, my thighs quivering, and I can't find my voice. My body seems to have come to the decision that I'm at his mercy, and now my brain is struggling to catch up.

Ghost is grinning at me, buried deep, purring, pumping into me.

"This is how it's meant to feel," he tells me as though he's having a conversation with himself. "Like we are one, like I can't bear to take a breath if you're not with me. This... fuck, this..." He unleashes a thunderous growl, then he kisses my neck, a rumble in his chest vibrating against me.

"Do you feel the connection?"

My stomach trembles, I'm sweating, and fuck, I sense my body changing, every inch of me burning up.

"Yes. What's happening?"

Every time he growls, my chest arches to be closer to him, and the vibrations all over me are centered around my core.

"You're starting to go into your heat, sweetheart, and I'm going to fuck you for as long as you need, knot you, breed you, show you what it's like to bond with a real Alpha."

The hackles on my neck rise, as his words terrify me. "Wait, what?"

"Has no one explained going into heat, little flame?"

"Of course I know what it is, but I'm not..." Suddenly, I remember the strange feelings in my body recently, my reaction around Ghost, the burning up. "No, it's too early. I'm not..."

He kisses my brow. "You're ready. I promise you." There's no harshness in his expression, just this handsome Alpha ready for my heat, more than me. All Omegas experience heat—a time when their bodies prepare to match with their Alpha, preparing for babies.

Panic curls through me because my life is chaos, and it's as if I'm watching my future unfold in front of me from a distance.

My womb suddenly cramps, then tightens, as I stare up at Ghost.

"No, you're wrong. That's just your knot."

He huffs with a grin. "If you say so." Suddenly, he peels back his lips over his teeth, sharper than normal; he's taken on part of his wolf teeth.

I'm not a fan of where this is going, yet that masculine scent of sex is strong, smothering me. Another tug of fire deep in my gut.

A sign of an Omega following her true Alpha's command—I know this, yet I fight it, meeting his gaze with steel in mine.

"There's only one way you're going to accept the change coming," he purrs, running his tongue over his top teeth, his canines gleaming dangerously sharp in the dim light.

"Ghost, don't think about it." My voice wavers.

"You're already mine, but now we need to seal it to lessen the pain of your oncoming heat."

"It doesn't have to happen now." My pulse hammers, and sweat trickles down the back of my neck. "Maybe next week? Your schedule must be packed with other Alpha things to do!"

"I made you a promise that I will protect you, so you need to trust me now."

I want to scream, to tear that self-assured smile off his face. The urge builds inside me like a storm about to break... until he leans in and his lips find my neck. The fight drains from me because I know he's right, but I fucking hate it. Am I ready to be locked to him for life?

A moan escapes before I can stop it, my body betraying me as my nipples harden and my heart races. The call of the Alpha is too strong to deny, and here I am, clinging to him, completely losing control of myself.

His teeth graze my skin. "I don't want to do it against your will, but you must see that this is needed?"

"I fucking hate this! And yet I'm going to say yes, as it seems I don't have a better choice," I relent, loathing that he's correct. Having seen it firsthand back in Denmark when girls went into heat. They experienced excruciating pain, where nothing truly sated them like their fated mate—fucking her, knotting her until her cycle of heat eased, and marking her as his.

When his fangs finally pierce my flesh, the pain is sharp and clean. I cry out, my fingers digging into his shoulders.

An addictive sensation flows through my veins like liquid, each heartbeat spreading the feeling through me until I'm convinced I'm floating. My eyes are shut, fluttering, my body shaking.

Ghost's scent surrounds me, and I crave him savagely. The bond snaps into place like a lock finding its key, and I shudder at the force that binds me to him. I cling to him and take deep inhales of his scent, unable to get enough.

My fear is still there, though, simmering beneath the surface, but it's joined by something I've never felt before—an overwhelming new emotion of being truly wanted, truly chosen by someone.

I'm not used to this sensation.

"Mine," Ghost growls against my neck, his tongue laving the bite mark. The word echoes through our bond, and I can't tell if I want to laugh or cry.

The world starts to blur at the edges, overwhelming and powerful, and darkness is creeping in. The last thing I feel is Ghost's arms tightening around me.

As consciousness slips away, one thought follows me into the darkness—I never stood a chance.

I wake to sunlight pouring into the bedroom, and for a moment, I'm wrapped in a contentment so foreign it takes me a moment to recognize it. Not the shallow kind of happiness I used to fake back home, but when I was younger and my brother, Ragnar, lived at home.

No, this feels... deeper. Real.

Then the word *mate* floats through my mind, and everything rushes back from last night.

My fingers find their way to my neck, to the spot where Ghost's teeth broke skin. The mark thrums like a heartbeat under my touch. The heat that used to feel like it was strangling me now purrs through my veins like warm honey.

"Well, this is new." I turn onto my back and find

that the other side of the bed is cold, Ghost-less, and I'm annoyed at how disappointed that makes me feel. Judging by the sunlight streaming through the windows, I've slept most of the morning.

I roll onto his side of the bed, and his scent surrounds me—pine needles, rain-soaked earth, wolf, and cocoa. His smell is filled with pheromones... of his seed, something so distinctly him it makes my wolf practically dance under my skin. "This is so not fair," I grumble, even as I bury my face in his pillow. My body feels as if it's been rewired to respond to him.

My arousal lingers. I snuggle deeper into the blankets, creating a nest of warmth that smells like him, like us, like safety—and isn't that a joke? Me, feeling safe?

Yep, for the first time in too long.

I curl in on myself, desperate to drown myself in his smell, all while slick pools between my thighs at the growing hunger for Ghost that sweeps through me.

My gaze drifts shut, and I might have dozed off again because the next thing I know, my bladder is protesting with a heavy pressure.

"All right, all right." I untangle myself from my blanket cocoon. The moment I stand, I feel the delicious ache between my thighs that makes me bite my lower lip. Memories of Ghost's cock deep inside me, his huge knot stretching me... it all floods back, and

I'm grinning like an idiot at how incredible it felt—his tongue, the orgasms—sending an excited shiver over me.

Take that, Jarl, you incompetent ass. All those times, he blamed me for his inability to knot, and it turns out that he was just... lacking.

I snicker to myself on the way to the shower, then yelp as cold water hits my skin. "Odin!" Nothing like arctic water to wake a girl up.

I raid the wardrobe Awa keeps stocked—bless that woman. I pull on riding pants, an oversized white button-down, and a leather corset that makes me feel like a warrior princess.

When I emerge from the bathroom, I spot a platter of muffins near the window. "Hello, beautiful," I purr, snatching one up. The first bite hits me with an explosion of banana, rum, and coconut that has me moaning. "Mara, you magnificent witch," I mumble around a mouthful of heaven. I grab a second one because I'm starving, and these are amazing. Much like my mate... Fuck, I have a mate now!

Speaking of Ghost...

Where is he?

"Down, girl," I tell my wolf firmly. "We're not going to be one of those clingy Omegas who can't function without their Alpha. Even if he does smell like sex and sin and— Nope, stopping that line of thought right there." But my heat is definitely coming.

I can feel it simmering under my skin, stronger than before but not yet urgent, and already my panties are drenched just from thinking of Ghost.

I walk out of the room to a quiet hallway. I'm surprised there are no guards today.

The stone hallway is oddly quiet as I head for the kitchen, and the sunlight pouring through the windows makes everything look deceptively peaceful. I pause at the balcony, drawn by movement near the tree line in the far distance. A figure darts into the woods, too quick for me to identify, and something about the movement makes my instincts heighten.

Footsteps sound behind me, and I twist around to find Eve. She joins me at the railing, her silence heavy, her forehead furrowed, shoulders curled forward. She stares out at the woods, tension radiating off her in waves.

"Everything okay?" I ask, though I shouldn't care. Yet, the way she's holding herself, it's like she's bracing for impact.

Somehow, I know whatever she's about to say is going to shatter this brief moment of peace I've found.

She turns to me but keeps glancing over her shoulder, as if expecting someone to materialize from the shadows in the hallway. She's wearing a simple cotton dress with an apron dusted with flour, probably from helping Mara in the kitchen. Though, the way her fingers keep worrying at the apron fabric makes me think she's not here to discuss breakfast.

"Listen, Hel." Her voice comes out barely above a whisper. "I don't hate you or anything, but sometimes we do things in life for pure survival." She lets out a bitter laugh. "This island is about surviving. Especially when you make the wrong decisions and trust the wrong people." Her lips pinch together, and there's something in her eyes that reminds me of a trapped animal.

I study her, tilting my head. Part of my brain is screaming that this is the same woman who tried to kill me, who I shouldn't give a damn about. And yet...

"Is someone going to hurt you?"

She shrugs. "Maybe. I don't know..." She swallows hard. "Anyway, I just wanted you to know that." She leans in closer. "I'm not interested in Ghost."

I can't help rolling my eyes and taking a step back. "Oh, this again? Because I distinctly remember you last night—"

"Shh!" She grabs my arm with surprising strength, dragging me to the far corner of the balcony where the shadows are deeper. Her nails dig into my skin.

"You are so stupid sometimes," she hisses.

"Oh, thanks," I drawl, trying to pull my arm free. "That really makes me want to listen to you. Really winning me over with the charm here."

"Would you just—" She makes a frustrated sound.

"Look, surviving here means making allies, and it's easy for you because you got Ghost from the get-go. Some of us have to work harder. I try to make out that I like him because I need his protection."

The genuine fear in her voice has me pausing. I search her face, trying to make sense of her behavior.

"Protection from what? What's going on?"

A sound echoes down the hallway, footsteps, maybe, or voices. Eve goes rigid, her face draining of color so fast I think she might faint.

"Just..." She licks her lips, glancing toward the sound. "Don't trust those closest to Ghost because nothing is as it seems. Nothing." The words tumble out in a rush, urgent and terrified. She turns to leave.

"Wait..." I grab her arm. "Where's Ghost now?"

But she's already pulling away, practically running down the corridor, her apron strings trailing behind her. The sound of her footsteps fades, leaving me alone with a growing sense of unease.

"Okay, that was fucking strange and disturbing." A chill races up my spine as her warning echoes in my head. Those closest to Ghost... My mind starts cataloging everyone.

Awa with her endless kindness.

Mara and her muffins.

Axel and Knut, who've been by his side for ages, it seems, but I don't really know them.

Or anyone else he's close to.

I'm still learning the ropes myself.

Movement catches my eye, drawing my attention back to the woods. Two men emerge from the tree line, dressed in black, like shadows. They pause at the edge of the clearing, scanning the land and remaining there.

I twist around to hurry to the kitchen and not be alone, but I slam straight into a solid chest. I jerk backward, managing to create just enough space to glance up and find a familiar face.

Axel.

Before I can speak, his hand clamps over the back of my head while shoving a chemical-soaked rag against my mouth and nose.

My blood turns cold as I react instantly, shoving against him.

The sharp, sweet smell burns my nostrils as I thrash harder, my hands clawing at his arms, my legs kicking out. But he's like steel, pressing the rag harder against my face as he pulls me tight against his chest. Black spots dance at the edges of my vision, and my movements become sluggish and uncoordinated. My legs give out, and the last thing I feel is Axel's arm around my waist, stopping me from hitting the floor as darkness claims me.

There's a bitterness coating my tongue that makes me want to gag. I snap open my eyes to find I'm no longer on the balcony. A yard surrounds me, and the rough bark of what I'm pretty sure is a tree digs into my spine. My shoulders ache from having my hands bound behind me.

I blink to clear my blurry vision as my head pounds, and I make out what looks like a graveyard of trees, stumps scattered everywhere. Random pieces of furniture are strewn about, too—cushions, half of what might have been a dining table once, even what looks like a bathroom sink lying on its side. But it's the roaming wolves, at least two dozen, that make my heart stutter in my chest.

They're everywhere. Some lounging in patches of sunlight, others pacing between the stumps with predatory grace in my direction. One massive gray beast lifts its head and stares right at me with amber eyes that are far too intelligent to be just an animal.

"This is just perfect," I mumble under my breath, testing the ropes around my wrists and tugging against them. They're tight enough to burn.

What in the world had Axel had me breathing, as my brain still feels foggy?

So, where the fuck am I?

In the distance, I spot makeshift homes. Some are just tattered tents held together by rope, while others are actual structures built into the trees themselves.

Platforms and rickety bridges connect some of the higher dwellings, where men lean against railings and stare down at me like I'm the main attraction at a particularly pathetic circus.

A black wolf, lean and scarred, slinks closer to me. Its lips pull back to reveal yellowed fangs, and a growl rumbles from its chest that makes every hair on my body stand on end.

Dread crawls up my legs, seeing there are lots of them, and I'm alone and tied up. My heart thunders against my ribs, and I'm trying my best not to freak out.

The wolf suddenly lunges, snapping at my leg. Pure instinct takes over, and I kick out, catching it right in the nose. It yelps and jumps back, shaking its head.

"Back off!" I shout, but my voice shakes too much. A few of the men in the trees laugh.

An explosion of snarls and the sound of flesh hitting flesh draw my attention to the right. Two wolves are locked in a fierce battle, rolling across the dirt in a fury of teeth and claws. Blood sprays as one catches the other's shoulder, and the injured wolf's howl of pain sends chills down my spine. Other wolves gather around to watch, some wagging their tails as if this is their favorite entertainment.

"Fuck!" I whisper, trying to look anywhere else to find out how to escape and what the hell they want with me. I notice a man walking in my direction, and my blood turns to ice in my veins.

I recognize him instantly.

It's the same fucking asshole who chased me when I first arrived on the island.

He's wearing nothing but black pants that hang low on his hips, showing off a torso covered in scars. His dark blond hair is wild.

His gray eyes lock on to mine as he approaches, and that's when I clearly notice the mark on his chest. His skin is charred, looking more like leather in the center of his chest—right where the lightning had struck him.

I break out in goose bumps and bite down hard on my lower lip to keep from making a sound. I know where I am now. Ghost warned me about the other half of Nightmare Island, about these wolves. The enemy pack.

He pauses right in front of me, close enough that I can smell perspiration on him.

"Welcome home." His crooked grin has my skin crawling.

I try to turn my head away, but his hand shoots out, gripping my chin. His fingers are too warm against my skin.

"Last time we met, you slipped away." His other hand tangles in my hair, yanking my head back. "But you're special, aren't you? And there's a rule on this island that that fuckwit Ghost seems to always forget." He leans in closer, his putrid breath making me gag. "Anything new belongs to whoever found it first. And that makes you mine, doesn't it, Omega?" He inhales deeply against my neck, and my stomach turns.

"Fuck you," I spit out.

"Oh, I like fighters." A laugh rumbles through his chest. "They're more fun to break."

Movement catches my eye, and I spy Axel striding toward us, looking like he owns the place. He doesn't even glance my way, the traitorous bastard. I grind my teeth but keep my mouth shut for now.

My mind races back to Eve's words, and suddenly, her actions make a horrible kind of sense. If she was using Ghost for protection, what kind of monster is she hiding from?

I stare at Axel.

"Sten," he states, and finally, I have a name to go with the nightmare in front of me. "Hel's yours. You got your side of the deal. Now you agree to mine."

Sten releases me and turns to face Axel. They take a few steps away from me as Sten cracks his neck, rolling his shoulders. Everything about him—from the way he moves, the calculated casualness, the barely contained violence—reminds me so much of my husband that I want to scream.

He taps his fingers against his thigh in a rhythm

that seems random but isn't. I know that tic, that false tell of nervousness hiding his real intention.

"Of course," he says, voice smooth. "A deal's a deal."

In a split second, Sten's holding a blade, and his arm swings, burying it into Axel's throat. Blood sprays, and Axel's eyes go wide with shock.

The wolves around us go wild, rushing around, howling, growling.

Sten laughs, the sound grating on my skin. "I don't fucking owe you or anyone anything, you fucking weasel."

A gasp tears from my throat as Axel falls to his knees, hands clutching his neck. Sten lets out a sharp whistle, and wolves of all sizes and colors emerge from the shadows.

"Have at it," Sten calls out, grinning. "I don't want any remains."

I want to look away but can't as the wolves descend. The sounds. Oh gods, the sounds—tearing flesh, cracking bones, Axel's gurgling screams cut short.

My whole body trembles, and I feel the familiar electric tingle in the air as clouds begin gathering overhead, responding to my fear.

But Sten's back.

"Don't touch me."

His hand is back on my chin, squeezing, forcing me to look at him.

"I see you're calling your storm." His grin is all teeth, no humanity. "So let's make this quick."

And a scream rushes past my mouth as I watch him lift his blade.

Fuck. Fuck. Fuck.

CHAPTER
FOURTEEN

HEL

My life flashes before my eyes as Sten lifts the blade, Axel's blood still dripping from its edge. The metallic scent of it makes my stomach turn, or maybe that's just the fear I'm trying desperately to swallow down. The rough bark of the tree digs into my back, the ropes cutting into my wrists, and all I can think is how stupid I was to end up here.

"Please." The word escapes before I can stop it, small and pathetic. "Don't—"

My breath hitches in my lungs as a memory crashes over me.

"Please, Jarl, I'm sorry." The marble floor is cold against my cheek, blood pooling in my mouth. "I didn't mean to—"

His boot connects with my ribs. "Fucking weak," he

214

spits. *"Begging like a dog. Is that what you are? A dog?"* *Another kick, and I scream, clutching at my middle.* *"Because dogs need to learn their place."*

That was the last time I ever begged. The last time I showed my belly to a predator. If he was going to beat me, then I'd fucking mouth off and tell him what I felt... something that slowly morphed into sarcasm. Jarl loathed it, and why I did it more and more. I guess, in the end, it's also why he decided to trade me in for a new Omega.

Sten's laugh yanks me back to the present, and before I can brace myself, the blade flashes toward me. I scream, expecting death, but instead feel a sharp sting across my arm. Blood wells up from the cut, trickling down my skin, then the sharpness of the pain digs into my arm.

"What the fuck?" I wince.

His hand cracks across my face, the force snapping my head to the side. Stars dance in my vision as he wipes his blade on my shirt, spreading Axel's blood across the fabric. Above us, thunder rolls across the sky like Thor clearing his throat.

Where's Ghost? The thought comes desperately. This morning, his scent had been everywhere, wrapped around me like a security blanket. I'd felt safe, protected, knowing he was close. I sensed it deep within me. Now I don't sense him at all... Does he know I'm gone? Does he sense it, too?

"Such a powerful Omega." Sten runs the back of his knuckles across my cheek. "We don't see many with such powers, do we? But none of that matters now because you're mine, and you're going to become my good little slave."

"I'd rather die." I spit at him, satisfaction blooming as it lands on his cheek.

He wipes the spit away slowly. "What I have in store for you is far worse than death, Omega."

A fat raindrop hits my nose, and I glance up at the roiling clouds. More drops follow, pattering against leaves and dirt. Around us, the wolves close in, their muzzles still wet with Axel's blood. My stomach lurches at the memory of them tearing him apart, the sounds of flesh ripping and bones cracking.

"Ghost's coming for you," I state, but the words ring hollow, even to my own ears. How could he find me when I can't even sense him anymore? When I have no damn clue where I am on the island.

"Here's the thing," Sten starts, then pauses like he's savoring what comes next. "How well do you think you know Ghost?"

I stare at him, trying for defiant but probably just looking scared.

"I'm guessing not much, then." He runs a finger down my cheek, and I try to bite it. He jerks back with a laugh. "Did he tell you that he came to the island because he killed his father in cold blood?"

I clench my teeth, remembering Ghost's words about his father's cruelty. "We all have family members we want to murder. Good on him for doing it."

"But did he tell you that, afterward, he was on such a savage rampage that he couldn't be stopped?" Sten's voice drops lower. "Murdered his mother and a neighboring whole family before he was taken down? The lunatic has something broken up here." He taps the side of his head. "So, how long before he goes feral on you? Or someone else close? He's a fucking time bomb."

My stomach twists. Ghost's control issues, his anger... I can understand his father, but the others? His mother? I swallow hard, trying to push down the doubt creeping in.

"Yeah, you see it now."

"Last I looked," I manage, "you're here for some horrendous crime, too."

"I'm not saying I'm innocent. Fuck, I'm not, and I own who I am. But I don't think Ghost is being honest with you." He shrugs, then studies the wolves around them like he might order them to attack me.

The rain is coming down harder now, plastering my hair to my face. Lightning flickers in the clouds, and the air feels heavy, charged with something more than just electricity. My skin prickles with it, and my wolf stirs restlessly inside me.

"Look," I say. "There are other ways of dealing with differences between us. It doesn't always have to resort to killings and torture. I mean, have you tried therapy? Managing your anger? A good massage?"

Sten laughs, and several wolves nearby make chuffing sounds that I'm certain are their version of laughter. The rain runs down their fur in rivulets, but they stand firm, watching me with hungry eyes.

"Have you forgotten where you are, Omega?" His eyes narrow. "Perhaps you have because I noticed you don't have the prison mark on your arm, so that means you aren't meant to be here. Tell me, were you on that jet that went overhead, smoking up the night I found you? Well, you've just had the worst luck of your day landing on this island, haven't you?"

"You know nothing about me."

"Oh, I know enough to understand that you have powers I need to finally take back the whole island."

I force out a laugh that sounds brittle even to my own ears. "Yeah, good luck with that. My powers come with a *fuck you* guarantee."

His smile darkens, almost evil in a way that makes my stomach clench and goose bumps race down my arms.

"Enough." He stands silent for a moment, eyes closed, murmuring something under his breath. When they snap open, they're completely white.

I flinch back, and even a few wolves retreat, as if sensing something very wrong with their Alpha.

The rain is sheeting down now, driven sideways by the wind that's picking up strength with every passing second. Lightning splits the sky every few seconds, thunder following so quickly it feels like the world is being torn apart.

Please strike him down again, but finish the job this time.

He pulls out his blade again and slashes his palm. I stiffen, but he doesn't even seem to notice the wound. He tucks the dirty blade away and gets in my face. I try to pull back, but there's nowhere to go.

"Okay, look, you don't—"

"Oh, but I have to." Those white eyes are like bottomless pits. "Are you ready to meet your roommate?"

"What the fuck are you talking about?"

"I control spirits, stupid Omega, and imagine what I can do to you if I force one into you and control the weather. I've been practicing and have mastered it."

I'm shaking now, rain running down my face like tears. Or maybe they are tears. I can't tell anymore. My wolf is pacing inside me, agitated, afraid. We both know something terrible is about to happen, but there's nothing I can do to stop it.

I glance up at the sky. Come on, I'm in a dire situation. Do something!

Sten lets out a roaring sound that makes me shudder, and with his bloodied hand, he's scooping at the air like he's trying to catch something invisible. In a heartbeat, his hand fists as if he's grabbed something, though I see nothing, and he slaps his bloody, now-open palm hard against my cut.

I scream, more from shock than pain, trying to squirm away, to kick him, but he might as well be made of stone. And then...

Oh gods.

Something moves inside me. Not like a physical thing, but like... like when I'm falling asleep and suddenly feel like I've missed a step and am dropping, except the sensation is spreading through my whole body. It's cold, so cold, seeping through my veins like liquid. My wolf thrashes inside me, snarling, terrified of this foreign presence.

Ice-cold fingers drag through my insides, touching places nothing should ever touch. I can feel it winding through me, probing, exploring, violating every part of my being. The violation of it makes me want to vomit, to claw my own skin off just to get it out.

"Get it out!" I scream, thrashing against the ropes until I feel them cut into my wrists. "Get it out, get it out, GET IT OUT!"

Sten just claps like a kid finally getting cake. "Oh, you feel it! Good, good! You know an interesting fact?

On this island, there are always spirits around us; you just don't see them. But I do."

Lightning flashes again, and in that brief illumination, I see the wolves watching me with something like pity in their eyes. They know. They know what's happening to me, and they're glad it's not them.

The sensation gets worse, spreading up into my mind. Memories start to blur, thoughts becoming harder to hold on to. It's like trying to think through static. Something is sharing my headspace, pushing against my consciousness.

Ghost's face flashes through my mind—the way he looked at me last night, like I was something precious, something worth protecting. But he's not here. I'm alone with this thing crawling through my mind, and I can't...

I can't...

Panic overwhelms me, and I thrash harder, crying out as the storm intensifies. The wind is howling now, strong enough to bend smaller trees. The sky has taken on an eerie greenish tint that makes everything look sick, diseased.

Wolves dart around us, but Sten stands unmoved, watching me with those terrible white eyes as I fight the battle in my own mind. It's like trying to hold on to myself while something else attempts to wear me like a costume, pushing me aside to take control.

A massive gust of wind makes everyone look up.

Above us, descending from the sickly green clouds, a thin funnel begins to form.

A fucking tornado.

"Oh, you are so impressive," Sten breathes, extending his hand toward me. Heat radiates from him even through the space between us, and I feel the thing inside me growing stronger. My thoughts get fuzzier, more distant, as though I'm slowly being pushed underwater.

And then I hear it—a voice in my head that isn't mine.

Hello, my bitch Omega.

The scream that tears from my throat doesn't sound human. My wolf howls in terror because we both know that voice. Know it like we know our own heartbeat.

It's Jarl.

My dead fucking husband.

I'm shaking, screaming, "Get him out of me, get him out!"

The thin tornado isn't just in the distance anymore. It's bearing down on us, ripping trees from the ground. The sound is deafening, roaring.

"What did you do?" I shriek at Sten, thrashing against the ropes as Jarl's presence grows stronger and colder, spreading through me like poison. "WHY DID YOU PUT *HIM* INSIDE ME?"

Sten just laughs, even as branches and debris fly past us. "I gave you the closest spirit I could grab."

Miss me, bitch?

I'm crying, and the tears are washed away. This can't be happening!

The tornado closes in on us, and Sten's expression finally furrows as he stares around him, the wind sending him stumbling on his feet. Branches are being thrown through the air like missiles, and the remaining wolves are running for their lives.

Suddenly, Sten is thrown sideways, shouting as his body is tossed into the woods. Objects are flung in every direction, and even the tree I'm tied to is starting to sway.

Wind beats against me, and I can't see straight from the rain coming sideways. I barely notice any of it because Jarl is in my head, in my body, touching me from the inside in ways that make me want to tear my own skin off. Memories of fists and boots and blood flood my mind. But they're not just my memories anymore. They're his, too.

The tornado hits the island somewhere in the distance, and the world explodes into chaos. Wood splintering, wind howling, Sten shouting something I can't hear. But nothing is louder than Jarl's laughter in my head.

This can't be happening. But it is. My dead

husband is possessing me, and a tornado is about to kill us all.

"Something's fucking strange. Why the hell show up, then run from us?" Knut quips beside me, his combat boots crunching over broken branches as we stride from our territory perimeter close to Sten's border. Dark stains mark his clothes where he'd thrown himself into the underbrush after Sten's men.

Yet, irritation gnaws at my gut as reality hits me hard. "They weren't there to attack us. It was a fucking decoy." My head pounds as I piece it together. "It had to be... they were distracting us from something. Why else run the moment they see us? Why were they just standing there?"

"Sten's never been fucking subtle," he adds. "This isn't his style—sending men to breach, then retreat?

He likes blood, chaos." He spits on the ground, and I catch the metallic scent of blood.

I exchange a dark glance with him, then we're both speeding up our pace to the mansion, fear clawing at my chest that we fell for his damn trap. My thoughts fly to Hel.

Barking over my shoulder, I instruct the rest of the guards to search the whole fucking perimeter urgently.

A grumble from overhead draws my attention.

I glance up at the unnatural green-black mass of clouds rolling in from Sten's side of the island. Lightning crackles within the darkness. I've never seen such a storm roll in so quickly, seeing as the morning was bright without a cloud in sight.

"What the fuck's up with the sky?" Knut mutters.

The truth is like a blade to my throat, and a dreadful fear sinks through me, turning my blood to ice.

Hel!

She's in danger! It has to be her calling the storm.

"I have to go," I bark at Knut, already moving. "Get all the men ready and head to Sten's. We're going to war today."

At the mansion, I shoulder past guards and servants, taking the stairs three at a time. There's a hollow feeling in my chest, an emptiness that shouldn't exist. The mating bite I gave Hel last night created a bond between us, one that lets me sense her presence in the mansion. Instead, there's nothing but a void where she should be.

An ache starts in my chest, and I run like a madman, praying I find her in my room and that I'm freaking out over nothing.

I slam my bedroom door open so hard it cracks the frame, but the sheets where I left her sleeping are empty. Her scent lingers. The pillow still holds the impression of her head, and my wolf howls at the memory of how she looked there just hours ago.

And where the fuck is Axel? I specifically ordered him to guard her. I rush out and find his room empty, too, bed made.

Something feels fucking wrong, and my head's spinning. Then I rush wildly through the mansion, not finding them, and no one's seen them.

The storm. No sign of Hel or Axel. The attacks.

"They were a fucking distraction," I snarl, putting my fist through a wall in the corridor. Blood drips from my knuckles, but I barely feel it. I promised to protect her.

Movement from my left catches my attention.

I glance over to Eve, freezing at having spotted me. She's fidgeting with her flowered dress, her brown curls tucked behind her ears.

"Eve." My tone is a pure Alpha command. I march over to her.

She lifts her chin to meet me, a half smile on her lips. "Ghost, is everything all right?"

"Have you seen Hel this morning?" The question comes out as a growl. "And where's Axel?" I'm going to wring his neck when I find him.

She bites her lower lip, and my patience snaps like a wire. Through the windows behind her, I spy that the storm has turned the day to almost night. Trees bend, nearly doubling in the wind. What the fuck?

"Hel's in danger," I snarl, closing the distance between us. The scent of her fear is cloying, suffocating. "And I can't wait. Fucking talk!"

"I saw her," she whispers, tears welling up. Her hands twist in her dress, wrinkling the fabric. "She was on the balcony alone, staring out, and she seemed fine, but..."

"But what?" I grab her arm, beyond caring about gentleness. My claws have partially extended, pricking through her skin.

"You're hurting me!"

"I'll hurt you a lot more if you're keeping anything from me." Another crack of thunder makes the windows rattle in their frames.

"She was alone when I left her, but I warned her to be careful." The tears spill over, rolling down her cheeks.

"Careful of what, Eve?" I square my shoulders, and I'm barely holding on to a thread of patience.

"Axel betrayed me... and you. He promised to make me his mate once he took over your pack and territory. Then he turned on me and threatened to kill me if I told you."

The words collide into me, knocking the air out of my lungs. "What the fuck did you say?"

My wolf howls for blood, and I struggle to think through the rage. My second-in-command wants my position? After everything I entrusted and shared with him? Everything I did for him?

A burning fire ignites in my chest, and with it comes a brutal fury.

Looking back, I can see some of the clues—his convenient absences, his probing questions in meetings, the times he seemed to vanish from the mansion entirely. The way he'd ask about our defenses, our patrol schedules. All under the guise of being my second, my brother in everything but blood.

The ones who'll stab you in the back are always the closest to you, boy. They know exactly where to slide the knife. My grandfather once whispered those words to me before he passed. Words that now sit heavily on my chest.

Axel, who's been by my side for three years. Axel, who helped me survive my first weeks here when I was nothing but a half-starved prisoner, dropped onto this hell of an island.

Odin, I'd been blind.

All of it lies. All of it preparation for this moment.

"Where the fuck is Hel?" I hiss through clenched teeth.

A nod as she wipes her face. "He took her to Sten."

The growl that tears from my chest feels like it might split me in two.

Running for the stairs, I shout back, "Don't you fucking leave the mansion! When I'm back, you're going to tell me everything, or I'll hunt you down until you're fucking dead!"

I burst out of the mansion at a dead sprint, my voice carrying to the guards over the howling wind.

"Get everyone together! Today, we paint this island with Sten's blood!"

The rain is coming down heavily as I burst into the woods, running ferociously.

I'll destroy the whole fucking island to rescue her, starting with Sten. And Axel? I'll save him for last, make him watch as I destroy everything he thought he could steal from me. Then I'll take my time showing him exactly what happens to traitors.

The rain soaks through my clothes while the forest around me groans under the storm's assault.

Hold on, Hel. I'm coming.

And may the gods help anyone who stands in my way.

CHAPTER
SIXTEEN

HEL

The bark scrapes against my wrists as I finally break free, the rope snapping from frantically rubbing it against the tree. I stumble free, blood trickling down where the bond bit into my skin.

Winds howl around me, rain pelting sideways, turning the world into streaks of gray. My hair whips around my face, stinging my eyes.

I can't hear myself think.

Sten's stumbling back toward me, fighting the winds, his face a mess of blood streaming down from his temple. But he's still standing. Still fucking terrifying.

He's bellowing something, but he's too far for me to hear, and I sure as hell am not waiting around. I shove against the blustering air and lunge toward the dense woods in the same direction where the storm is lighter, where Ghost's mansion lies.

Yet the sickening pulse of energy inside me, the one belonging to my fucking dead husband, crawls under my skin like thousands of insects, making my stomach heave.

You fucking bitch, you're going to pay. His voice slithers through my mind like oil on water. *Remember how I used to make you pay, Omega?*

"Shut up," I yell, running madly through the storm hammering into me, trying to get the tornado as far behind me as possible.

Look at you run. Jarl's voice oozes through my thoughts. *Fat little Omega, always running.*

"Fuck off." My feet slip in the mud as I bolt for the tree line. "You're fucking dead, and I danced on your grave."

Did you? Or did you cry, knowing deep down you deserved everything I gave you?

"The only thing I deserved was to kill you myself." My lungs burn as I run, branches whipping past my face. The mountain looms ahead. That massive stone wall is somewhere beyond, where I know Ghost's mansion waits.

Kill me? I should have cut out your filthy tongue.

His laugh rattles through my skull. It's like being stabbed behind my eyes. I stumble, catching myself against a tree, waiting for the ache to pass. I use the canopy overhead for some protection from the weather.

Behind me, I can barely see Sten's settlement from the storm. Then I'm off again. I know he won't stop until he comes for me. And right now, I need to find Ghost and work out how to get this fucker out of me.

Hours blur together as I keep going, exhaustion close to making me collapse, and the rain doesn't relent. I'm too busy trying to breathe to pay any attention to Jarl's insults.

"Hel!" Someone's calling my name, his deep, familiar voice cutting through the storm. My heart lurches until I see him. Ghost. He's running down the mountain slope toward me, and just the sight of him makes my chest ache. His black clothes are soaked through, clinging to muscles that ripple as he moves. The mask is askew on his face, showing a slice of his jaw—strong, stubbled, clenched with worry.

Who the fuck is that, whore?

"Shut up, shut up, shut UP!" I didn't mean to scream it out loud, but Ghost hears. He runs faster.

Soon, you'll give me full control... I'll find a way to take it.

My stomach turns at the idea, terrifying me, but I don't respond, don't reward him with my fear.

"Ghost!" The cry rips from my throat, desperate to drown out Jarl's voice. Ghost reaches me, strong arms lifting me off my feet. Through the rain, I can see his eyes filled with fury that would terrify me if I didn't know it wasn't aimed at me.

"I'm so sorry," he says, voice rough with emotion. His hands are gentle on my waist. "I should have done more to keep you safe, should have—"

I don't let him finish. My fingers find the edge of his mask, pushing it up onto his head and tossing it aside as I kiss him hard. His lips are warm despite the rain, soft against mine, and for a moment, I forget everything else.

Pain explodes through my chest and stomach. I cry out, doubling over.

"Hel, what's going on?"

You disgusting whore. You think you can kiss him with the same mouth that begged me for mercy?

Ghost lowers me to my feet but keeps his arms around me. Rain streams down his face and drips from his full lower lip. A face that would be beautiful if it weren't twisted with worry.

"What's wrong? Are you hurt?"

Tell him, Jarl taunts. *Tell him how damaged you are. How used. How worthless.*

I stare up at Ghost, hating the tears that mix with rain on my face.

"I'm in huge trouble."

"What? I'll fix it, whatever it is." His thumb brushes my cheek, so tender it makes my heart crack.

"I hope you can." My voice breaks. "Sten can

control spirits. Did you know that? And he put one inside me to control my power. He put... he put..."

Say my name, bitch. Say it.

"He put Jarl inside me." The words taste like ash. "My husband. My dead fucking husband is inside me."

Ghost's face morphs into pure rage. Lightning flashes, illuminating the sharp planes of his features, the murderous gleam in his eyes. "That fucking—" He cuts himself off, hands gentle on my shoulders even as his voice drops to a deadly growl. "Is it hurting you?"

Tell him how much you like pain. Tell him how you used to thank me for it.

"Can you remove it?" I grip Ghost's shirt, desperate. The wet fabric bunches in my fingers, and I feel his heart pounding under my hands. "You said you can see spirits. Take it out of me, please take it out—"

I'm going to enjoy this. Breaking you all over again. Making you destroy everything you love. Just like before.

Ghost's face falls. "I can't. I see them, they come to me, but I can't manipulate them."

My heart sinks. "So who the hell can on the island?" I scratch at my arm, trying to erase the phantom sensation of Jarl's touch—the memory of fingernails leaving tracks on my skin. "Fuck."

"Only Sten that I know of," Ghost answers slowly. His arms tighten around me, protective, grounding. "I have an idea... somewhere that might help."

He can't help you. No one can. You're mine, Omega. Forever mine.

I lean into Ghost, breathing in his masculine scent, his wolf, the forest, and that sweet cocoa that's all him. I let myself get lost in it, trying to smother Jarl.

"Please, let's do it. Anything's better than having him as a permanent brain roommate."

We'll see how long you can pretend to be strong before I break you again.

Pressing closer to Ghost, I let his warmth fight back the cold, dead thing inside me. I've survived Jarl once. I'll survive him again. Even if I have to drag his ghost ass back to hell myself.

Hell's too good for you, Jarl hisses. *But don't worry. I'll make Earth so much worse.*

The rain continues to fall as we start moving, Ghost's arm strong around my waist, supporting me. Each step takes us farther from Sten, but Jarl's laughter follows, echoing through my mind.

The trek uphill is endless, each step a reminder that my body wasn't made for this shit. Rain pelts us sideways, turning the ground into a muddy obstacle course from hell. My thighs burn, my lungs aching, but Ghost's hand is firm in mine, warm despite the cold, anchoring me to something real while my dead husband whispers his poison.

"So, anyway, you can switch off the storm," Ghost

half jokes with me, running a hand down his face to wipe away the rain.

"I wish I knew how. I've tried so often, but nothing responds, only my emotions, and in situations like this, I'm struggling to calm down."

The forest feels alive in the worst way possible. Ancient pines loom overhead, their branches creaking and swaying.

You should be happy we're back together. We just need to get rid of this schmuck, then it's just us again, Omega.

"In your fucking dreams," I whisper.

"Are you doing all right?" Ghost asks.

"Peachy. Just sharing headspace with Satan's favorite asshole."

Jarl laughs.

I glance back toward Sten's territory, down below, barely visible through the curtain of rain and mist. There's no sign of the tornado I summoned, leaving just angry storm clouds.

But something about Ghost's presence seems to calm me and the weather—or maybe it's just me, feeling safer, despite everything. He walks fast, those long legs eating up the distance while I half jog to keep up. He holds my hand and is dragging me along with him, helping me.

"The weather's settling," I say, partly to drown out Jarl. "Guess I'm not as out of control."

Ghost's thumb traces circles on my palm. "You were never out of control."

Listen to him butter you up, Jarl sneers. *Like anyone could want damaged goods like you. He's using you, stupid bitch. Just like everyone else.*

The path in front of us winds higher, bordered by ferns that seem to glow an impossible green in the strange storm light. Moss covers everything, thick and soft. Ghost keeps me close, watching every time I flinch at Jarl's words.

"Talk to me," he says suddenly. "What's he saying?"

I laugh, but it comes out bitter. "Trust me, you don't want to know."

You think you're so fucking clever.

My face must show something because Ghost stops, turning to face me.

"Hey." His hand cups my cheek, thumb brushing away rain and tears. "I'm going to get him out. I promise."

Tell him about the closet, Jarl purrs. *Tell him how you used to beg. How you promised to be good if I just let you out.*

"The forest opens up ahead," Ghost says, clearly trying to distract me. "There's a plateau where we can rest."

We emerge onto a rock platform jutting from the mountainside. The view would be spectacular if I could see more than twenty feet through the rain. Ghost guides me to a relatively dry spot under an over-hanging boulder.

Getting tired already? Jarl mocks. *Always were weak.*

I dig my nails into my palms, focusing on the pain instead of his voice. Ghost notices and gently uncurls my fingers.

"You're bleeding," he says softly.

"Better than listening to him." I lean against the boulder, the cold stone grounding me. "Distract me? Tell me how you ended up on Nightmare Island."

Ghost's jaw tightens, but he nods. "When I first arrived, Sten kept me prisoner. Months of beatings, starvation, mind games. Typical Alpha bullshit, trying to break me down." He looks out into the rain. "The worst part wasn't the pain. It was feeling helpless again, just like when I was back home."

"Sten told me things," I say carefully. "About why you ended up here. Different from what you told me before."

Ghost's brow furrows as he glances at me. Rain runs down his face, dripping from his jaw.

"I didn't tell you the truth earlier because I didn't want to show you the ugliness of my past. I didn't want to scare you away. But back home..." His voice darkens. "My father wasn't the only monster. Mother watched it all and never lifted a finger. Neighbors

239

thought it was fine to lock me in cupboards for days, keep me quiet so no one would ask questions."

He runs a hand through his wet hair, making it stand up wildly.

"I'm not justifying what I did. But there's only so many times you can be broken before something inside you snaps." His laugh is hollow. "So, yeah, I deserve to be here. Did things that can't be forgiven, but I can't say I regret them."

I reach for him with my hand, fingers tracing the edge of a scar on his cheek. "I don't judge you. Living with monsters..." I swallow hard. "It pushes you to limits you never thought you'd reach."

Stop whining, bitch. You deserved everything I gave you.

"I used to lie awake, imagining all the ways I could kill my husband," I say, and for once, Jarl goes quiet. "Poison in his whiskey. Push him down the stairs and make it look like he fell while drunk. Again."

Ghost pulls me close, his lips finding mine. The kiss is deep, desperate, tasting of rain and something wild. His hands cup my face as though I'm something precious, not the broken thing Jarl always claimed I was.

Fuck, stop that! Jarl roars, and pain explodes behind my eyes like shattered glass. I cry out, pulling back.

"Fuck off, Jarl!" I snarl out loud, clutching my head.

Ghost catches me before I fall over, scooping me into his arms. "I've got you," he murmurs, lifting me into his arms. His chest is solid against my cheek, heartbeat steady under my ear.

"Keep talking," I beg. "Your voice... It helps drown him out. Tell me more about you and Sten."

"A challenge," Ghost continues, his breath warm against my hair as he carries me up the path. "Sten had this fucking stupid rule about doing it over the Gravewater pool. Some ancient bullshit about proving worth."

"Come again?"

"This island?" His laugh rumbles through his chest. "It used to belong to the fae before wolves came and slaughtered them all. Left their magic behind, though. That pond up ahead where we're going is the most powerful spot on the whole damn island."

Fuck, he can talk. Sure he's not an Omega in hiding?

I ignore him, watching rain drip from Ghost's jaw.

"What happened in the challenge?" I ask.

"We both fell in during the fight. Killed each other right there in those waters." His arms tighten around me. "That's how I got these—" He jerks his chin toward his scarred eye. "Before the spirits could take us completely, the pack dragged us out and revived us. But we came back... different. Both seeing shit that should stay dead."

The path grows steeper, rocks slick with moss and

rain. Ghost navigates them like he's done this a thousand times, never loosening his grip on me.

"You actually died," I murmur, the words feeling strange on my tongue. "That's got to fuck with your head."

"Don't remember much. Just darkness, then waking up feeling wrong. Like something got in my head while I was gone." He kisses my forehead. "Think you can walk from here? Ground gets tricky in this area."

"For sure. I can manage. Thanks."

He sets me down but keeps an arm around my waist. "Prefer you close where I can't lose you." His voice drops lower. "Fair warning... what you're about to see? It's not natural. Try not to freak out."

"My freak-out meter is pretty much maxed out."

We round a sharp corner, stepping onto a narrow ledge, and I freeze. The scene before us can't be real. A vast pond spreads out in a perfect semicircle, bordered by jagged rocks. But that's not the impossible part.

The rock face that forms the back wall bears an enormous skull, easily the size of a house. Water pours from its eye sockets like endless tears, creating twin waterfalls that feed the pond below. The bone-white stone seems to glow with its own light, casting everything in an eerie pale sheen.

"Please tell me I'm hallucinating this." I gasp at the sight.

Ghost leads me closer to the water's edge, his grip firm as we pick our way over slick rocks. That's when I see white shapes swirling beneath the surface like smoke underwater. Faces form and dissolve, hollow black eyes staring up, reaching with ghostly hands that dissipate just as quickly.

"Odin!" I step back, but Ghost holds me firm.

"The Gravewater pool," he says grimly. "Jarl's dead. The water is where the dead on this island go, so it should pull him out naturally."

Fuck that! I'm not leaving until you're dead with me, Jarl hisses.

"Well," I say, lifting my chin and stepping forward. "Guess it's time for an official divorce, asshole."

Ghost's lips twitch despite the tension. "I'm right here. Won't let anything else happen to you."

I step onto a submerged ledge, the water icy against my legs.

He watches the spirits swarm toward me.

The deep, freezing touch hits first—not normal cold water, but something that seeps straight into my bones. White tendrils wrap around my calves like silk scarves, but when I try to move, they hold firm. My heart beats against my ribs as they pull, and—

Something's wrong.

The cold spreads through my chest like frost, crawling up my throat. I'm being pushed back into my own head, trapped behind my eyes like I'm watching through a window. Everything goes dark except for a small square of vision.

Panic wraps around me, and I'm fighting to move my legs again, to get out.

Fuck yes, you little bitch. Jarl's voice booms through what used to be my head. *Now I control you. Now you get to watch while I destroy everything you love.*

Horror floods through me as I realize the truth. The water didn't pull him out.

It pushed me in.

And now I'm trapped in my own body, watching as my dead husband takes control.

Shit!

I feel my lips curl into a smile and see my hand reach out as if practicing how to use it again.

Watch closely, Omega, Jarl purrs in our shared mind. *I'm going to make you hurt him in ways you never imagined. And the best part? He'll think it's you doing it.*

I scream, but the sound stays trapped in the darkness with me. On the outside, my body just smiles wider.

"Ghost," my external voice says, but it's all wrong —Jarl's inflections, Jarl's cruel amusement. "I feel so much better now."

I can't even scream to warn Ghost.

I'm locked in the dark, and Jarl is in charge.

CHAPTER
SEVENTEEN
GHOST

J ust a little longer. Even as Hel sinks to her knees in the Gravewater pool, the first convulsion rocks through her body. When she cries out my name, it takes everything I have not to lunge forward. Every instinct I possess—wolf, warrior, mate —screams at me to grab her, to pull her to safety. But I can't. Not if we want this to work.

The spirits are crawling up her legs now, tendrils wrapping around her thighs like pale smoke, dragging her deeper. She's panicking—I can smell it rolling off her in waves.

This has to work.

That fucker inside her needs to come out, and the spirits, they're trying to help. They have to be.

"Ghost," she calls me again.

But something's off. Her voice isn't quite hers. My

blood turns to ice, every hair on my body standing on end. This is wrong. So fucking wrong.

"I feel so much better now," she continues, and something inside me shatters. That voice coming from her lips—it's like watching someone puppeteer her body, and the wrongness of it triggers something primal in me.

Pure panic hits me like a sledgehammer to the chest, and suddenly, I'm moving without conscious thought. My hand snaps out to grab the back of her neck while the other fists in her shirt. I yank her out of the water like she weighs nothing. The fear coursing through me makes my movements savage, desperate —I know I'm being too rough, but I can't stop myself. Not when every second she's in that water feels like another second I might lose her.

She stumbles as I drag her onto the bank, coughing up water that looks too dark, too thick, to be natural. But I can't give her a moment to recover. My fingers find her chin, probably leaving bruises as I force her face up to mine. Her skin is ice cold, and fuck if that doesn't send another spike of fear through me.

"Sweetheart, tell me he's gone!" The words come out more like a growl than actual speech.

"Ghost, it's me." The words that escape her are pure Hel—all sass stripped away by fear, leaving behind something raw and vulnerable that makes my chest ache. "But... but he took me over completely. I can't go in the water. It gives him strength over me."

My chest feels as though it's being ripped apart as I watch her struggle. She's trembling in my arms, soaked to the bone, and there's a war being waged behind her eyes. And I'm standing here fucking useless.

The rain beats down on us as I grasp her close, feeling her shiver against me. Memories I'd rather forget claw their way to the surface, triggered by her pain. Each tremor that runs through her body is like a knife in my gut.

But I know spirits. An idea forms—desperate, probably stupid, but when has that ever stopped me? In this new world, sometimes the worst plans are the only ones we've got.

I take her hand, skin cold against mine. "Come to the water."

She jerks back as if I've burned her, eyes wide with terror. "No! Are you fucking insane?"

There's an edge of hysteria in her response that cuts me to the bone.

"Because I've got to tell you," she begins. "Swimming with spirits once today was enough for my quota. Actually, it's enough for my lifetime. Maybe even in my next lifetime."

"Do you trust me, Hel?" The words come out rougher than intended as I take a step into the water.

The cold bites at my ankles, then my knees, and the spirits are already reaching for me.

Memories flash—drowning, dying, the cold taking me under, the feeling of life slipping away as water filled my lungs. I push them back, but my hands are shaking.

"Take my hand," I say.

"Ghost, get out of there!" The fear in her voice nearly breaks me, but I stretch my arm toward her, trying to project my confidence.

"This can work. You use me as a conduit." The words tumble out fast. Every second in this water brings back memories of my death, of the darkness and cold. "Maybe I'll be stronger with the spirits, so Jarl can come into me and the pool."

"Are you sure about this?" She edges closer, shaking, and fuck if the trust in her eyes doesn't make me want to howl with both pride and fear. "Because you look about as sure as I feel, which is somewhere between 'fuck no' and 'hell no.' And I've got to say, your track record with spirit water isn't exactly stellar."

"Yes. Now, hurry, please, as I fucking hate this water." Every second I stand here is another second fighting the urge to run, to get away from the cold that once claimed my life.

The moment her hand touches mine, it's like getting hit by lightning. Energy races up my arm, the spirits at my legs going absolutely ballistic, tearing at my flesh with ethereal claws. Then I feel him—her dead husband's spirit pouring into me like acid, filling every corner of my consciousness with his hatred. It's like having ice water injected directly into my veins.

Get away from my wife, you mongrel, his voice echoes in my skull. *She's mine. She'll always be mine. You're nothing but an animal playing at being human.*

The disgust rises in my throat. Having another consciousness inside me is like being infected. It's worse than dying was—at least then, I only had to deal with my own pain.

But who gives a fuck when my idea worked—Hel's clear of the fucker, though the pain on her face when I let go of her hand nearly brings me to my knees.

I turn toward the deeper water, ready to drag this bastard down with me, to end this once and for all, when a growl freezes me in place. The sound reverberates off the rock walls, and my heart sinks.

On the ledge across the pond, Sten and his wolves emerge from the shadows, their eyes reflecting the dim light like burning coals.

"Not fucking now!" The words escape through gritted teeth as they start moving into our space. Hunters who've done this a thousand times before. I know their type—I am one of them. They're not here to talk.

Hel's scanning for escape routes, and fuck, I can't

leave her alone out here. Not for a second. Not with them. Protecting my fated mate takes priority over everything.

You can't have my whore. I'll watch them tear you apart, then I'll take her back. She belongs to me. She's always belonged to me.

"Shut the fuck up," I growl. Then I bark at Hel, "Run! Around the back of the rock face."

She's already backing away from Sten's approaching pack but hesitates. Her huge eyes meet mine, and I see the war there—the need to run is fighting with the need to stay, to help. That's my girl, brave to the point of stupidity sometimes.

"Are you sure? Because this looks like one of those times when running away from the guy with the spirit possession might be a bad call. Just saying."

"Go, now! I have this," I tell her, marching out of the water, pulling against the damn spirits clinging to my legs, but they don't have a strong enough hold of me yet. "I'll deal with you later, prick," I murmur to Jarl.

She runs, and I turn to face Sten as he stalks forward. The rain never ends, and the sky is dark. The odds are shit—I'm outnumbered, possessed, and still half frozen from the spirit water. But I don't have a choice. Hel's life depends on me winning this fight.

And I've never been good at losing, especially not when it comes to her.

You think you know her? I MADE her. Every scar, every fear, every nightmare—those are my marks on her soul.

The spirit claws at my consciousness, trying to force memories into my mind—memories of Hel crying, bleeding, broken—but I shove them down. Not now. Not fucking now.

Sten's massive frame blocks my path, his shoulders hunched forward. The rain streams down his face, but it can't wash away the hatred etched into every line.

Let me show you what she looks like when she begs, her husband whispers. The images he forces into my mind make me want to tear my own head off. *She always begs so prettily.*

"Focus," I growl to myself, planting my feet wider.

Sten's lips curl into something violent.

Good. I'm fucking ready to end this shitshow.

"Funny how we ended up here." His voice rolls across the space between us like thunder. "Where it all started... and where, today, it's all going to end."

His wolves—six of them, all battle-scarred and hungry-looking—start to spread out.

I glance back, and my heart slams against my ribs.

Hel is scaling the rock face, her small form barely visible through the rain. She's found handholds in the black stone, pulling herself up inch by treacherous inch. My throat closes up as I watch her foot slip, then catch again. Every instinct screams at me to fly up

251

there and grab her before she falls, but I understand why she's done it. More of Sten's wolves have emerged from the tree line behind us, cutting off any escape route on the ground. They've cornered us.

Look at her climb. Like a scared little rat.

Desperation and fury bleed through me. This ends now. All of it.

"Like old times," I growl at Sten, baring my teeth. "You and me, you piece of shit."

The wolf inside me howls for blood, and I don't hold back.

The transformation rips through me in seconds, clothes falling away. The world sharpens, sounds becoming crisp, smells intense. I don't wait for Sten to complete his own change—I launch myself at him, catching him mid-shift. We hit the ground hard, and my teeth find his throat. I clamp down hard, fangs sinking into flesh. Blood coats my mouth, and I go deeper.

He whines, thrashing beneath me, finally trans- forming into his wolf but making horrible gurgling sounds. I love the sound of his suffering.

Amateur, Jarl sneers in my head. *You should have gone for the spine.*

The momentary distraction costs me. Sten's back leg catches me in the gut, claws raking through flesh. Pain explodes across my abdomen, and I flinch—just enough for him to writhe free. Blood mars his neck as he scrambles away, but he's fully wolf now. Some of his wolves close in, growling and howling, drunk on the violence.

I risk another glance at Hel. My blood runs cold when I spot two men in human form climbing after her. She's too high now. If she falls...

Sten slams into me like a freight train, knocking me off my feet. We roll across the stone ground and in the rain, a chaos of teeth and claws. Years of hatred fuel every bite, every slash. This isn't just a fight—it's vengeance. For the way he tortured me, for every person he's killed on the island.

You fight like a bitch, Jarl taunts as Sten's teeth graze my shoulder. *I'd have killed him by now. You're pathetic —no wonder she lets you fuck her. She always did have a thing for weak men.*

My concentration splinters between the fight, Hel's precarious position, and the poison being spewed in my mind. I miss a dodge I should have seen coming, and Sten's teeth suddenly find purchase in my side, crunching down with bone-crushing force. I howl as he tears at the wound, pain shooting through me.

The husband's laughter echoes in my skull. *You pussy. I could take him so easily. You'd be dead by now if I were fighting.*

Something clicks in my mind as I snap at Sten's

head, my teeth tearing at his ear. He snarls, releasing me, shaking his head. I scramble to get up.

Fine, you fucker, I mumble back at him. *Show me. You and me... let's fight. Winner gets Hel.*

Jarl goes quiet.

That's what I thought, I snarl internally.

How? Jarl's voice is suspicious but interested. Hook, line, and sinker.

You go into Sten's body and take over. Then, the real fight begins.

I'm going to fuck you up so good, he growls.

Sten comes at me once more, and with every ounce of strength left in my battered body, I rush at him, head low, slamming Sten in the chest. The force throws him off me, and I scramble to his side before he can recover. Then I lunge forward with all my strength and crash into his side as he gains his composure. He's stumbling over the water's edge and hits the shallow pond with a splash that sends spirits scattering.

Go, you fucker, I growl at Jarl. *Show me what you're made of.*

I leap into the water, driving a paw against Sten, batting to get up over the slippery rocks underneath. The spirit moves through me with speed, flowing backward through my veins. It's a violation, a wrong-ness that makes me want to claw my own skin off, but then... blessed relief as it leaves my body through my paw touching him. I retreat instantly, pulling back my wolf, flesh rippling as I return to human form.

Sten stumbles in the water, shaking his massive wolf head. Confusion clouds his eyes as the possession takes hold. He growls, stumbling about. I don't waste a heartbeat.

I wade in, ignoring the spirits swirling around my legs, and slam both hands into his side. He loses his footing, his massive body crashing into the dark water.

I leap back onto solid ground as the spirits surge forward like a tidal wave. They swarm him, dozens, then hundreds, of forms drawn to the dead soul now trapped in living flesh. The sight turns my stomach. It's like watching sharks in a feeding frenzy.

Sten thrashes in the water, his wolf form melting away as panic overtakes him. His human face breaks the surface, mouth open in a scream that bubbles through the water. His eyes are wide with terror—he knows what's happening. The spirits aren't just coming for Jarl—they're claiming Sten, too, dragging them both down to whatever darkness waits below.

His hands claw at the water's surface, desperate for purchase, but the spirits pull harder. Dark water floods his mouth as he screams. Then, with a final, violent convulsion, he goes under. Bubbles rise to the surface, then nothing.

Satisfaction burns through me as I turn to face his

pack. "You bow to me now," I roar, letting every ounce of Alpha power fill my voice. "Or you die!"

They drop to their knees as one, even those still in wolf form, lowering their bellies to the stone. The sight sends a surge of primitive pleasure through me, but it's short-lived as I whirl toward Hel.

She's frozen halfway up the rock face, the men who were pursuing her having stopped to watch their leader's death.

"Hel!" I call out, already rushing toward the wall.

She looks down, calling to me, sounding terrified. She's wedged herself into a precarious position where she could easily slip right into the pond. I don't waste time with words—I frantically climb, taking the diagonal path that follows the edge of the rock face. The stone is slick with rain, and one wrong move could send me plummeting into the spirit-filled water below.

The other men scramble down as I climb past them, their eyes cast downward in submission. Good. They've learned quickly.

When I reach Hel, she's trembling so hard I can hear her teeth chattering.

"Is he..." she mumbles, staring past me at the pond where Sten's body floats facedown, spirits still circling like vultures.

"They're both gone, sweetheart," I say, reaching for her. "I told you I'd protect you."

"My hero," she says, managing a weak smile despite her terror.

"Climb on my back," I instruct, turning carefully on my narrow perch. "Slowly."

She moves like she's made of glass, her arms wrapping around my neck, legs around my waist. I feel every shake, every hitched breath as she clings to me. The climb down is worse than going up—one slip and we'd both fall. I take it methodically, testing each hold before trusting it with our weight.

When we reach the bottom, I maneuver us toward the far edge where she can step onto dry land without touching the water. The moment her feet touch the ground, I turn and pull her into my arms. My lips find hers, tasting rain and tears and blood. She melts against me, her small form fitting perfectly against mine, as if she was made for me.

"You are mine forever now," I murmur against her hair. "Nothing will ever hurt you again."

She's smiling. Covered in scratches and cuts, tears in her eyes, she whispers, "I've had enough of danger. I want a boring life now."

I chuckle.

The sound of approaching voices makes me tense, but when I turn, it's Knut arriving with more of my men. He surveys the scene—the kneeling wolves, the floating body, the blood-stained ground—and grins.

"Well, you had to take all the glory for yourself,

didn't you?" Knut lifts his hand, grasping my mask. "And I found this discarded. Figured you'd want it back."

I bark out a laugh, keeping Hel tucked against my side.

"We need to collect all the Alphas on the island. No rogues. Everyone falls under our line now, and we teach them our ways. Then I'll update you on everything."

Knut nods at the assembled wolves. "You got it, boss." Then his expression turns serious. "Just thought you should know... seems Axel betrayed us to Sten. I found his body."

"Good," I growl, even if my stomach turns for the years I trusted him and lost who I thought had been a friend. But I push those thoughts down. "He saved me the trouble of killing him myself."

Knut nods and begins barking orders at our new recruits.

I turn back to Hel. She looks up at me, those fierce blue eyes that first caught my attention now soft with something that makes my heart stutter.

"You know," she says, trailing a finger down my chest. "For a big bad wolf, you're actually kind of sweet. Don't worry, though. Your secret's safe with me."

I pull her closer, inhaling her delicious scent, bathing in her warmth and the simple fact that she's alive and safe in my arms. Everything I've done, everything I've become—it was all for this. For her.

"Better keep it that way." I wink, and she smiles so beautifully. I never imagined finding someone to give my heart to, but it's happening...

The rain starts to ease, and somewhere in the distance, thunder rumbles. But here, at this moment, with Hel in my arms and our enemies defeated, I finally feel at peace for the first time.

EIGHTEEN

4 Weeks Later

It's been four weeks since Sten died in the Gravewater pool up on the mountain and when Ghost took over as Alpha of the entire island. Now every shifter bows to him, and I still can't wrap my head around it. The man I'm falling for—okay, who am I kidding, the man I've already fallen for but was too stubborn to admit it—holds absolute power over this place. Yet somehow hasn't let it go to his head. Though the hungry way he looks at me sometimes makes me wonder if all that power finds... other outlets.

"Are you ready?" His voice comes from the doorway, and my heart is suddenly racing. He's leaning there like some kind of sinful god in low-hanging jeans and boots, a tight black T-shirt riding up just enough to show a strip of those abs that make me lose all brain function. One arm is propped against the door frame, muscles flexing in a way that should be illegal.

Meanwhile, I'm wrapped up in our bed, wearing his shirt that smells like him. Lately, I've been craving his scent like it's an addiction, to the point where I actually caught myself sniffing his laundry yesterday. Yes, I've officially become that Omega. Someone should just put me out of my misery now.

"You look so adorable nesting," he says, his good eye glinting with amusement. "Are you thinking of me in there with you? Touching yourself?"

"Ha, you wish." I'm a terrible liar because my inner thighs are soaked. "And don't say the *nest* word," I grumble, burrowing deeper into my blanket fortress. "I'm not nesting. I'm... strategically arranging comfort items."

His chuckle is dark honey as he shuts the door and strides into the room, all broad shoulders and predatory grace. He's not wearing his mask today, and lately, these maskless days have become more frequent. The scar tissue around his dead eye doesn't seem to bother him as much, or maybe he just cares less about the stares. Not that many people dare to stare anymore—not since they saw what he did in the

Gravewater pool. Now they whisper that he's part ghost, which would be funny if it weren't partially close to the truth.

"Hard not to think you're nesting when you've literally wrapped yourself in our blankets and buried yourself in my clothes," he points out.

"Well, then you shouldn't have been away from me for so long." The words come out needier than I intended, but fuck it. Four weeks of this growing heat inside me has stripped away most of my pride anyway.

He crawls onto the bed, moving with the grace that reminds me he's all animal inside. My body reacts instantly, fire racing down my body, my pussy already tingling at the idea of him pleasing me, desire crackling along my skin like electricity. It's ridiculous how little control I have around him, but at least I'm not dealing with a psychotic Alpha. Instead, I've got one who looks at me like I'm both prey and goddess, who treats me like a queen while making it clear he could devour me at any moment.

His lips find mine, and I melt fast. My hands slide around his neck, pulling him closer, trying to crawl inside his skin. But before I can get too comfortable, his hands scoop under me and suddenly I'm airborne.

"No!" I protest laughingly as he lifts me out of my nest—damn it, now he's got me saying it.

"Do you know how impossible it is to resist you?" His tone is rough, hungry. "Your scent is driving me insane. It's like you were crafted specifically to torment me, and you haven't even hit full heat yet."

I glare at him for bringing that up again. I prefer ignorance. "Can we not discuss my impending hormone apocalypse?"

"My little flame," he growls, and the possessiveness in his voice makes my toes curl. "You can sass all you want, but we both know what's coming. I can smell it on you, can see it in the way you're surrounding yourself with my scent. You're getting ready to be claimed, to be bred."

"I am not—" I start to argue, but he cuts me off with a kiss that melts my bones.

"Come on," he says, unwrapping me from my blanket cocoon. "I have something to show you. It's urgent."

I blink up at him, trying to focus through the haze of desire. He grips my chin, tilting my face up, and licks my bottom lip in a way that makes me whimper.

"You're mine," he purrs against my mouth. "Every inch, every breath, every storm you create. And soon, everyone will know it."

His smile is all predator. "Now get dressed before I change my mind and keep you in this bed all day."

I scramble for clothes, very aware of his burning gaze on my skin. The way he watches me dress is almost as intimate as watching me undress—like he's memorizing every movement, every inch of skin before it's covered.

"I can't wait to see you pregnant," he murmurs darkly, making me freeze with my shirt half on. "To watch your belly swell with our child, your breasts grow heavy with milk. I'm going to worship every new curve, fuck you every moment I get, taste your milk."

The raw hunger in his voice makes me shiver. "Getting a little ahead of ourselves, aren't we?"

He stalks toward me, backing me against the wall. "Am I? Your heat is coming, little flame. And when it does, I intend to make sure it takes." His hand splays possessively across my stomach. "I want to see you round with my pup, to know that everyone who looks at you will see that you're mine in every possible way."

"Ghost..." I whisper, caught between desire and surprise at the intensity of his words.

His smile is knowing, dangerous. "You have no idea how crazy your scent is making me."

"Deep breath," I tease him, and he's got me in his arms, his face in my neck, inhaling, licking me. He's relentless.

"What I'm going to show you will change a few things and will ensure that none of those Alphas out there can reach you when you're in full heat."

I smooth down my clothes, trying to regain some composure. "Okay, then let's do this." Anything to get him to calm down... For a moment there, I wasn't sure we were going to leave the room today. Not that I would have minded.

Ghost takes my hand, leading me out of the room. His fingers intertwine with mine, warm and callused. "This room is too small for both of us."

"Are you moving me out of your bedroom?" I tease, watching his face. Without the mask, I can see every micro-expression, the way his good eye darkens at my words. "Now that you're the big Alpha, you need your space?"

He drags me close, so fast I stumble against his chest. His arm locks around my waist like an iron band. "The opposite, little flame. I can't get enough of you and need to keep you all for myself." His lips brush my ear. "But we need change. Just like the pack has evolved, with new huts and better facilities, we need more, too."

"I'm curious to see what you have for us, then."

His lips curl at the corners, that dangerous smile that makes my knees weak. We stroll down the corridor, his hand still claiming mine. He leads me toward the fourth floor—a mysterious level I've only recently discovered exists on one side of the mansion, watching Ghost and others disappear up there the last few weeks while I've been firmly prohibited from exploring. Until now, apparently.

At the base of the steps, he pauses. "Wait here for two seconds and I'll come get you." His excitement is adorable, though I'd never tell him that. "Don't go anywhere."

"Because there are so many other places I could go on this island?" I quip.

He growls playfully, nipping at my lower lip before darting up the stairs.

Moments later, Eve strolls past, bowing her head respectfully. The gesture toward me still throws me off. The world really has gone mad.

"How are you feeling?" she asks, smiling. "Any changes? Cravings? Mood swings?"

I groan. "Why is everyone so obsessed with my heat lately? The pack's acting like they're taking bets on when I'll pop out a pup."

Eve laughs, the sound lighter than I remember from when I first arrived. "You know that's what happens during heat, right? Especially a mating heat with a powerful Alpha."

"I'm choosing ignorance," I huff. "Because thinking about being a mother really terrifies me."

"You're not alone," she answers softly, smiling freely. More than I've seen since the whole debacle with Axel's betrayal. I've forgiven her for her part in almost getting me killed—fear makes people do desperate things. But forgiveness doesn't mean forgetting. I know exactly who I'm dealing with.

She heads off with a skip in her step, but I'm not fooled. We're still on Nightmare Island, still surrounded by dangerous Alphas who'd rip out throats. But at least I have the most dangerous one of all on my side.

Ghost returns, taking my hand and pressing his lips to my knuckles. "Are you ready?"

"Always, my dangerous ghost."

His answering smile makes my heart skip. He leads me up the stairs, and I can't help but wonder what he's been plotting these past weeks. Whatever it is, that gleam in his eye tells me my life is about to change again.

Then again, that's what I signed up for when I let myself fall for the Alpha of Nightmare Island. Boring was never in the cards.

Ghost guides me up the final steps, and my heart pounds with anticipation. We reach a wooden door, carved with intricate wolf designs.

He opens the door and I step inside, then my world stops.

The room is enormous, easily three times the size of our current bedroom. But it's not the size that steals my breath; it's the massive four-post bed that dominates one wall, the dark wood carved with running wolves. The posts spiral upward, treelike, their branches reaching toward a ceiling that takes my breath away. It's painted with constellations, so realistic I feel like I could fall up into that star-filled sky.

"Ghost," I whisper, but he squeezes my hand, urging me to look more.

The walls are covered in painted murals—scenes from the island. Wolves race along the shoreline, their forms caught mid-stride. The mountains rise majestically, and... "Is that us?" I point to two wolves, one white, one black, standing on the cliff where we first met.

"Awa painted them," he says proudly. "She has many hidden talents."

A walk-in wardrobe is through one door, already filled with clothes. An ancient couch, reupholstered in rich fabric, sits near towering bookshelves that reach almost to the ceiling.

"Are those..." I move closer to the shelves, running my fingers along leather spines. Books. Dozens of them, hundreds maybe. Most are old, all precious on an island where I had no idea books existed.

"I had them brought in from the old library in Wreckage," Ghost explains.

Around the bed, blankets in perfect disarray, surrounding bowls on a nearby table overflowing with island fruits, fresh-baked bread, and so many more baked goodies. The scents make my mouth water—coconut cakes, honey bread, even those little pastries Mara makes that I love so much.

"You did this for me?" My voice cracks, tears welling up. "All of this?"

Ghost's hand cups my face, his thumb catching a tear. "Everything I do is for you, little flame." His voice drops lower, darker. "Your heat's coming. I can smell it getting stronger every day. I want you to have somewhere that's just ours, where I can lock that door and take my time with you."

The tears won't stop now, and I blame my out-of-control hormones. He lifts me into his arms, licking the tears away with gentle swipes of his tongue. "Don't cry, little flame."

"These are happy tears," I choke out. "No one's ever... I never had anyone do something just for me. This shows me you truly care for me, that you—"

"That I love you," he finishes. "I love you so fucking hard, Hel. More than I thought possible. More than is probably safe."

Now I'm really crying, cupping his scarred face in my hands as I kiss him. "I love you so much. Even if you are a dramatic, possessive Alpha who probably traumatized half the pack getting this room ready."

He grins against my lips. "Only half? I'm losing my touch." Then his expression softens. "I have something else to show you."

He sets me down, leading me to billowing white curtains that stir in the breeze. Beyond them, a massive balcony stretches out, overlooking the entire island. The beach curves down below, the ocean endless. There's seating and a lounge, and I already love it out here.

"Oh," I breathe, moving to the railing. From up here, the island almost looks peaceful. Almost looks like home.

He hugs me from behind, his chest solid and warm against my back. "This is just the start," he murmurs into my hair. "We may be on Nightmare Island, but we're making it ours. Creating something new from all this darkness."

His arms tighten. "And we'll find a way for you to see your brother. I swear it. I just need to figure out how to deal with my mark." He touches the brand on his inner arm that keeps him bound to the island.

I lean back against him, still crying, when something cold hits my nose. We both look up as white flakes drift down from the sky, getting heavier by the second.

"What is it?" Ghost asks as we both reach out to catch the falling pieces that melt instantly on our skin.

"Snow?" I laugh in disbelief. "I'm making it snow on a tropical island."

His deep chuckle rumbles against my back. "Looks like we've discovered another trigger for your powers, little flame. Happy crying equals snow. Should I be worried about blizzards during sex?"

I laugh and elbow him, but we're both staring at

the snow that falls harder, dusting the balcony in white.

That's when it hits—a deep ache in my stomach that steals my breath, liquid heat flooding between my thighs. My laugh turns to a gasp as desire slams into me with the force of a tidal wave. Every nerve ending comes alive, my skin suddenly too tight for my body.

Ghost goes still behind me, his grip tightening until it's almost painful. "I smell you," he growls, his voice pure Alpha. "Your heat's starting." The words rumble through me.

"Ghost," I whimper, turning in his arms. "I need—"

"I know exactly what you need." He sweeps me into his arms. "Time to bless our new bed, little flame. I'm going to make you forget there was ever anyone before me."

He carries me toward our bed, snow still falling outside, and the moment is perfect. In Ghost's arms is the only place I want to be.

And as his lips meet mine, I realize something. Home isn't a place. It's a feeling. It's this—his arms around me, his heart beating against mine, and the knowledge that no matter what comes next, we'll face it together.

Even if it means making it snow in paradise.

Ghost

"I'd almost forgotten how you taste, sweetheart," I purr against her dripping wet pussy.

My little flame is on her back, legs spread, just how I love her, panting for breath. "You went down on me yesterday, and you forgot?" She cranks her head up to glance at me before collapsing back onto the bed, her body writhing.

Laughing, I lean in to lap at her juicy lips. She's so swollen, her clit engorged. Her heady scent intoxicates me, her taste faint but sweet, and it's going straight to my dick. It throbs hard while I gently nudge her legs wider, and then, with my fingers, press open her lips, stretching her entrance, giving me a perfect view of that gorgeous little hole I'm going to enjoy.

Slipping my tongue into her, she cries out, bucking her hips, and she's so beautifully sensitive to every touch.

"Please..." Her voice hitches as another wave hits her. "I swear you're enjoying watching me suffer."

"Maybe a little. You're fucking breathtaking like this—all spread, desperate, and needy for me." My fingers ghost along her bikini line, drawing a long whimper. "But don't worry, little flame. I'll take good care of you."

She arches up again, pupils blown wide. "Then stop being such a damn tease! Do I have to spell it out? I need cock. Yours!"

I bark with laughter, adoring her directness, but my own control is fraying from watching her.

"And where do you want my cock?"

She bares her teeth at me. "Ghost!"

Her tongue darts out, wetting kiss-swollen lips. "Okay, fine. I have a better idea." She tries to push herself up on shaky arms.

I grin. "Oh?"

"Get on the bed. Let me—" Her demand ends in a cry as her body betrays her, trembling so hard she collapses back into the pillows.

"That's not how this works, little flame." My voice drops lower, rougher. "Your heat is calling for me to take charge. To rut you, to claim you."

She manages to shoot me a glare despite being barely able to string two thoughts together. "Then why are you taking your time?"

"Because I'm not rushing to knot you, not yet. First, I'm going to take my time fucking you every which way, fulfilling every fantasy and sating your heat. So you might as well lie there and enjoy it."

"Shut up," she groans, but there's a smile playing on her lips as she reaches down to those gorgeous tits, plucking at her nipples. "I hate that you're... coherent right now. My head's foggy, and I'm so turned on that it hurts."

I purr, finally climbing onto the bed, over the top of her. "I promise to tame those fires. And begging always helps." My mouth closes around a tight nipple, sucking down on it, flicking it with my tongue. She's writhing beneath me, wrapping her legs around my hips. She's rocking those sweet hips, trying to push herself toward my cock.

A protesting sound tears from her throat, but no words form, and I adore her submissive body.

Her body is burning up, her scent heavier, and she's so wet that I know she's more than ready. Kissing my way to the other breast, I growl low in my throat, the sound ripping from my chest.

"Gods, you're beautiful like this." I relish each shiver.

"Please, Ghost."

"Please what?" I drag my teeth lightly across her skin. "Use your words."

"Fuck me!" she purrs, her thighs around me quivering. My dick hardens, desperate to be inside her. So I pull back, her hands chasing after me, and I catch one, kissing her fingers.

"Get on our belly for me," I command, and there's no hesitation as she rolls over, then lifts that stunning round ass into the air. She's spreading her legs and I take her in, reaching over, rubbing my thumb across her entrance, at her stickiness, which pulls away with my touch.

She's purring, and her hands are grasping a pillow tightly, while a primal roar rolls through my chest.

I grasp my cock and push into her, slowly working my way in, pressing her open, my breaths racing to shove into her.

A moan bleeds from her throat, and I slide in deeper, her pussy gripping my cock so fiercely that it has me hissing.

"Fuck, Hel!"

Her hips move against me as if she's fucking me, but I hold those hips, fingers digging in, and I take charge, drawing out and then thrusting into her.

Hard.

Fast.

Savagely.

My sweetheart is crying out for more, her core dripping out of her and onto my balls. She has no idea how beautiful she is this way or that it might last for days, maybe even a week or more. I'll tell her later.

Right now, I'm ramming into her, hissing, eyes rolling back from the hottest fucking experience of my life. With my thumb, I slide up between her cheeks, finding her little puckered ass. She's silky wet and I inch into her.

She groans but isn't stopping me.

"I'm going to fuck you, sweetheart, just as you begged me. And I'm going to claim every hole." That's when I slide my thumb in all the way, and she cries out breathily, the sound seeming to reverberate around the room.

"Why does that sound so good?"

"Because you're so fucking horny for me."

She's half laughing, half moaning. "Please, please, don't you dare stop."

"I don't plan to." And I smile to myself because I'm the luckiest son of a bitch in this fucked-up world. And I'll never get enough of Hel. She's got her spell on me, and I'll give myself willingly to her.

But right now, my focus is clear.

Fuck her.

Love her.

Breed her.

Because I'm ready to start my own family.

BONUS SCENE

WHAT'S IN THE BASEMENT?

Hel

Two Weeks After Ghost Took Over Nightmare Island

"Are you sure?" Ghost asks for the dozenth time, and I roll my eyes just as many. "I've lived here for years, spent a lot of time in Wreckage, and not once have I seen a locked basement door in that town."

"Yes, I'm certain," I insist. "I saw it right before I fell into that pit with the zombie." The memory alone makes my skin crawl, but I push it aside.

"Okay, then we're going to check it out." We're strolling through the woods behind the mansion, along a path that looks completely different now that it's sunny and wolf-free. The memories of that terrifying night I ran through here alone still linger, but I can laugh about them now. It's wild how things turned out—with me now living on Nightmare Island with my fated mate after he killed Sten. The place feels so much more peaceful without that crazy bastard around. Though, seeing the wolf shifters from Sten's old pack trying to integrate with Ghost's is like watching a perpetual fighting match. Ghost insists it's *normal behavior* for them, but I have my doubts.

Ghost's thumb strokes the back of my hand as we walk, and I catch him studying me with that intense stare of his. "So why are you so curious about this basement?"

I shoot him an incredulous look. "Are you kidding me? It's a mysterious locked basement in a ghost town. You're telling me you're not dying to know what's inside?"

"Have you heard of Pandora's box?" His voice is serious, but I hear the amusement behind his words.

I chuckle and bump into him on purpose, loving how solid he feels against me. "Aww, is the big bad Alpha scared of a little basement?"

"I'm appropriately cautious of anything that's managed to stay locked up this long," he growls playfully, tugging me closer. "Someone has to look after you."

I love the way his eyes darken behind his mask.

The ruins of Wreckage emerge through the trees, looking even more decrepit in the daylight. The old road, now more stone than pavement, cuts through the center of town like a jagged scar. Remnants of old buildings gape at us with broken windows, and vines crawl up everything. I lead Ghost toward the mansion, past the massive pit I fell into that night. I peer inside, and a yellowed bone catches my eye—all that's left of my zombie friend. Lovely.

"And you're not afraid of encountering another zombie?" Ghost asks, his hand tightening on mine.

"Well, that's why I brought you along, right? My own personal zombie slayer." I flutter my eyelashes at him dramatically.

He just chuckles but doesn't deny it.

We round the side of the mansion, the same one that had given me major creeps when Ghost was being an ass and trying to scare me. But all thoughts of that night vanish when I spot the metal door set into the ground right next to the house, leading down into what has to be the basement.

"There it is!" I call out, picking up my pace. But Ghost stops, his brow furrowing.

"Where? I don't see anything."

"Oh my gods, it's literally right there!" I point directly at the door, but he's still staring around like

I'm speaking another language. Is he doing this on purpose?

He huffs.

"Do you even know what an underground door looks like?" I tease, but there's something unsettling about the way he's looking—or not looking—at it.

"I seriously don't see anything, only grass, stones, and a broken house," he says, and the playfulness is gone from his voice.

I blink in confusion, then walk over to the door and tap it with my boot. The metallic clang echoes slightly. Ghost's eyes follow the sound, and he reaches down to touch where my foot just was. The moment his fingers make contact, he jerks back like he's been shocked, eyes going wide.

"Fuck me," he breathes. "I swear to Odin, that was not there moments earlier. It just appeared."

"Then how come I saw it the whole time?"

"Fuck if I know, but something's wrong here." His eyes narrow.

"Okay, so you don't want to check it out, then?" I ask, already knowing the answer.

A slow grin spreads across his face. "Fuck, I do now! A magic invisible door that only you can see? That has me curious. Especially the part where it seems to have been hidden from me."

I'm giggling as I watch him wrestle with the lock.

He finally grabs a piece of metal debris, shoves it through the lock loop, and puts his supernatural strength to good use. The lock snaps with a satisfying crack.

My stomach does an excited flip as he pulls open the door, revealing a set of stairs descending into darkness. The musty smell that wafts up makes my nose wrinkle. Before I can take a step, Ghost's arm blocks my path.

"Stay here. I'll check it first."

For once, I don't argue. The zombie memories are a little too fresh to play hero. I wait at the top of the stairs, straining to see or hear anything in the darkness below. No sounds of fighting or cursing come up, which I take as a good sign. Finally, Ghost's head appears around the corner.

"All clear, sweetheart. Come on down."

I practically race down the stairs. The basement is about the size of our bedroom back in the mansion, with dusty shelves lining the walls. Most are empty, covered in years of grime, but Ghost is standing by one particular shelf, completely still. When I join him, I see why.

He's holding a wooden box about the size of his head, maybe a bit larger, and carefully rubbing decades of dust off the top with his thumb.

"What is that?"

"Treasure," he suggests with a half smile, but we're both transfixed by this box that somehow hasn't decayed like everything else down here. With another display of strength, he snaps off the small lock and lifts the lid.

I lean in close, curiosity burning, and we both stare at what's inside: a deep, blood-red stone, its surface covered in tiny craters that make it look almost organic. It sits nestled in what might have once been velvet, now faded and worn.

"What the hell?" I whisper.

"I feel an electric current coming off it." Before I can protest, he's already reaching for it.

"Should you touch it, then?"

"How else are we going to find out what it is?" His logic makes a certain amount of sense, but still...

His fingers wrap around the stone, and there's an instant spark against his arm. He flinches back, but I'm too busy staring at his inner arm, where his mark—the one that's kept him prisoner on this island—is rapidly fading away.

"Oh my gods!" I gasp. "Your mark, it's gone!"

He stares at his arm incredulously, running his fingers over the now-unmarked skin. Without a word, he bolts for the stairs, and I chase after him.

"What is it?"

He bursts into the sunlight, holding his arm up. "Is

this real? Are you fucking kidding me? This whole time, there's been a solution to the mark right under my nose?"

"Maybe," I say slowly, my mind racing to keep up. "Maybe this is what keeps you locked to the island, not just the mark itself…"

He turns to stare at the open basement door. "And maybe why I couldn't see the door but you could. It was hidden from me, from all of us with marks, by some kind of cloaking magic. Until you made me really look and see it."

"You can leave the island with me," I blurt out. He's free. Suddenly, I'm in his arms, his mask pushed back, and he's kissing me with a passion that makes me blush, his tongue in my mouth, reminding me how easily he brings me to his mercy. When we finally break apart, I'm grinning like an idiot.

"We can go see your brother," he says, excitement making him sound younger. "Once you work out how to lure a boat to us with the weather…"

I laugh at the absurdity of it all, but I'm going to find a way to finally go to him, the one person in my family who protected me as much as he could against my father.

"I'm dying to see my brother, Ragnar," I murmur. "You'd get along well with him."

His grin widens and he pulls me close again,

pressing a kiss to my forehead. "We will. I promise you."

A thought occurs to me. "What about the others on the island? And their marks? They'll want them removed, too."

His face darkens. "You know most are dangerous assholes here for a good reason?" He shakes his head. "I don't think it'd be wise to tell them about this... at least not for a... long time. The last thing we want is to draw attention from those in Denmark who will hunt us all down if they think everyone escaped. First, we find a way off the island. Then, we deal with everything else."

"For now, time to close this up." His voice drops lower. "You're the only one who gets to see this side of me, you know that? The one who makes me want to be better, even if I'm still an asshole."

I smile up at him. "You're a sweetheart to me."

"Damn right I am." He pulls his mask back down, but not before I catch his grin. "Now let's get this locked up before anyone else stumbles on our little secret."

Ghost wrestles with the broken lock, trying to bend it back into something usable, but after a few frustrated attempts, he gives up. "Wait here," he growls, disappearing into the basement once more. He returns moments later with lengths of dusty rope, meticulously weaving them through the door handles and securing them with knots.

"No one else should be able to see the door while they have their mark," I say, studying him as he works.

"I may bring Knut for a walk here one day and see if he notices it or not... just to be sure," he adds, giving one final tug. I nod.

"So... aren't you now glad I'm a curious cat?"

His laugh is low and dangerous, and before I can blink, he has me pressed against a tree, his cheek brushing mine. "You're my cat," he growls, and his hand travels down between us. I gasp as it slips under my dress. "Maybe we should play a bit with your sweet pussy?"

I laugh and push away from him, darting between the trees. His growl as he pursues me sends shivers down my spine—the ridiculously good kind.

It's funny how life works out sometimes. I found him while running for my life, terrified and alone, in these same woods. Now I run because I love what he'll do to me when he catches me. And he always catches me. That's the best part.

Ragnar

Savage Sector

. . .

Three nights without sleep, and still no word about my sister. She was being transported to Romania, so she should be here by now, but the waiting is fucking brutal.

Something's wrong.

The rain hammers against the windows, but inside, the crackling fire keeps the darkness at bay. I lean back in my leather chair, a glass of whiskey untouched in my hand. Somewhere upstairs, my mate and pup sleep soundly with her three other mates, unaware of the storm.

But I can't rest my mind... Worried like fuck about Hel.

My sister, my wild girl who was forced into an arranged marriage by our father. I vowed to her that I'd come save her one day, but it seems she got to me first. But now... this silence gnaws at my gut.

A sharp knock cuts through the thunder.

"Enter," I bark, setting my glass down on a nearby table.

A young man I've seen before opens the door. He's a messenger sent to me often by Dušan, the Alpha of the Ash pack down in Shadowlands Sector, the southern side of Romania. While I control the northern half.

"Sorry for the late arrival," he groans, lips tight.

"No apology needed. One day, I'll get Dušan to finally get a damn phone." Though, setting up an electricity grid in his part of the country is close to impossible.

The young man is wet, though not dripping, so I pour him a generous glass of whiskey.

"What brings you during such shit weather, my friend?"

His hands shake slightly as he accepts the drink. "I have urgent information from Dušan that he received from Alpha Ander. The plane your sister was in went down. But thankfully, she escaped in a pod."

I'm on my feet in seconds, my heart thundering into my ribs. "Where?" The word tears from my throat, every muscle in my body turning to stone. "Is she alive?"

He shrugs, eyes downcast. "No one knows where she landed or in what state. Only thing they said was that she went down in Exiled Sector, maybe somewhere near Nightmare Island."

"What the fuck!" Exiled Sector is where most around the world send the worst kind, the most depraved, where even the strongest wolves fear to tread. But *near* Nightmare Island—that could also be dozens of places.

Dread rushes through me. I curl my hands into fists.

"Sorry I couldn't bring better news," he says with a bow of his head.

"It's not on you," I manage through clenched teeth. "Rest here tonight, until the rains pass."

As I arrange for someone to show him to a guest room, my mind darkens with worry.

But I remind myself that Hel is tenacious. She's survived shit that would break lesser wolves. But Exiled Sector is different. That's where nightmares are born.

Back in the room, I down my whiskey in one burning gulp. I'll hire every tracker, every hunter worth their salt. I'll tear apart those islands one by one if I have to.

My sister is out there, and nothing—not storms, not distance, not even the monsters that prowl Exiled Sector—will stop me from bringing her home.

Even if I have to paint those islands red with blood.

Thanks for reading Nightmare Island

Curious about what happened to some of the other Omegas?

Check out their stories:

Venom Island (Caja's story) by Lexi C. Foss

Outcast Island (Guðrún's story) by Jennifer Thorn

Want to know about the Savage Sector and Shadowlands Sector?

Start the complete series today by Mila Young, available on Amazon or her online book store, **www.milayoungshop.com**

BANANA CLAW CRUNCH MUFFINS

Muffin Ingredients:

4 Tbsp butter (can sub 4 Tbsp applesauce)

¾ cup brown sugar

2 large eggs

1½ cups mashed bananas

2 Tbsp spiced rum

½ tsp vanilla extract

¼ cup buttermilk

2¼ cups cake flour

2½ tsp baking powder

½ tsp baking soda

½ tsp salt

Icing Ingredients:

1 can of cold coconut cream (just the cream on top, not the liquid)

⅓ cup heavy whipping cream

1 oz. coconut rum

1 tsp vanilla bean paste (or clear vanilla extract)

2+ cups powdered sugar (sweetness preference)

Toasted coconut for topping

Directions:

1. Preheat your oven to 350° F (180° C)

2. Start by creaming your butter and sugar together until creamy. Add in your eggs, mashed bananas, rum, extract, and buttermilk and mix until combined.

3. In a separate bowl, whisk together your dry ingredients.

4. Add half the dry mixture into the bowl of wet ingredients and mix until combined, then continue adding the rest of the dry ingredients into the batter, mixing until just combined.

5. Line a cupcake tin with liners or nonstick spray and spoon batter into each, filling ¾ of the way.

6. Bake for 15–20 minutes (depending on your oven). When the toothpick or cake tester inserted comes out clean, it is done.

7. Let cool for 2 minutes before removing from the pan and transferring to a cooling rack.

8. While the muffins cool, start assembling your icing.

9. In a bowl, combine the cold cream of the coconut (not the liquid), heavy cream, rum, vanilla, and powdered sugar. Use a hand mixer to mix it together until it forms a thick icing. You want it to drizzle off a spoon but not like a complete liquid.

10. You can add more powdered sugar for sweetness preference.

11. Spoon on top of muffins and top with toasted coconut.

Enjoy!

VENOM ISLAND
AN EXILED SECTOR NOVEL

Welcome to the Exiled Sector, home to the most lethal Alphas on the planet.

These beings don't play nice with others. They've been banished.

And a plane full of Omegas just crash-landed in their isles.

We're being hunted.

Their feral growls follow us.

Their howls haunt us.

Their knots call to us.

And their savagery terrifies us.

Some will escape.

Some will be caught.

Three will be *claimed*.

My name is Caja. And this is the story of how an Alpha named Enrique saved me from the horrors of Bariloche Sector...

Only to end up crash-landing our plane on Venom Island...

OUTCAST ISLAND
AN EXILED SECTOR NOVEL

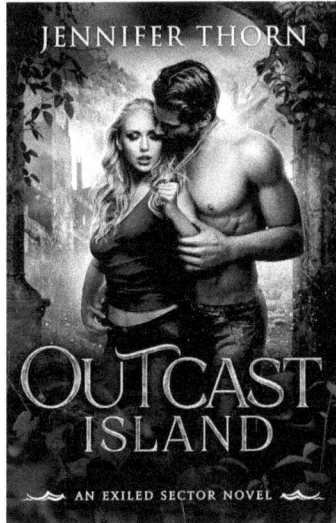

They're hunting me.

And I didn't even get a chance to run.

But it doesn't mean I won't *bite*.

When I was sold into slavery, I made sure I wasn't worth
bedding. I bit. I fought. I made such a snarl of things, they
drugged me to try and calm me down.

They would have eventually won, had I not been rescued.

Silly me, thinking that was the end of it.

Of course I would crash land on an island.

And now I'm being hunted on this exiled sector of brutal vampires.

They're after my body and my blood.

Magnus is one of them.

I should be terrified of the gorgeous male who has taken me to his lair. Yet, when the blood has washed off and the moon turns red from his dark deeds, I realize he's not like the others.

He's darkly beautiful.

He's patient in his form of hunting me.

He's powerful in the way he says he'll claim me.

But he's waiting for something.

I'm not entirely sure what.

Because I'm not like the females he knows.

There's no way I can go into heat and take his knot like he wants.

There's no way I can take his seed.

... Right?

About Mila Young

Find all Mila Young books at
www.milayoungbooks.com
www.milayoungshop.com

Best-selling author, Mila Young tackles everything
with the zeal and bravado of the fairytale heroes she
grew up reading about. She slays monsters, real and
imaginary, like there's no tomorrow. By day she rocks
a keyboard as a marketing extraordinaire. At night she
battles with her mighty pen-sword, creating fairytale
retellings, and sexy ever after tales.

Ready to read more and more from Mila Young?
www.subscribepage.com/milayoung

Join Mila's **Wicked Readers group** for exclusive
content, latest news, and giveaway.
www.facebook.com/groups/
milayoungwickedreaders

For more information...
mila@milayoungbooks.com

www.ingramcontent.com/pod-product-compliance
Ingram Content Group UK Ltd.
Pitfield, Milton Keynes, MK11 3LW, UK
UKHW031029120325
456161UK00005B/316